The State of Māori Rights

The State of Māori Rights

Margaret Mutu

First published in 2011 by Huia Publishers
39 Pipitea Street, PO Box 17–335
Wellington, Aotearoa New Zealand
www.huia.co.nz

ISBN 978-1-86969-437-1

National Library of New Zealand Cataloguing-in-Publication Data
Mutu, Margaret.
The state of Māori rights / Margaret Mutu.
Includes bibliographical references and index.
ISBN 978-1-86969-437-1
1. Maori (New Zealand people)—Civil rights. 2. Maori (New
Zealand people)—Government relations. [1. Kāwanatanga. Reo.
2. Mana motuhake. Reo] I. Title. II. Contemporary Pacific.
323.1199442—dc 22

We gratefully acknowledge Ngā Pae o te Māramatanga for its provision of a
Publications Support Grant, which assisted in the publication of this work.

NGĀ PAE O TE MĀRAMATANGA

Contents

List of Abbreviations

ABS	Aotearoa Broadcasting Systems
ACT	Association of Consumers and Taxpayers
ANZAC	Australia and New Zealand Army Corps
BIL	Brierley Investments Limited
CA	Court of Appeal
CEO	Chief Executive Officer
CERD	(United Nations) Committee on the Elimination of Racial Discrimination
ERMA	Environmental Risk Management Authority
Hon.	Honourable
HSBC	Hong Kong and Shanghai Banking Corporation
MA	Master of Arts
MLR	*Māori Law Review* edited by Tom Bennion
MMP	Mixed Member Proportional representation
MP	Member of Parliament
NZLR	New Zealand Law Reports
NZPA	New Zealand Press Association
OECD	Organisation for Economic Co-operation and Development
OTS	Office of Treaty Settlements
PhD	Doctor of Philosophy
QSM	Queen's Service Medal
SFO	Serious Fraud Office
TPK	Te Puni Kōkiri – The Ministry for Māori Development
TWOA	Te Wānanga o Aotearoa
UNDRIP	United Nations Declaration on the Rights of Indigenous Peoples
USPGA	United States Professional Golf Association

CHAPTER 1:

Introduction

This book brings together a series of annual reviews of issues affecting Māori that have been published over the past fifteen years. In 1994, the editor of *The Contemporary Pacific*, a journal of Pacific Island affairs published out of the Centre for Pacific Island Studies at the University of Hawai'i (Mānoa), asked me to provide a review of issues affecting Māori over the past year. Ranginui Walker had been providing annual reviews for the journal for several years and wanted to pass the role over to me. There was plenty to write about; during 1994 and 1995 Māori were once again at loggerheads with the New Zealand government, this time as we battled them over their iniquitous fiscal envelope policy for settling Treaty of Waitangi claims. So I agreed, and found it cathartic to be able to review and record our experiences over the previous twelve months, having participated in many hui not only amongst my own people of Te Hiku o te Ika (the Far North) but also on marae throughout the country. I had been actively involved in our own land issues and then our Treaty claims for nearly two decades and had the benefit of many hours of discussion with my own Ngāti Kahu kaumātua and kuia, as well as many others around the country, about what was happening to the Māori world.

Issues and events as viewed through Māori eyes
Every year after that *The Contemporary Pacific* asked me to review the previous twelve months from July to the following

June and that format has been retained here. Every year there were far more issues and events to report on than could be included in the review. Those I included were those I had heard being discussed on marae, in other hui, in Māori news media such as *Mana* magazine and on the Māori radio stations which had operated since the 1980s and then, since 2004, on Māori Television. Even so there were still several important issues that I did not cover. The approach I took was to try to capture as best I could the wide range of thinking expressed by Māori on issues and events affecting us as Māori. And while many of the events and issues I reviewed were covered in the mainstream (Pākehā) media, the way they were reported there rarely, if ever, reflected Māori thought on the matter.

Approach based on He Whakaputanga and Te Tiriti
My approach was strongly influenced by the teachings of my kaumātua. Much of what I reviewed dealt with our relationship with Pākehā and the ongoing struggle to free ourselves of their domination, oppression and discrimination. For my kaumātua, the relationship we entered into with the British in the nineteenth century was that set out first in He Whakaputanga o te Rangatiratanga o Nu Tireni: The Declaration of Independence of 1835, where our mana and tino rangatiratanga – our sovereignty, our ultimate authority, control and ownership of the country – was recognised and confirmed, followed by the formalisation in Te Tiriti o Waitangi of our relationship with the tino rangatira, the ultimate chief of the British: the Crown.[1] Both those documents solemnly undertook that our mana and tino rangatiratanga would be upheld and respected by the British Crown if we allowed her subjects to live amongst us on our lands and, in Te Tiriti, that the British Crown would take responsibility for and govern over her own hitherto lawless subjects who had already arrived in, and would continue to come to, Aotearoa-New Zealand. Te Tiriti also guaranteed that the British Crown would guard

against Māori being harmed by the lawless behaviour of her subjects.

Yet the British Crown has never been able to control her own subjects who came to live in our land, and for far too long they behaved in a manner that severely demeaned not only her mana, but also that of her descendants right down to today. For my kaumātua, setting that relationship right and, in doing so, upholding both He Whakaputanga and Te Tiriti, were the single most important aims they pursued in respect of our relationships with Pākehā and passed on to my generation to pursue after them.[2] Many of the events and issues reviewed in this book came about as a result of numerous and repeated violations not only of the official and internationally authoritative Māori language treaty, Te Tiriti o Waitangi, but also its English version, the Treaty of Waitangi.[3]

The underlying problem of racism in New Zealand

The underlying cause of the violations of Te Tiriti was invariably racism, that deeply embedded notion of white supremacy which imbued the incoming British with a belief that they could dispossess Māori as and however they chose. Racism can be defined as the attitudinal or ideological phenomenon that accepts racial superiority, and, when present in those with power, justifies them using that power to discriminate against and deprive others of what is rightfully theirs on the basis of their race.[4] It arrived in New Zealand with the first European visitors and remains to this day. Moana Jackson, writing for *Mana* magazine, explains: '… colonisation after 1492 was based on the belief of most of the White States in Europe that they had a right to dispossess most of the non-White Indigenous Peoples of the world. Colonisation was driven by racism, and efforts to "improve" race relations in this country will fail unless we address that, and try to deal with the constitutional, social and economic injustices which it creates'.[5]

Racial discrimination was not formally outlawed in New Zealand until 1971 with the passing of the Race Relations Act. However the main reason for passing the law was so that New Zealand could ratify the United Nations' International Convention on the Elimination of All Forms of Racial Discrimination. While the Office of the Race Relations Conciliator established by that Act conducted various education programmes aimed at reducing overt racism, it was unable to cure the deep-seated prejudice that had seen the country proudly adhering to a White New Zealand policy until the Second World War.[6] As such, racial prejudice against Māori, and particularly institutionalised racism,[7] continues to be widely practised by many Pākehā institutions and large numbers of New Zealand Pākehā, who are well represented in Parliament. One past prime minister, Sir Geoffrey Palmer, commented to a conference of judges, lawyers and Māori leaders (convened to discuss 'Treaty Claims: The Unfinished Business' a few days after the Waitangi Day debacle at Waitangi in 1995) that racism remains the 'unpleasant underside to the New Zealand psyche whenever there is debate of Māori matters'.[8] Māori efforts to combat racism are usually met with denial of its existence and personal threats to those who dare to raise the issue publicly.

Reoccurring issues and themes
The Waitangi Tribunal

From 1994 to 2009, common issues and themes reocurred. The work of the Waitangi Tribunal has involved many thousands of Māori throughout the country as we fight to take back our lands and resources. It is rare for the Tribunal not to uphold our claims, and its reports largely rewrite the history of the country. Yet Pākehā find it unbearably painful to have to come to terms with the true history of this country and react angrily to being told that their claims to ownership and control are not legitimate.

The Waitangi Tribunal – Te Roopu Whakamana i te Tiriti o Waitangi – was set up in 1975 under the Treaty of Waitangi Act as a permanent commission of inquiry, to inquire into and make recommendations on alleged breaches of the 'principles' of the Treaty of Waitangi.[9] For the first eight years of its existence it was ineffectual, rejecting Joe Hawke's fisheries regulations claim, and seeing only seven claims registered by the end of 1983. Then in 1983, three years after Edward Taihākurei Durie,[10] a Māori, was appointed to chair the Tribunal, the Motunui-Waitara report[11] was released. It upheld Te Ātiawa's claim in respect of the likely pollution of traditional fishing reefs near Waitara by the proposed Synfuel plant if it went ahead. Then in 1984, and again in 1985, Māori proprietary rights and environmental concerns were upheld in the Kaituna River and Manukau Harbour claims.[12] In 1986 the Tribunal recommended that te reo Māori be given the status of an official language.[13]

In 1985 the Tribunal's jurisdiction was expanded to allow it to inquire into claims back to 1840. Its membership was also expanded to seventeen in 1988 as claims started increasing in number. Specific provision was made for approximately equal numbers of Māori and Pākehā members, with a kaumātua usually appointed to each inquiry.[14] The Tribunal went on to uphold numerous historical claims to lands taken by the Crown throughout the country in violation of the Treaty.[15] It was the investigations and subsequent reports into these claims, which challenged the legitimacy of Pākehā settlement in New Zealand, that created the significant Pākehā backlash.[16] The Tribunal came under threat as politicians sought to abolish it or downgrade its powers, particularly those to make binding recommendations in respect of Crown forest and state-owned enterprise lands. The threat of the removal of these powers should they ever be used has hung over the Tribunal ever since.[17]

The fiscal envelope – side-stepping the Tribunal to extinguish Treaty claims

In an effort to marginalise both the Tribunal and the Treaty, and to extinguish Māori claims, the National Party government in 1994 launched its discriminatory fiscal envelope policy for settling Treaty of Waitangi claims by Māori. Despite its total rejection by Māori, successive governments have clung to it, imposing many 'settlements' in the last fifteen years on various tribal groupings desperate to rise above the poverty and deprivation they have suffered for over a century. The disruption and divisions amongst Māori caused by the Crown's 'settlement' activities have been widespread and featured in my writing repeatedly over the years.

The fisheries allocation debacle

The longest-running dispute was that over the fisheries settlement allocation. It dragged on for more than eleven years after the Waitangi Tribunal produced its report, with allocation only taking place after iwi throughout the country had become exhausted fighting the gross injustices perpetrated by the settlement. It became another theme, featuring throughout the reviews up until 2003.

Racism and Pākehā media

Racism against Māori in New Zealand is perpetuated and encouraged by Pākehā media. Numerous examples of it occurred over the years and it too became a recurring theme throughout the book.

Those who have perhaps suffered most publicly from racist attacks are those of our MPs who are proud to acknowledge their Māori descent. Prior to 1996 there were very few Māori in Parliament and they were largely invisible, marginalised and unable to speak out for their people. In 1996, the year of the first MMP election, fifteen MPs of Māori descent entered the House. Media attacks on them were merciless from the outset and eventually resulted in all but one or two of them maintaining very low profiles and remaining marginalised. This was another recurring theme until 2005, when the Māori Party won four seats and became the first independent voice of Māori in the New Zealand Parliament. From 2005 Parliament reeled under repeated onslaughts from the Māori Party publicly attacking racism against Māori whenever it occurred. But it still took three years and a government staring down inevitable defeat in the 2008 general election before Māori started to see any significant changes of attitude.

International criticism of government treatment of Māori

The government's ongoing racism and discrimination against Māori has not gone unnoticed in international circles. Another reoccurring theme is the United Nations' criticism and increasing condemnation of the treatment of Māori in New Zealand that has resulted in many Māori immigrating to Australia. For years the New Zealand government has reported to the United Nations that race relations in New Zealand are good and that only a few non-representative radical Māori were saying otherwise. Yet the facts speak for themselves in respect of Māori poverty, deprivation and marginalisation, and when the New Zealand government voted against the United Nations Declaration on the Rights of Indigenous Peoples in 2007 it could no longer sustain its 'good race relations' façade. In the year following the period covered in this book, in April 2010, the Māori Party finally persuaded the New Zealand government to support the Declaration. While Māori were jubilant that their human rights were now formally recognised, the Prime Minister played down its significance and was dismissive of its potential impact.[18]

Loss of key leaders

Along the way we lost many great leaders and icons. While it was not possible to note all our leaders who had passed on I have reported on those who had made particularly noteworthy and valuable contributions towards our struggle for freedom from oppression.

Bright spots

And in amongst the gloom and depression we always look for the bright spots, the great successes – the great Māori international sporting and fashion achievements, an award-winning film about us, an amazing survival against impossible odds, Māori Television and so on. I have included far too few of these but where we have had cause to celebrate a truly exceptional Māori achievement, I have recorded it.

Added references

In compiling the reviews for this book I have significantly expanded several of them in order to provide background material. I have also added in references to allow the reader to pursue matters in greater detail than I was able to find space for in a book that aims primarily to review issues and events, rather than to provide an in-depth analysis of them.

Acknowledgements

I am hugely indebted to and wish to thank the very large numbers of my whānau, my kuia and kaumātua, my hapū, Te Whānau Moana, and my iwi, Ngāti Kahu, who trained me and guided me over many years and have been my backbone and shelter as we have fought to maintain, uphold and enhance our mana and tino rangatiratanga. Ahakoa te nui o koutou kua mene atu ki te pō, e kore koutou e warewaretia. Ko tātou ngā kākano i ruia mai i Rangiātea, ā, ka ū, ka mau. Ki a tātou ngā waihotanga iho o rātou mā, ngā mihi whānui, ngā mihi aroha. He taonga tēnei mō koutou me ā koutou tamariki, mokopuna, ngā uri hakatupu.

It was my kuia and kaumātua who first took me outside our own iwi territories and throughout the country to meet and listen to hundreds of our whanaunga who work tirelessly for their whānau, hapū and iwi. It has been an honour to have learnt so much not only in hui, but also in discussions with so many of you over the years, and particularly in respect of the issues and events covered in this book. Tēnei te mihi nui ki a koutou katoa.

To my colleagues over the past three decades in Māori Studies at the University of Auckland who taught me so much about the fascinating world of Western academia and the manner in which it can help us in our pursuit of te mātauranga me māramatanga, and to my colleagues in Māori Studies in all the other New Zealand universities and at our Whare Wānanga, I extend warm greetings and thanks for your tautoko and scholarly fellowship. Our discussions in the various hui we have been able to convene have also been invaluable. Likewise to my colleagues in Hawaiian Studies at the University of Hawai'i at Manoa, Native Studies at the University of Saskatchewan, Saskatoon, Canada, Native American Studies at Dartmouth College, New Hampshire, thank you for your support and assistance as I tried to make more sense of our situation by comparing it to yours.

To Brian and Robyn Bargh and the meticulous editors at Huia Publishers, my thanks for your on-going support and mentoring for this project. For the photographs, ka nui aku mihi ki a Gil Hanly, ki a Katherine Findlay i *Mana*, ki a Sally Nicholas, ki a Josie McClutchie. Gil's enthusiasm and patience with my fascination for her marvellous collections of photographs; Katherine's generous sharing of her extensive knowledge of the *Mana* photographs; Sally's painstaking work preparing the photographs; Josie's technical insights and skills relating to the design. All of immeasurable help as I tried to capture in photographs the determination of Māori to be recognised as the first and indigenous people of Aotearoa-New Zealand and to have our rights upheld. I am also grateful to and thank Ngā Pae o te Māramatanga: the National Māori Centre for Research Excellence for its provision of a publication grant, which assisted in the publication of this work. Thanks also to the Faculty of Arts at the University of Auckland, which also provided financial support.

---

1 See Appendices 1 and 2.
2 McCully Matiu and Margaret Mutu, 2003, *Te Whānau Moana: Ngā Kaupapa me ngā Tikanga: Customs and Protocols*, Auckland, Reed, p. 179–181.
3 Margaret Mutu, 2010, 'Constitutional Intentions: The Treaty of Waitangi Texts', in Malcolm Mulholland and Veronica Tawhai (eds), *Weeping Waters: The Treaty of Waitangi and Constitutional Change*, Wellington, Huia Publishers, p. 13–40.
4 Paul Spoonley, 1995, *Racism and Ethnicity*, Auckland, Oxford University Press, p. 3.
5 Moana Jackson, 1998, 'The Good, the Bad and the Ugly', *Mana* no. 25, December 1997–January 1998, pp. 16–17.
6 Te Ara Encyclopedia of New Zealand, 'The end of a 'white New Zealand' policy', http://www.teara.govt.nz/NewZealanders/NewZealandPeoples/HistoryOfImmigration/15/en. For an outline of the background and history of racism or White Supremacy in New Zealand see Spoonley, 1995, *Racism and Ethnicity*; Angela Ballara, 1986, *Proud to be White? A Survey of Pakeha Prejudice in New Zealand*, Auckland, Heinemann.
7 Ranginui Walker, 2004, *Ka Whawhai Tonu Matou: Struggle Without End*, Auckland, Penguin, p. 277.
8 Sir Geoffrey Palmer, 1995, 'Where to from Here?' in Geoff McLay (ed.), 1995, *Treaty Settlements: The Unfinished Business*, Wellington, New Zealand Institute of Advanced Legal Studies and Victoria University of Wellington Law Review, p. 151.
9 The Waitangi Tribunal was left to define the principles of the Treaty. However both the Court of Appeal in *New Zealand Maori Council v Attorney-General* [1987] 1 NZLR 641 in particular, and subsequently the government have also attempted to define the principles (Paul Hamer, 2004, 'A Quarter-century of the Waitangi Tribunal', in Janine Haywood and Nicola R Wheen (eds), 2004, *The Waitangi Tribunal: Te Roopu Whakamana i te Tiriti o Waitangi*, Wellington, Bridget Williams Books, p. 6). Māori on the other hand have argued that the words of the original and internationally authoritative Māori language version of the Treaty, often referred to as Te Tiriti o Waitangi, are what Māori agreed to and as such it is what should be adhered to. This document is eschewed by governments because it states clearly that tino rangatiratanga, which encompasses sovereignty, remains with Māori and that the Crown has a much lesser kāwanatanga or governance role. All New Zealand governments have always asserted the complete sovereignty of Parliament over New Zealand and refused to acknowledge Māori sovereignty.
10 Now the Honourable Doctor Sir Edward Taihākurei Durie.
11 Waitangi Tribunal, 1983, *Report of the Waitangi Tribunal on the Motunui-Waitara Claim* (Wai 6), Wellington, Waitangi Tribunal, http://www.waitangi-tribunal.govt.nz/reports/
12 Waitangi Tribunal, 1984, *Report of the Waitangi Tribunal on the Kaituna River Claim* (Wai 4); 1985, *Report of the Waitangi Tribunal on the Manukau Claim* (Wai 8), Wellington, Waitangi Tribunal, http://www.waitangi-tribunal.govt.nz/reports/

13 Waitangi Tribunal, 1986, *Report of the Waitangi Tribunal on the Te Reo Maori Claim* (Wai 11), Wellington, Waitangi Tribunal, http://www.waitangi-tribunal. govt.nz/reports/

14 See the website of the Waitangi Tribunal, http://www.waitangi-tribunal.govt.nz/ about/wtmemb/

15 See the Waitangi Tribunal website at http://www.waitangi-tribunal.govt.nz/ reports/ for the large number of reports upholding historical claims.

16 Hamer, 'A Quarter-century of the Waitangi Tribunal', p. 7.

17 Hamer, 'A Quarter-century of the Waitangi Tribunal', p. 7.

18 Tracy Watkins, 20 April 2010, 'NZ Does U-turn on Rights Charter', Stuff: http:// www.stuff.co.nz/national/politics/3599153/NZ-does-U-turn-on-rights-charter.

CHAPTER 2:

1994–95 – The Year of the Fiscal Envelope

During 1994 and early 1995, the New Zealand government sorely tested Māori patience in respect of settling their grievances arising from breaches of the Treaty of Waitangi. Come Waitangi Day on 6 February 1995, Māori anger boiled over for all the world to see and the commemorations at Waitangi had to be truncated. In the months that followed, more than twenty instances of different tribal groupings taking over and reoccupying lands that had been stolen from them were reported in the national media. Many more took place quietly and away from the glare of media attention.

It was the first time in many a decade that Māori had been almost totally united on an issue.[1] The country watched the government's stance move from a swaggering confidence that they had finally found the solution to Māori grievances, to hurt and bewilderment as one by one each of the major tribal groupings in the country totally rejected the government's proposals for settlement of past grievances, to outbursts of indignation at increasingly vocal Māori demands for recognition and acknowledgement of Māori sovereignty, to, finally, a very quiet admission that they had totally misread and underestimated Māori.

Sealord deal controversy – settling fisheries claims by removing rights

Seeds of Māori discontent with the National Party government had started to mature in 1992, over the settlement of Māori claims to the full, exclusive and undisturbed possession of their fisheries that is specifically guaranteed in the Treaty of Waitangi. The Waitangi Tribunal had already upheld fisheries claims in Te Hiku o te Ika (the Far North) and in the South Island.[2] The Māori negotiators were men chosen by the Crown.[3] They had no mandate to act on behalf of all iwi or all Māori and for some, their mandate within their own iwi or organisation was not even sure.[4] And although the Māori negotiators called hui to consult, they disregarded significant opposition and made positive recommendations to the Crown.[5] Negotiations were reported as being conducted with strong emotional overtones. Simple commercial considerations such as the size and value of the fishing resource, and a careful examination of the viability of either the international fishing industry or the fishing company purchased as part of the settlement deal, were accorded very little attention. Moana Jackson of the Māori Legal Service was reported as noting that instead of grabbing what was offered, the fundamental difficulties with the quota management system, the guidelines and instructions for negotiations, the disbursement of the income and the mandate of the negotiators should have been worked out first, before negotiations began.[6]

The settlement deal, dubbed the Sealord deal, exchanged the exclusively Māori right to an economic base that so many Māori had relied on for centuries, our multi-billion dollar fishing resource, for

- a $150 million half share in the Sealord Products fishing company;
- the promise of 20 percent of quota on all new species brought under the quota management system

(although most commercial species were already under the system);

- a Crown appointed commission to allocate the quota amongst the tribes; and
- the reduction of customary fishing rights from full protection under the law, to regulations to be promulgated by the Minister of Fisheries.[7]

Despite a huge outcry from many iwi once Māori gained access to the Deed of Settlement, the government and the Māori negotiators remained firm and the Treaty of Waitangi (Fisheries) Claims Settlement Act 1992 was rapidly put in place preventing any further legal action by Māori against the Crown in respect of commercial fishing rights. Several Māori groups opposed to the deal unsuccessfully sought help from the Waitangi Tribunal, the High Court and the Court of Appeal.[8] The Waitangi Tribunal, though not dismissing the deal outright, considered it wrong that Treaty-based fishing rights would be extinguished. It recommended that the settlement legislation should provide for Treaty fishing interests, rather than extinguishing them. However it also took a wait and see approach, considering it would be more reasonable to have a twenty-five-year moratorium on Māori fishing claims rather than banning them completely.[9] Furthermore neither the deal nor the legislation resolved the very complex question of how the government-appointed Treaty of Waitangi Fisheries Commission would allocate the quota to Māori. From 1992 arguments over allocation were being fought out on marae, within whānau, hapū and iwi, between iwi, and between iwi-based and urban-based Māori. The task of applying a solution derived from tikanga to a problem caused by the Crown's greed and determination to extinguish that tikanga proved insurmountable. Starting in 1994, disaffected parties turned to the courts[10] in what would be years of hugely destructive and expensive litigation as Māori fought Māori in a Pākehā forum.[11]

Māori electoral option – government reluctance to ensure Māori participation

Early in 1994, Māori had the option of enrolling on the Māori electoral roll. In the past large numbers of Māori had simply not taken part in general elections and were not registered voters.[12] The advent of Mixed Member Proportional representation was seen as an opportunity to improve Māori participation in the electoral process and increase the number of Māori seats in Parliament from four (out of ninety-six) to possibly twelve or so (if all eligible Māori adults were to register) out of one hundred and twenty.[13] However, the opportunity for Māori to register was very poorly advertised and a very short period of only two months between February and April was allowed for enrolment. Māori protested and took a claim to the Waitangi Tribunal. The *Maori Electoral Option Report*[14] of February 1994 recommended increased funding as a matter of urgency to ensure maximum enrolment of Māori. The government rejected the Tribunal's recommendation, citing other spending priorities.[15] In the event, the number of enrolments increased from 104,414 to 136,708 (31 percent), which was sufficient to allow only one extra seat.[16] Māori then took the matter to the High Court, which, while critical of the disadvantage caused to Māori and encouraging of the government to remedy the situation, did not find against the government.[17] The government refused to reopen the option and provide the resources needed for the enrolments to ensure proper coverage of the Māori population and so the matter was appealed unsuccessfully to the Court of Appeal and the Privy Council.[18] Māori discontent with the government's attitude was increasing.

The fiscal envelope debacle – unilaterally determined government policy on extinguishing Māori Treaty of Waitangi claims and rights

Throughout 1994 rumours were emanating from Wellington about Crown proposals for the settlement of Treaty of Waitangi claims being drawn up. Alarm grew as very oppressive and divisive parts of the proposals were leaked to the media. Questions in the House drew little information. One Cabinet paper, however, revealed that the government was intent on excluding the lands administered by the Department of Conservation from any Treaty claims settlement process, despite the large number of claims over almost all of those lands.[19] More than seven million hectares of land, which is more than one third of the country, had been placed under the administration of the Department of Conservation in 1987 at the time the government's corporatisation and privatisation programmes were attempting to put Crown lands that should be returned to Māori out of their reach.[20] Then, in the Waitangi Tribunal, counsel for the Crown revealed that 'the Crown is developing an approach to negotiations with respect to natural resources policy generally.'[21] The Chairman of the Tribunal warned of the danger of including only state nominees in important and influential positions in Māori policy formulation,[22] which would result in policy that served Crown interests instead of those of Māori.

In the event there was negligible Māori input into the development of the proposals. The chief executive of Te Puni Kōkiri at the time was later to complain bitterly about the manner in which his staff were ostracised and marginalised by ministers and other 'free marketeer, conservationist and environmentalist' public servants, and their policy advice on the content of the proposals was ignored. He wrote that he and his officials had opposed a large number of the major features of the government's policies.[23] It appeared that the government looked elsewhere for Māori advice that would support its own views. The *Maori Law Review* revealed in February that 'discussions have been held with some Māori leaders'.[24] At least some of the Māori negotiators for the Sealord deal, for whom the Minister in Charge of Treaty of Waitangi Negotiations wrote that he had the greatest admiration, were involved.[25] They had been well rewarded for delivering Māori consent for the fisheries deal[26] and could be relied on to support the government again. However, Māori had been stung by their betrayal in the Sealord deal and they were not about to see their land claims head off in the same direction.[27] Pressure was mounting to curb decision-making on behalf of all Māori by this small cabal of Māori leaders.[28]

On 28 October, the anniversary of the signing of the Declaration of Independence acknowledging Māori sovereignty in 1835, Mike Smith, an ex-government servant from the large northern iwi Ngāpuhi, successfully brought the matter to the nation's attention by taking a chainsaw to a very prominent tree on the Auckland skyline, the lone (non-indigenous) pine tree which stood on One Tree Hill.[29] It, and the memorial obelisk beside it, are symbols of British colonisation and oppression and the denial of Māori rights.[30] The chainsaw attack enraged Pākehā in Auckland in particular but the media also gave good coverage of the reasons for the protest.

Although some Māori reportedly condemned the action, some of Smith's elders took a light-hearted approach and berated him for not having felled the tree, offering to teach him how to use a chainsaw properly.[31] Many Māori indicated strong support for the political statement it made about the government's refusal to give proper consideration to the settlement of the more than 500 claims then before the Waitangi Tribunal. Only approximately 15 percent of these claims had been investigated and reported on. The overwhelming majority of the reports from the Tribunal had been a great embarrassment to the Crown and they clearly wished to avoid any further information about breaches of the Treaty being publicised through this forum. More telling, however, was the increasing number of successful actions against the Crown that Māori were starting to accrue in the Courts.[32] The inclusion of references to the Treaty in twenty-one statutes was making it much more difficult for the Crown to keep evading its responsibilities to Māori.

Thus, in early December 1994, the government published its *Crown Proposals for the Settlement of Treaty of Waitangi Claims*. The worst fears of Māori were confirmed. The 'proposals' were presented as an ultimatum rather than a negotiable idea.[33] The Minister of Treaty Negotiations, Doug Graham, later admitted that it was not the intention of the government that Māori agree with the parameters set by government.[34] Rather their intention was to reduce hard-won Māori Treaty rights to the point where settling claims would have little or no impact or repercussions on non-Māori,[35] thus freeing them and the Crown from their Treaty obligations. As such the government sought to restrict the investigation into and settlement of all Treaty claims to a process of direct negotiation between Māori and the Crown. They sought to settle all claims without utilising natural resources[36] or land currently administered by the Department of Conservation[37] and to declare all settlements to be full and final,[38] removing the jurisdiction of the courts or the Waitangi Tribunal to hear any further claims of iwi who 'settled'.[39] It was a deliberate strategy to return Treaty issues from the Waitangi Tribunal and the courts to the political arena, where the Crown had far greater control. Its aim was to reduce the Crown's exposure to recommendations of the Waitangi Tribunal and decisions in favour of Māori in the courts.[40] And although the proposals talked about the settlement of claims, the process outlined aimed to extinguish rather than settle claims.

The proposals stated that the Crown would completely control the settlement process[41] and that essentially, once the

Crown had decided what each iwi could have in compensation for breaches of the Treaty throughout their particular territory, that would be the end of the matter.[42] Claimants who had lodged specific claims on behalf of individual whānau and hapū of an iwi would have their claims extinguished by the settlement of the wider iwi claim.[43] That was a sure recipe for conflict between whānau and hapū whose lands would be returned and the wider iwi grouping in whom the lands would be legally vested. Whānau and hapū who had successfully fought for the return of their lands would find them returned not to themselves, as the rightful owners, but to some wider iwi body to manage on their behalf. There was no guarantee at all that they would benefit from their own lands, and that the vesting of the lands in the wrong people would not, in fact, simply create yet another injustice.[44]

Māori would have to forgo any and all legal remedies once they started to talk to the Crown,[45] but would have to accept that before the Crown started talking to them, it would have already decided what the settlement would be.[46] Iwi, however, would not know what that was before they talked to the Crown.

Then to ensure that all iwi settlements would be full and final, legislation would be introduced removing the settlements from the jurisdiction of the Waitangi Tribunal and the courts so that iwi could not return in later years once further breaches were uncovered.[47] This condition was proposed even though most tribes had yet to carry out research on the full extent of the breaches in their areas.

The Crown would then consult with different tribal groupings over what they thought the extent of another iwi's settlement should be,[48] a clear attempt to set iwi against iwi. Furthermore, although the present policy only allows Crown land to be used to settle claims,[49] most of that would not be available to be used for settlement. The proposals simply decreed that, in general, lands held for 'conservation purposes' (lands administered by the Department of Conservation) would not be available for settlement.[50] It is no coincidence that most tribal claims include large areas which are 'conservation' lands. Likewise the Crown would not return natural resources such as water, river and lake beds, geothermal energy, the foreshore and seabed or sand, shingle and minerals, even though the Treaty guaranteed Māori full, exclusive and undisturbed possession of all their properties.[51] Similarly lands which Māori had gifted in the past for certain purposes but which had been sold or used for other purposes by the Crown would not be returned unless certain restrictive conditions were applied.[52]

To cap it all off, a fiscal limit of $1 billion was put on the total value of all assets returned (including the 1992 fisheries settlement) plus the expenses associated with bringing the claims and reaching a settlement.[53] By the time the proposals were published, over one third of that budget had already been expended. Within four months an iwi settlement of $170 million reduced the available settlement pool to just over half a billion dollars.

Māori reaction to the fiscal envelope – initial silence at the magnitude of the insult followed by firm, repeated and unanimous rejection

The government naively misread the initial silence over their proposals as indicating a measure of acceptance. The fact that prominent Māori iwi leaders declined the government invitation to attend the launch of the documents at the Prime Minister's residence in December 1994 ought to have signalled Māori displeasure.[54] Late in January 1995, one of those leaders, the ariki of Ngāti Tūwharetoa of the central North Island, Sir Hepi te Heuheu, convened a national hui of all iwi and hapū to discuss the proposals at Hīrangi Marae near Tūrangi. More than a thousand tribal representatives from throughout the country attended. At that hui Māori leaders indicated very clearly that they found the proposals most insulting. They unanimously rejected them because of:

- the poor consultation in the formulation of this proposal, which did not accord with court requirements;[55]
- the principles used and the lack of reference to the Treaty in these principles;
- the denial to Māori of legal rights that are available to other New Zealanders (such as access to the courts and the normal legal entitlement for full restitution based on the value of the property at the time of the loss, plus compound interest);
- the imposition of non-Māori processes and structures on claimants;
- the government's non-negotiable stance on several aspects of the policy;
- the government's assumptions and claims of ownership of natural resources and lands administered by the Department of Conservation; and
- the billion dollar cap.[56]

They called for some fundamental changes to the country's constitution so that these matters could be properly dealt with.[57]

The government in response referred to the people who attended the hui, who included a great many of Māoridom's elder statesmen and women, as a bunch of radicals. Those leaders chose not to respond to the insults. Instead they carried the message from the hui back to their marae and iwi.[58] But the insults were not taken lightly and Māori anger boiled over for all to see at the Waitangi Day celebrations the following week. Protestors successfully disrupted the proceedings, replaced the New Zealand flag with three Māori sovereignty flags and taunted and insulted the Prime Minister and other members of his cabinet and officials in attendance until the Minister of Internal Affairs finally cancelled the rest of the proceedings.[59]

The inevitable media frenzy produced wildly varying reports of what had happened.[60] The Prime Minister vowed to abolish Waitangi Day and attacked Māori for not keeping their radicals under control.[61] Threats of prosecutions against protestors resulted in only one arrest. A conviction for spitting at the Governor-General was later secured by the Crown and the protestor jailed for six months.[62] Māori commentators noted that it appeared that this one person had had to bear the brunt of Pākehā anger for what had happened at Waitangi and that scant regard had been had for the far worse indignities and atrocities that Māori had experienced at the hands of the Crown over the past 150 years when deciding the sentence. Some more insightful media commentators warned that the government had bought itself a fight with Māori with its fiscal envelope, and that it needed to change its stance and understand that while Treaty claims remained unresolved, protest at Waitangi would continue.[63]

In the months following Waitangi Day a series of occupations took place, during which different tribes in different parts of the North Island publicly repossessed lands that had been stolen from them.[64] Once again there was media frenzy with demands that occupiers be removed.[65] Initially some authorities signalled that they would use heavy-handed tactics. All that achieved was huge influxes of supporters, both Māori and Pākehā, from all parts of the country, to assist the occupiers.[66] At one site, however, in Auckland, occupiers were forcibly removed in full view of the media. The result was that private purchasers whom the government had offered the land to refused to complete the purchase.[67]

Yet the government's refusal to acknowledge and comprehend the obvious outrage of Māori at the proposals was quite breathtaking. Nine days after the debacle at Waitangi the government embarked on a series of consultative hui around the country to get a 'true' gauge of Māori opinion. It was only at this stage that the government considered that its Māori state servants could assist. Their job was to organise and facilitate the 'consultation' process with Māori.[68] Staff of Te Puni Kōkiri were sent ahead of Ministers in an attempt to smooth the path for them. These staff came under severe attack wherever they went. The Chief Executive of the Ministry, Wira Gardiner, later described the trauma suffered by his staff as 'combat stress'.[69] Within six weeks of the end of the consultative round, he announced his resignation.

At every one of the thirteen hui called, the proposals were once again rejected. In a subjective and emotive account of the hui published the following year in the aptly named book *Return to Sender: What Really Happened at the Fiscal Envelope Hui*, Gardiner detailed how each of the hui dealt with the proposals. Despite attacking the credibility of many of the Māori spokespeople who articulated their opposition prior to and at the hui, Gardiner did not deny the clear message of total rejection of the proposals. He wrote 'The emotion, anger and frustration associated with Māori opposition to the proposals was a stunning blow to a government committed to settling the major historic Treaty claims by the end of the century.' [70]

Slowly, the Minister of Treaty Negotiations started to concede that maybe the government had misread the situation. He acknowledged that Māori did not accept that conservation lands could not be used for settlement, nor that gifted lands should only be returned under certain conditions. He also appeared to accept that the Crown alone could not determine and control the settlement process. At the final consultation hui on 25 March in Christchurch he conceded that he had made mistakes, and that he would now retire to a quiet corner and think.[71] The Prime Minister's response, on the other hand, was to try to squash any notions of Māori sovereignty that were raised repeatedly during the hui,[72] stoutly declaring that there could only ever be one Parliament and one law for all.[73]

A report on the submissions made on the proposals indicated that they were generally attacked and that 'very few positive comments appear to have been received'.[74] Even so, no changes were made and once again, the fears of Māori were confirmed. The policy had in fact already been decided before the proposals were launched and the 'consultation' hui were merely an exercise in distributing information.[75] The *Māori Law Review*, commenting on the 1995–96 Financial Year Budget, reported that $525 million had been allocated over the next five years for the settlement of Māori claims in accordance with the fiscal envelope policy. The editor commented that this 'reinforces the impression that, like it or not, the fiscal envelope is the only game in town for the foreseeable future'.[76]

Waikato-Tainui Settlement – Crown-determined and a dangerous precedent

By late May 1995, the government had started to settle some of the bigger claims. Again it chose to seek the support of the fisheries negotiators it had chosen in 1992. For Waikato-Tainui, that led to a settlement being concluded in May 1995 for the confiscation of 1.2 million acres (486,502 hectares) in 1863. Waikato-Tainui's whakataukī relating to the confiscations was well-known: 'I riro whenua atu me hoki whenua mai, ko te moni hei utu mō te hara' ('As land was taken so must it be returned, the money is acknowledgement of the crime.')[77] Many other iwi and claimants have used this whakataukī over the years.

The settlement included three main components: the return of 47,048 acres; an apology from the British Queen; and monetary compensation of approximately $70 million to bring the total value of the package up to $170 million.[78] The

Deed of Settlement sets out that Waikato-Tainui has forgone full redress for the raupatu lands, which they estimated to be valued at $12 billion. In other words, they were knowingly settling for 0.14 percent of the true value of their settlement. Furthermore they would give up all claims concerning confiscations, claims to lands under state enterprises and Crown forests, claims to any minerals and forests, and claims to all lands administered by the Department of Conservation and natural resources with the exception of the Waikato River, the West Coast Harbours, and the Wairoa and Waiuku blocks which would be negotiated later.[79] However the chief Waikato-Tainui negotiator Sir Robert Mahuta is on record as saying it was a Crown determined offer made on a take-it-or-leave-it basis.[80] The fiscal envelope was here to stay whether Māori liked it or not.

These were very dangerous precedents, not least because they did not appear to fulfil the whakataukī. There was strong objection from some Waikato groups, whose criticisms included lack of adequate consultation, use of the fiscal envelope policy and loss of rights to minerals.[81] Other iwi had tried to establish a minimum benchmark agreeable to all tribes for settlement but were stymied by Waikato signing before they could reach a decision.[82] Although Sir Robert was at pains to point out that Tainui did not consider it had set a benchmark against which all other settlements would be measured,[83] as far as the government was concerned they had.[84]

Attempts to repeat Waikato-Tainui in Te Hiku o te Ika create uproar

While the government was able to settle Waikato-Tainui's claims under the fiscal envelope within six months of announcing it, attempts to apply the policy in Te Hiku o te Ika (the Far North) failed spectacularly. During the 'consultation' hui it had been noted that the mandate for the negotiators of the Sealord deal would be invalidated by the mandate requirements under the government settlement proposals.[85] By mid-1995 the media was reporting major upheavals among some tribal groupings as they tried to rein in leaders who no longer held the tribal mandates they may have had five or ten years before. In Te Hiku o te Ika, several hui-ā-iwi considered the performance of the two Sealord negotiators from their region, Matiu Rata and Graham Latimer, at considerable length during 1995. The decisions of the people to remove Rata's mandate and to reject Latimer's claim to an automatic right to speak for whomever he chose were decisive and very clear.[86] Neither of the men ever accepted the decisions. The result was lengthy, bitter disputes involving hugely expensive, divisive and exhausting litigation which, after two years, simply confirmed the people's decision.[87]

A bright spot – Whale Watch Kaikoura wins international acclaim

In February 1995 the whale watching commercial venture set up and controlled by Takahanga Marae in Kaikōura in the South Island and their iwi, Ngāi Tahu, was named the global winner of the British Tourism for Tomorrow Award.[88] The hapū of Kaikōura had initiated and developed the business, drawing on their knowledge of the large number of whales that had frequented their particular part of the coast for many generations. Visitors were taken in boats to see the whales as they dived and surfaced off the Kaikōura coast, at the same time experiencing the traditional hospitality of this Ngāi Tahu hapū. From very small and modest beginnings they built the operation into a major tourist attraction, finding innovative solutions to the racism used in attempts to stop them succeeding in their commercial ventures.[89]

1 Wira Gardiner, 1996, *Return to Sender: What Really Happened at the Fiscal Envelope Hui*, Auckland, Reed, p. 12.
2 Waitangi Tribunal, 1988(a), *Report of the Waitangi Tribunal on the Muriwhenua Fishing Claim* (Wai 22), and 1992(a), *Ngai Tahu Sea Fisheries Report* (Wai 27), Wellington, Waitangi Tribunal. All Waitangi Tribunal reports are available at http://www.waitangi-tribunal.govt.nz/reports/
3 Moana Jackson, 1997, 'What do Maori Want?', *Mana* no. 16, June–July 1997, p. 20.
4 Mason Durie, 1998, *Te Mana, Te Kāwanatanga: The Politics of Māori Self-Determination*, Auckland, Oxford University Press, pp. 154–9; Gardiner, *Return to Sender*, p. 199.
5 Durie, *Te Mana, Te Kāwanatanga*, p. 157.
6 Jackson, 'What do Maori Want?', p. 20.
7 Jane Kelsey, 1993, *Rolling Back the State*, Wellington, Bridget Williams, pp. 261–2; Douglas Graham, 1997, *Trick or Treaty*, Wellington, Institute of Policy Studies, p. 70; Durie, *Te Mana, Te Kāwanatanga*, p. 56; Margaret Mutu, 2005(a), 'Recovering Fagin's Ill-gotten Gains: Settling Ngāti Kahu's Treaty of Waitangi Claims against the Crown' in Michael Belgrave, Merata Kawharu and David Williams (eds), *Waitangi Revisited; Perspectives on the Treaty of Waitangi*, Melbourne, Oxford University Press, p. 193.
8 Durie, *Te Mana, Te Kāwanatanga*, p. 158
9 Durie, *Te Mana, Te Kāwanatanga*, pp. 158–9.
10 *Maori Law Review* (MLR) December 1994–January 1995, edited by Tom Bennion, Wellington, Esoteric Publications, p. 5.
11 Durie, *Te Mana, Te Kāwanatanga*, pp. 163–71.
12 Mason Durie, in *Te Mana, Te Kāwanatanga* (p. 100) notes '... a lack of confidence in the parliamentary system to deliver to Māori ...'
13 Durie, *Te Mana, Te Kāwanatanga*, p. 99.
14 Waitangi Tribunal, 1994, *Māori Electoral Option Report* (Wai 413), Wellington, Brooker's.
15 MLR, February 1994, p. 3.
16 MLR, May 1994, p. 7.
17 *Atawhai Taiaroa and Others v The Hon. the Minister of Justice, The Chief Registrar of Electors and the Attorney-General*, High Court, McGechan, J, CP No 99/94, 4 October 1994; MLR, October 1994, p. 5; Durie, *Te Mana, Te Kāwanatanga*, p. 100.
18 *Taiaroa v Minister of Justice* [1995] 1 NZLR 411 (Court of Appeal); MLR December 1994 – January 1995, p. 6; Durie, *Te Mana, Te Kāwanatanga*, p. 100; for a very brief description of the Privy Council, see 'The Privy Council', *Mana* no. 2, April–May 1993, p. 61.
19 MLR, June 1994, pp. 4–5: the 'conservation estate' is made up of all Crown lands not transferred to State Enterprises from the New Zealand Forest Service, Lands and Survey Department, Department of Agriculture, Ministry of Agriculture and Fisheries, Department of Internal Affairs, Marine Department, Ministry of Transport and Transport Department (Conservation Act 1987). Apart from administering national parks, conservation parks, reserves, conservation areas, marine reserves, inland waters, and rivers, it also administers many farms, camping grounds, and other areas with little or no conservation value (Graham, *Trick or Treaty*, p. 61).
20 The government's attempt to assign Crown lands to state owned enterprises drew decisive action from Sir Hepi te Heuheu and a delegation he led to have the Prime Minister add a Treaty of Waitangi section (section 9) to the Bill (see chapter 5, 1997–98). The Waitangi Tribunal which commenced its hearings in Te Hiku o te Ika in December 1986 had also addressed an urgent memorandum containing recommendations which led to the inclusion of section 9. This was the section relied on in the famous Lands case (*New Zealand Maori Council v Attorney-General* [1987] 1 NZLR 641). It resulted in an arrangement where the government promised to return the SOE land or interests in the land should the

Waitangi Tribunal so recommend in the future (Kelsey, *Rolling Back the State*, p. 213). However, all subsequent governments have gone to extraordinary lengths to prevent the Tribunal ever making such recommendations (for example, see MLR, August 1998, p. 2).

21 MLR, June 1994, p. 2.

22 E T Durie, 1994, 'Keynote Address', in *Kia Pūmau Tonu: Proceedings of the Hui Whakapūmau*, Department of Māori Studies, Massey University, p. 19.

23 Gardiner, *Return to Sender*, pp. 44–5, 49.

24 MLR, February 1994, p. 8.

25 Graham, *Trick or Treaty*, p. 70; Gardiner, *Return to Sender*, p. 31.

26 Durie, *Te Mana, Te Kāwanatanga*, p. 157.

27 Mutu, 'Recovering Fagin's Ill-Gotten Gains', p. 201.

28 Gardiner, *Return to Sender*, p. 13.

29 Aroha Harris, 2004, *Hīkoi: Forty Years of Māori Protest*, Wellington, Huia Publishers, p. 127.

30 Harris, *Hīkoi*, p. 127.

31 Michael Stone, 1995, 'Reflections: A House Divided Against Itself', *Mana* no. 9, Winter 1995, p. 84.

32 See Walker, *Ka Whawhai Tonu Matou*, p. 300 for a list of eight successful actions as at 1991, and Kelsey, *Rolling Back the State*, pp. 212ff, 254–5.

33 Harris, *Hīkoi*, p. 126; Alan Ward, 1999, *An Unsettled History: Treaty Claims in New Zealand Today*, Wellington, Bridget Williams Books, p. 52.

34 Graham, *Trick or Treaty*, p. 59.

35 Office of Treaty Settlements (OTS), 1994, *Crown Proposals for the Settlement of Treaty of Waitangi Claims*, Wellington, Office of Treaty Settlements, p. 5.

36 OTS, *Crown Proposals*, p. 21.

37 OTS, *Crown Proposals*, pp. 6, 19.

38 OTS, *Crown Proposals*, p. 27.

39 OTS, *Crown Proposals*, pp. 28–9.

40 Durie, *Te Mana, Te Kāwanatanga*, p. 188.

41 OTS, *Crown Proposals*, p. 7.

42 OTS, *Crown Proposals*, pp. 16, 17, 24ff.

43 OTS, *Crown Proposals*, pp. 13–15.

44 For example, in April 1995 members of Ngāti Wairere hapū of Tainui occupied the Department of Māori Studies at the University of Waikato in protest that their lands on which the university now stands were being returned to the Tainui Trust Board rather than to Ngāti Wairere (Radio New Zealand news item, 7 April 1995, available in Radio New Zealand Sound Archives located at http://www.radionz.co.nz/popular/treaty/events-1990s#1990; Adam Gifford, *Nga Korero o te Wa*, 15 April 1995, vol. 8 no. 4, p. 4.

45 OTS, *Crown Proposals*, p. 16.

46 OTS, *Crown Proposals*, p. 16.

47 OTS, *Crown Proposals*, pp. 28–9.

48 OTS, *Crown Proposals*, p. 28.

49 Land stolen from Māori was often sold to private individuals and then arbitrarily deemed to be unavailable for return to its Māori owners. For example the Waitangi Tribunal can investigate private land but cannot make recommendations in respect of it. Māori nevertheless continue to seek its return. Some private owners have gifted back land to its Māori owners, for example parts of the Māheatai block at Taipā in the Far North were returned to Ngāti Kahu in 1974 and 1986 by Pākehā who had lived on it for three generations (Waitangi Tribunal, 1988(b), *Mangonui Sewerage Report* (Wai 17), Wellington, Waitangi Tribunal, section 3.6, http://www.waitangi-tribunal.govt.nz/reports/).

50 OTS, *Crown Proposals*, pp. 19–20.

51 OTS, *Crown Proposals*, pp. 21–2.

52 OTS, *Crown Proposals*, pp. 23–4.

53 OTS, *Crown Proposals*, p. 24.

54 Durie, *Te Mana, Te Kāwanatanga*, p. 190; Harris, *Hīkoi*, p. 126; Gardiner, *Return to Sender*, p. 29.

55 For example, *Wellington International Airport v AVR NZ* [1991] 1 NZLR 671.

56 Mutu, 'Recovering Fagin's Ill-Gotten Gains', p. 200.

57 Durie, *Te Mana, Te Kāwanatanga*, pp. 190–1; Harris, *Hīkoi*, p. 126; Walker, *Ka Whawhai Tonu Matou*, p. 303.

58 Durie, *Te Mana, Te Kāwanatanga*, p. 190.

59 Gardiner, *Return to Sender*, pp. 23–8; Radio New Zealand Sound Archives, 1995(a), 'Waitangi Day – 1995', *Treaty of Waitangi: Events – 1990s*, 7 February 1995, http://www.radionz.co.nz/popular/treaty/events-1990s, part 3; Stone, 'Reflections: A House Divided Against Itself', pp. 82–5.

60 Gardiner, *Return to Sender*, pp. 24–5.

61 Harris, *Hīkoi*, p. 126; Durie, *Te Mana, Te Kāwanatanga*, p. 126; Radio New Zealand, 'Waitangi Day 1995', part 1.

62 Gardiner, *Return to Sender*, p. 230.

63 Radio New Zealand, 'Waitangi Day 1995', parts 1, 3; Gifford, *Nga Korero o te Wa*, vol. 8 no. 1, 14 January 1995, p. 1.

64 Harris, *Hīkoi*, p. 134; Radio New Zealand's interviews on Māori land occupations at the University of Waikato, Whakarewarewa, Pākaitore, Tāmaki Girls' College, Takahue School, and Pātea: Radio New Zealand Sound Archives, 1995(b), 'Māori Activism', *Treaty of Waitangi: Events – 1990s*, April–May 1995, http://www.radionz.co.nz/popular/treaty/events-1990s, parts 1–4; reports on the occupations of Ngāwhā (Northland), 'Takahue Occupiers Support Ngawha Stand', *Northland Age*, 27 April 1995, p. 1; Rangiāniwaniwa (Far North), 'Occupation Ends with Abuse and Arrests', *Northland Age*, 15 August 1995, p. 1; Maunganui Bluff (Northland), Gifford, *Nga Korero o te Wa*, vol. 8 no. 4, 15 April 1995, p. 4; Tāneatua (Bay of Plenty), Gifford, *Nga Korero o te Wa*, vol. 8 no. 5, 13 May 1995, p. 5; Otorohanga (Waikato), Gifford, *Nga Korero o te Wa*, vol. 8 no. 5, p. 5; Mangamuka Gorge (Far North), Gifford, *Nga Korero o te Wa*, vol. 8 no. 6, p. 5; Taemāro (Far North), Gifford, *Nga Korero o te Wa*, vol. 8 no. 7, 15 July 1995, p. 6; Huntly (Waikato), Gifford, *Nga Korero o te Wa*, vol. 8, no. 7, pp. 6–7.

65 Pat Snedden, 2005, *Pakeha and the Treaty: Why it's our Treaty Too*, Auckland, Random House, pp. 102, 106.

66 Snedden, *Pakeha and the Treaty*, p. 105.

67 Radio New Zealand, 'Māori Activism', occupation round-up part two: interview with Yoon Lee, legal advisor for the New Zealand Chinese Christian Church, on 7 April 1995; Gifford, *Nga Korero o te Wa*, vol. 8 no. 4, 15 April 1995, pp. 4–5.

68 Gardiner, *Return to Sender*, pp. 40-50.

69 Gardiner, *Return to Sender*, p. 143. Throughout the book Gardiner compares his experiences during the fiscal envelope hui to his experiences as a soldier serving in the New Zealand Army in the Vietnam war. See for example p. 49.

70 Gardiner, *Return to Sender*, p. 12.

71 Gardiner, *Return to Sender*, pp. 206, 210.

72 Gardiner, *Return to Sender*, p. 213.

73 Hone Harawira, 1995, 'Te Reo o te Kawariki: Sovereignty must come soon', *Northland Age*, 18 May 1995, p. 3; Gifford, *Nga Korero o te Wa*, vol. 8 no. 6, 10 June 1995, pp. 7–8; Gifford, *Nga Korero o te Wa*, vol. 8 no. 10, 7 October 1995, p. 8.

74 MLR, December 1995–January 1996, p. 12; see also New Zealand Government, 1995, *Report of Submissions: Crown Proposals for the Treaty of Waitangi Claims*, December 1995, Wellington, New Zealand Government.

75 Durie, *Te Mana, Te Kāwanatanga*, p. 191.

76 MLR, June 1995, p. 6.

77 Paul Diamond, 2003, 'Sir Robert Mahuta', in *A Fire in Your Belly: Māori Leaders Speak*, Wellington, Huia Publishers, p. 114.

78 MLR, May 1995, p. 9.

79 Graham, *Trick or Treaty*, pp. 76–77; MLR, December 1994–January 1995, pp. 12–3; MLR, May 1995, p. 9; Diamond, *A Fire in Your Belly*, p. 138.
80 Diamond, *A Fire in Your Belly*, p. 137.
81 Derek Fox, 'No Difference from the Tauiwi', *Mana* no. 8, February–April 1995, p. 36; Derek Fox, 'Te Raupatu Number Two?', *Mana* no. 8, February–April 1995, p. 37.
82 Walker, *Ka Whawhai Tonu Matou*, pp. 304–5.
83 Durie, *Te Mana, Te Kāwanatanga*, p. 187–8.
84 Graham, *Trick or Treaty*, p. 78.
85 Gardiner, *Return to Sender*, p. 199.
86 1995, 'No confidence vote in Matiu Rata', *Northland Age*, 22 June 1995, p. 1; Tuhoe Manuera, 1995, 'Ngati Kahu Spokesmen', *Northland Age*, 29 June 1995, p. 2.
87 Mutu, 'Recovering Fagin's Ill-Gotten Gains', p. 194; 1995, 'Muriwhenua claimants "treated like mushrooms"', *Northland Age*, 1 June 1995, p. 1; 1995, 'Hone Harawira a lone voice says Rata', *Northland Age*, 6 June 1995, p. 9; 1995, 'Taemaro not part of Muriwhenua claims', *Northland Age*, 6 June 1995, p. 9; 1995, 'No mandate from Te Rarawa', *Northland Age*, 15 June 1995, p. 1; 1995, 'Te Rarawa's version of Waimanoni hui', *Northland Age*, 6 July 1995, p. 1; Kaio Rivers, 1995, 'Future Maori leadership', *Northland Age*, 18 July 1995, p. 2; 1995, 'No mandate from five tribes', *Northland Age*, 20 July 1995, pp. 1–2; 1995, 'Te Rarawa moves to conduct own land claims', *Northland Age*, 19 September 1995, p. 6; 1996, 'New hopes for settlement of Muriwhenua claims', *Northland Age*, 11 January 1996, p. 1; 1996, 'Auckland claimants support new order', *Northland Age*, 20 February 1996, p. 1; 1996, 'Three tribes press ahead with Tribunal claims', *Northland Age*, 15 February 1996, p. 1; 1996, 'Ngati Kuri votes for Muriwhenua', *Northland Age*, 22 February 1996, p. 1; 1996, 'Support for Runanga and Rata', *Northland Age*, 28 May 1996, p. 1; 1996, 'Ngati Kuri votes to stand alone', *Northland Age*, 28 May 1996, p 1; 1996, 'No renewed faith for Te Rarawa', *Northland Age*, 30 May 1996, p. 1.
88 NZPA, 1995, 'Tourism Coup for Kaikoura Whales', *New Zealand Herald*, 10 February 1995, p 5; Kip Brook (NZPA), 1995, Kaikoura on Whale's Back', *New Zealand Herald*, 18 February 1995, p 24.
89 Personal communication, Whale Watch Kaikoura Ltd, August 2003.

CHAPTER 3:

1995–96

The Taranaki Report – laying bare 155 years of Crown atrocities

In June 1996 the Waitangi Tribunal issued its ground-breaking *Taranaki Report*. Using unusually strong language[1] they recounted not only the historical atrocities perpetrated by the Crown against the iwi of Taranaki, which have carried on so cruelly right up to the present day,[2] but also the on-going desire of British settler governments to destroy Māori autonomy or tino rangatiratanga (which is often translated as Māori sovereignty) in the face of Māori determination to maintain it.[3] Government-appointed bodies such as the Waitangi Tribunal are usually more circumspect in their criticisms of government treatment of Māori. This has enabled successive governments to ignore Māori grievances. However, it is no longer internationally acceptable to subject indigenous peoples to atrocities such as those that successive New Zealand governments have perpetrated against Māori. In this report the Tribunal was clear that international standards do apply in New Zealand, that they were not being applied in respect of Taranaki Māori and that this situation could not be tolerated any longer.

From the outset the Crown got it wrong in Taranaki. The Tribunal found that claims that it had purchased 75,370 acres around New Plymouth between 1844 and 1859 were invalid. And then having detailed the repeated breaches of the Treaty of

Waitangi from 1841 to 1995 when the report was written, the Tribunal attacked the then-government's Treaty of Waitangi claims settlement policy requirement that Māori must make full and final settlements of the claims for a fraction of that due.[4]

The *Taranaki Report* is an interim report on their investigations into the loss of 1,922,200 acres of land and 155 years of associated government atrocities. It provides an overview of the main aspects of the Taranaki claims. It is worth quoting at considerable length a large number of excerpts from the introduction and the conclusion to illustrate the tone and depth of feeling expressed in the report.

In its introductory overview the Tribunal reports:
The [Taranaki claims] could be the largest in the country. There may be no others where as many Treaty breaches had equivalent force and effect over a comparable time … The real issue is the relationship between Māori and the Government. It is today, as it has been for 155 years, the central problem.[5]

In respect of what the Tribunal calls 'The Never-ending War':
Land conflict has continued in Taranaki, with little amelioration, for 155 years … The nub of the Taranaki complaint is the land confiscations during the 1860s wars …

… in Taranaki, conflict with the use of arms was spread … over a staggering 40 years …

… The confiscations came with an undertaking that lands necessary for hapu survival would be returned without delay, but the promise was not maintained … many hapu were left with nothing of their own to live on and became squatters on Crown land … It was only after more conflict that some reserves were eventually defined, but they were given over to administrators to hold for Māori and the 'promotion of settlement'. They were then leased to [European] settlers on perpetual[ly renewable leases], with the result that Taranaki Māori, and they alone, have still to receive the right to occupy lands promised after the war.

Legislation is now proposed to terminate those leases within 63 years [of the present] ... over 180 years after they were made...

... If war is the absence of peace, the war has never ended in Taranaki, because that essential prerequisite for peace among peoples, that each should be able to live with dignity on their own lands, is still absent and the protest over land rights continues to be made ...[6]

In respect of continuing expropriation:

The confiscation of tribal interests by imposed tenure reform was probably the most destructive and demoralising of the forms of expropriation. All land that remained was individualised, even reserves and lands returned. No land was thus passed back in the condition in which it was taken; it came back like a gift with an incendiary device.

... The mood to capture as much Māori land as possible permeated through to today ... The Treaty principle that each hapu should possess sufficient land endowments had long ceased to exist in Government policy, if it had ever been part of that policy at all. There was no change of attitude until the land march of 1975, when the catch-cry 'Not one more acre ...' drew attention to what had been happening continuously for over 100 years ...[7]

In respect to Māori autonomy:

We see the claims as standing on two major foundations, land deprivation and disempowerment, the latter being the main. By 'disempowerment' we mean the denigration and destruction of Māori autonomy or self government [which] is pivotal to the Treaty ... The international term of 'aboriginal autonomy' ... describes the right of indigenes to constitutional status as first peoples, and their rights to manage their own policy, resources, and affairs, within minimum parameters necessary for the proper operation of the State. Equivalent Māori words are 'tino rangatiratanga', as used in the Treaty, and 'mana motuhake', as used since the 1860s.[8]

... Through war, protest, and petition, the single thread that most illuminates the historical fabric of Māori and Pakeha contact has been the Māori determination to maintain Māori autonomy and the Government's desire to destroy it. The irony is that the need for mutual recognition had been seen at the very foundation of the State, when the Treaty of Waitangi was signed.

At no point of which we are aware, however, have Taranaki Māori retreated from their historical position on autonomous rights. Despite the vicissitudes of war and the damage caused by expropriation and tenure reform, their stand on autonomy has not changed.[9]

In respect of the muru (confiscations) perpetrated by the Crown against Taranaki:

Few Māori have been as inhumanely penalised for standing by their rights as the Taranaki hapu. Perhaps this was because ... it was in Taranaki that a Māori ascendancy was most maintained.

... Eventually, military expeditions traversed the length of Taranaki to destroy all homes and cultivations in the way.

Then, in the last years of the wars, Titokowaru emerged from the slopes of Taranaki mountain to clear the land of

Waitangi Tribunal Chairman Edward Taihākurei Durie and Tribunal member Paul Temm at Ōrākei Marae in the early 1980s. (Gil Hanly)

Ngāti Te Ata's Maioro Wāhi Tapu. (Gil Hanly)

Members of the Waitangi Tribunal at Ōrākei Marae, November 1986. From left: Professor Keith Sorrenson, Georgina te Heuheu (Tūwharetoa), Chief Judge Eddie Durie, Bishop Manuhuia Bennett (Ngāti Whakaue, Ngāti Pikiao, Ngāti Rangitihi), Sir Monita Delamere (Te Whānau a Apanui), Professor Gordon Orr. (Gil Hanly)

Ngāneko Minhinnick (Ngāti Te Ata) took the Manukau claim to the Waitangi Tribunal because of the pollution and environmental degradation to the Manukau harbour caused by local government; fought the New Zealand Steel iron sand mining company, who were desecrating and destroying wāhi tapu, ancient burial grounds at Maioro; and pursued these matters through the United Nations, where she worked on the Declaration on the Rights on Indigenous Peoples. As a result the United Nations Rapporteur-Chairman of the Working Party on Indigenous Populations, Professor Erica-Irene Daes, visited New Zealand and issued a report critical of the New Zealand government's treatment of Māori (Daes 1988). (Gil Hanly)

Sir Hepi te Heuheu (Ngāti Tūwharetoa). (Mana)

Niko Tangaroa (Te Āti Haunui-a-Pāpārangi, Ngāti Kahungunu, Rangitāne), one of the leaders of the Pākaitore occupation in Whanganui. (Mana)

The Hon. Justice Sir Edward Taihākurei Durie (Rangitāne, Ngāti Kauwhata, Ngāti Raukawa), first Māori Chief Judge of the Māori Land Court, Chairman of the Waitangi Tribunal 1983–1999, High Court Judge 1999–2009. (New Zealand Herald)

Professor Sir Mason Durie (Rangitāne, Ngāti Kauwhata, Ngāti Raukawa), secretary to the National Māori Congress during the 1990s. Congress played a major role in the Hīrangi hui of 1995–96. (Courtesy of Massey News)

Sir Harawira (Wira) Gardiner (Ngāti Awa, Whakatōhea, Te Whānau-a-Apanui). (New Zealand Herald/Mana)

Syd Jackson (Ngāti Kahungunu, Ngāti Porou) and Deirdre Nehua (Ngāpuhi) at one of the Fiscal Envelope hui in April 1995. (Gil Hanly)

The flags of Te Whakaminenga (Māori Independence and sovereignty), Kotahitanga (Māori Unity) and Te Tino Rangatiratanga (Māori sovereignty) flying at Waitangi, 6 February 1995. (Mana)

Climbing up the pole at Waitangi to replace the New Zealand flag, Waitangi Day 1995. (Gil Hanly)

Flying the Tino Rangatira flag higher than all the others at Waitangi, at the top of a Norfolk pine. (Gil Hanly)

A large police contingent guarding the flagpole at Waitangi and fending off Māori activists as a result of the successful 1995 replacement of the New Zealand flag with Māori flags. (Gil Hanly)

Mike Smith (Ngāti Kahu, Ngāpuhi). (Gil Hanly)

A whale off the coast of Kaikōura. (Whale Watch Kaikoura)

Te Miringa Hohaia (Taranaki), who played a leading role in Taranaki's successful Treaty of Waitangi claims against the Crown. (Mana/Rowen Guthrie)

Moana Jackson (Ngāti Kahungunu, Ngāti Porou), legal expert and activist, author of the 1988 report Maori and the Criminal Justice System: He Whaipaanga Hou – A New Perspective, *(Wellington, Ministry of Justice), who worked for many years with other indigenous peoples to draft the United Nations' Declaration on the Rights of Indigenous Peoples and played a leading role in the constitutional debate in the Hīrangi hui of 1995 and 1996. (Mana)*

Mereana Pitman (Ngāti Kahungunu, Ngāti Porou, Ngāti Wai), National Māori Chairperson of Women's Refuge and activist dedicated to working for Ngāti Kahungunu and all Māori, led workshops at the Hīrangi hui. (Gil Hanly)

Whale Watch Kaikoura. (Whale Watch Kaikoura)

Taranaki, part of the successful Treaty of Waitangi claims against the Crown by the iwi of Taranaki to the Waitangi Tribunal. (Dan Csontos)

Dr Huirangi Waikerepuru (Ngāpuhi and Taranaki Whānui: Parininihi ki Matemate-ā-Onga, Waitōtara ki Taipake, Tangahoe, Ngāti Ruanui, Ngā Rauru, Ngā Ruahine), standing by Te Whiti's monument at Parihaka. He lodged Ngāti Ruanui's successful Treaty of Waitangi claims against the Crown. (Mana/Rowan Guthrie)

Hone Harawira (Ngāi Takoto, Ngāti Kahu, Te Aupōuri, Ngāpuhi) and his wife Hilda Halkyard-Harawira (Te Rarawa, Te Aupōuri, Ngāti Whātua) at Waitangi. Hone pursued accountability from Crown-appointed Māori leaders who supported the government's loathed fiscal envelope policy in 1995, led the national Hīkoi against the foreshore and seabed legislation and is the MP for Te Taitokerau. (Gil Hanly)

Sir Tipene O'Regan (Ngāi Tahu) led the settlement of the Ngāi Tahu Treaty of Waitangi claims against the Crown. He also chaired the Treaty of Waitangi Fisheries Commission. (Mana/Southand Times)

all soldiers and settlers for a distance of over 40 miles. ...
In 1869, while flushed with victory, and for reasons that
have never been clear, Titokowaru and his forces packed
up and left.

That is how Taranaki Māori ended their fighting. Never
again did they raise arms in aggression ... They placed
their faith in the pacifist prophets of Parihaka, Tohu and
Te Whiti ...

Māori protested but, true to a new policy of peace,
did not resort to arms ... Protest came after no less than
12 years when, with the whole of their lands confiscated
and their habitations given over to settlers, they were still
waiting for promised reserves. The protest that then came
took the form not of arms but of ploughing settler land.

... As the ploughmen were arrested, Titokowaru
among the first, others took their place, until over 400
Taranaki ploughmen swelled the gaols of Dunedin,
Lyttelton, Hokitika and Mount Cook in Wellington ...

... [N]o resistance was offered when the Armed
Constabulary took possession of the remaining Māori
land to divide it and sell it for European settlement.
Included was the very land that Māori were cultivating or
had planted in crops and on which whole communities
depended in order to survive. When the army broke the
fences ... Māori simply re-erected them ... new fencers
replaced those who were incarcerated, until over 200
Taranaki fencers joined the ploughmen in the South
Island gaols.

At all times Māori protest had been peaceful, when
eventually a force of 1589 soldiers invaded and sacked
Parihaka, the prophet's home, dispersed its population
of some 2000, and introduced passes to control Māori
movements. This large prosperous Māori settlement,
rumoured to have been preparing for war, had not one

fortification, nor was there any serious show of arms. That was a fact the Government knew full well before the invasion began. There were official reports to say so.

... All that could have been done was done to destroy the land base for Māori autonomy and representation. In the governance of the Taranaki province, since the Treaty of Waitangi was signed, land has been reserved for the bush and the birds but not one acre could be guaranteed as a haven for Māori.[10]

As to the validity and legality of the Crown's actions:
The wars, in our view, were not of Māori making. The Governor was the aggressor, not Māori ... Of the numerous Treaty breaches, we believe none was more serious than the Government's failure to respect Māori authority. ... The Governor assumed that his own authority must prevail and that of Māori stamped out, when the principles of the Treaty required that each should respect the other ...

In terms of strict law, ... the initial military action against Māori was an unlawful attack by armed forces of the Government on Māori subjects who were not in rebellion and for which, at the time, the Governor and certain Crown officers were subject to criminal and civil liability.

... The Governor was in rebellion against the authority of the Treaty and the Queen's word that it contained. Māori were not in rebellion ...

It follows that, in Treaty terms, the confiscations were not valid.

... [I]t seems almost certainly the case that the confiscations in Taranaki were unlawful ... For Māori the consequences were horrendous. There was nothing left for them to live on. Far from ending the war, the confiscations became the cause of its continuance and forced Māori to unaccustomed levels of desperation.[11]

In respect of the raupatu perpetuated by the Crown against Taranaki:

The raupatu (marginalisation) was effected through a reconstruction programme to make Taranaki Māori subservient to Government control.

... For over 100 years, Māori protested the Government's assumed right to administer the lands reserved for Māori, lease those lands without Māori consent, and make those leases perpetual.

... The leases in perpetuity were the unkindest cut of all, the twist to the blade of the raupatu ... as each generation of Māori succeeded to lands they could never walk on, they inherited the history of war, protest, imprisonment and dispossession ... The perpetual leases have been the subject of protest for a century. They are not past history but a live issue in the present ...[12]

As to the prejudice caused:

Taranaki Māori were dispossessed of their land, leadership, means of livelihood, personal freedom, and social structure and values. As Māori, they were denied their rights of autonomy, and as British subjects, their civil rights were removed. For decades, they were subjected to sustained attacks on their property and persons.

... With regard to the so-called 'returned' land ... most of the land was not returned to Māori possession; it was leased to Europeans and is held by Europeans to this day.[13]

In its conclusions the Tribunal reminded the government of the international understandings of the rights of indigenous peoples that had been encapsulated in the United Nations' Draft Declaration on the Rights of Indigenous Peoples.[14] It then found:

The whole history of Government dealings with Māori of Taranaki has been the antithesis of that envisaged by the Treaty of Waitangi. The Draft Declaration on the Rights of Indigenous Peoples affirms the relevance of the Treaty's principles for the global environment of today, defines the required relationship between governments and their indigenes, and emblazons in vivid relief the many respects in which the ability of Taranaki Māori to develop in their own country was removed from them ...

... The right of Māori to make their own decisions about who controlled the disposition of land and the nature of interests held was negated, and the immediate result was war. The long-term consequence was that the Government enforced a plan to alter Māori land tenure and to destroy, by stealth and by arms, the capacity of Māori to manage their own properties and to determine rights within them. The relationship the Government imposed was that of dominance and subservience ...

... [T]he confiscation plan was immoral in concept and unlawful in implementation throughout the length and breadth of the land...

... The protests of the landless were protests of desperation, but for their actions they were imprisoned in their hundreds, at will, without trial, and with all civil rights suspended. The ultimate consequence, the invasion and sacking of Parihaka, must rank with the most heinous action of any government, in any country, in the last century. For decades, even to this day, it has had devastating effects on race relations. There was not a tribe in the country that did not learn of it, for Parihaka had been open to them all ...

... [W]ithout Māori consent, the administration of such lands as were returned to Taranaki Māori was passed by the West Coast Commission to the Public and Native

Trustees ... the bulk of those lands were then tendered to Europeans on perpetually renewable leases ... most of the lease lands were sold by the trustees. The remainder are still under perpetually renewable leases. Over 100 years have passed since the wars, but Māori have still to gain possession of the promised land, and in the interim, their society crumbled as development opportunities passed them by.

... The perpetual leases ensured the pain of dispossession, which prolonged the war and imprisoned the protestors, was formally passed down in succession orders through every generation to the present.

... We cannot begin to describe the resentment that welled up at every hearing, founded not on factual research but on the reality of inherited opinions. There is a conviction that from first [European] settlement to the present there has been a concerted and unending programme to exclude Māori from land ownership throughout Taranaki. Law and order are not readily maintainable in that situation. Similar views are held by Australian Aboriginals and Canadian Indians, and it seems to be relevant that the three are the world's most imprisoned races. The prejudice must be overcome. The opinion that the world is no longer theirs to behold must stop with this generation.[15]

As to the size of the claims:

... [T]he gravamen of our report has been to say that the Taranaki claims are likely to be the largest in the country. The graphic muru (confiscation) of most of Taranaki and the raupatu (marginalisation) without ending describe the holocaust of Taranaki history and the denigration of the founding peoples in a continuum from 1840 to the present.[16]

The Tribunal's use of the word 'holocaust' here prompted an acrimonious public debate[17] as it deliberately challenged the amnesiac tendencies of the large sections of the Pākehā population about the atrocities committed as they took control of huge tracts of Māori land.

And as to full and final settlement required by the government's 'fiscal envelope' Treaty of Waitangi claims settlement policy:

> ... Based on legal principles, the Taranaki claims may be assessed in billions of dollars, yet claimants appear to be required to settle for a fraction that is due. Some billions of dollars would probably result were loss based only upon the value of the land, when taken with compound interest to today, leaving aside exemplary damages or compensation for loss of rents and the devaluation of annuities ... it seems to us that a full reparation based on usual legal principles is unavailable to Māori as a matter of political policy, and if that is so, Māori should not be required to sign a full and final release for compensation as though legal principles applied. How tribes can legally sign for a fraction of their just entitlement when they have no other option is beyond us. To require Māori leaders to sign for a full and final settlement in these circumstances serves only to destabilise their authority. If a full pay-off for the past on legal lines is impractical, it is more honest to say so and to reconsider the jurisprudential basis for historical claims settlements.
>
> ... [I]t appears to us that generous reparation is payable, and if the hapū are to waive further claims to the Waitangi Tribunal in future, it must be subject to the Government maintaining a commitment to the people's restoration and adhering thereafter to the principles of the Treaty of Waitangi.[18]

The Hīrangi hui – strategising for constitutional change through decolonisation and scrutinising Māori leadership qualities

Although the Minister of Māori Affairs welcomed the report and hoped that others would read it,[19] it was issued in a climate of increasing animosity between Māori and the government. During 1995 and 1996, Māori continued to seek effective ways of ensuring that they could once again exercise the tino rangatiratanga guaranteed to them in the Tiriti o Waitangi. Well over a thousand Māori from a wide range of tribal, political and intellectual backgrounds came together for each of the two national hui which followed the initial fiscal envelope hui at Hīrangi. They were convened, once again, by Ngāti Tūwharetoa's ariki, Sir Hepi te Heuheu. The first had been held in January 1995, the second was convened eight months later in September 1995, and the third in April 1996. Māori pooled their energies and expertise to help develop robust strategies to enable them to take back control of their own lives. The strategies aimed to enable Māori to manage and control their own policies, resources and affairs.

Yet the drawing up of the policies, which inevitably focused on how to achieve constitutional change and entrench the Treaty of Waitangi in the constitution, exposed the fact that the current government is no different from any other New Zealand government in its determination to prevent Māori from being afforded the recognition and respect owed to them.[20] In a campaign whose thinly-disguised aim was that of orchestrating anti-Māori sentiment, the Prime Minister, Jim Bolger, led a sustained attack on Māori aspirations articulated by Māori leaders, ridiculing calls for recognition of Māori sovereignty.[21] Furthermore, his government's refusal to consider abandoning its claims settlement policy, which Māori throughout the country unanimously rejected in early 1995, sent a clear message that Māori policy would continue to be developed and determined by those who know little or nothing about the realities of Māori history, culture and social circumstances. It also guaranteed ongoing demonstrations of Māori anger and frustration.

By mid-1995 the government was smarting from the dual humiliation of the fiasco at Waitangi in February 1995 and continued unanimous Māori rejection of the government's loathed fiscal envelope claims settlement proposals. Despite legal (including judicial) and political opinions to the contrary,[22] the Prime Minister continued to assert as an unquestionable and undebatable truth that parliamentary sovereignty is indivisible and the will of the (Pākehā) majority must prevail.[23] His confidence became arrogance when he also started declaring that in fact the fiscal envelope policy was really the best thing for Māori and that current Māori rejection was simply Māori not understanding what it was really about. He was reported as asserting that Māori did not know what they were talking about, especially when they used words like Māori sovereignty, decolonisation and tino rangatiratanga.[24] The fact that Māori debates over and calls for recognition of Māori sovereignty, tino rangatiratanga, or mana motuhake were well over 130 years old was conveniently ignored and avoided by the Prime Minister. However the point was not lost on the Waitangi Tribunal, whose reports deal directly with these matters.

In the face of the Prime Minister's onslaught Māori remained unmoved. Different hapū throughout the North Island continued to occupy lands taken from them in breach of the Treaty of Waitangi although media interest in them declined. Then, at the second national hui, not only was the fiscal envelope policy unanimously rejected yet again, the Prime Minister's invitation to select four Māori to assist and advise the government on how to implement that policy was also rejected.[25] (In his letter to Sir Hepi, Mr Bolger had emphasised the magnanimity of his offer but warned that he was only prepared to talk to Māori if they did not challenge the sovereignty of the present Parliament and stopped focusing on concepts such as tino rangatiratanga.) The hui went on to condemn the ongoing sales of government assets that are under claim by Māori and confirmed the unanimous resolution of the first national hui that the Treaty of Waitangi be entrenched as the constitution for New Zealand to enable tino rangatiratanga to be realised for Māori.[26] However decolonisation was emphasised as an important prerequisite and hui participants went home to start setting up decolonisation programmes for their whānau, hapū, marae, iwi, kura and any other group that brought their people together in a safe environment for such matters to be discussed.[27]

The third national hui, convened in April 1996, discussed several models for recognising mana Māori as the basis for constitutional change. However it became clear that for such change to be supported by Māori communities throughout the country, much more decolonisation work and revival of the knowledge of Māori values and identity was required in those communities.[28] Once again hui participants returned home to conduct wānanga for their people. The re-empowerment of Māori was starting at the level of the whānau and marae and in kōhanga reo and kura kaupapa Māori around the country. It included Māori being much more assertive about who their true leaders were, rather than accepting those imposed on them by governments and state agencies.[29]

Challenges to Crown-appointed Māori leaders

Traditional leadership qualities of openness and accountability, willingness and ability to listen to the people, honesty and integrity were insisted on and the ability of leaders to keep the people together was emphasised as paramount.[30] Unilateral decision-making, autocratic leadership styles and lack of accountability, which are inimical to good leadership,[31] were strongly condemned and rejected.[32] Indications of the determination of Māori to remove leaders of this ilk had been delivered to the Governor General, Crown Ministers, international diplomats and government officials on Waitangi Day 1995 at Waitangi by the spokesperson for the Taumata Kaumātua o Ngāpuhi (Ngāpuhi Council of Elders), Kīngi Taurua. *Mana* Māori news magazine reported him telling the government in the formal speeches of the day "'the time of the Sir Graham Latimers of the Māori world has come to an end. Ngāpuhi have new leaders and there will be no more Latimers'".[33] With so much at stake and the mistakes of the Sealord deal splitting the people asunder, Māori leadership came under intense scrutiny, with some earning strong rebuke and rejection by their own iwi.[34]

Nelson Mandela visits and criticises the government's racist attitude

The Prime Minister's attitude towards Māori also drew severe criticism from several Pākehā opposition members, with charges of racism being levelled at him and other government members on more than one occasion in the House. Support for Māori outside the House came from a range of sources including many churches, the Combined Trade Unions, Federated Farmers and several international visitors. In particular, the South African president, Nelson Mandela, went out of his way during his time in New Zealand (for the Commonwealth Heads of Government Meeting in November) to acknowledge Māori as the indigenous people of New Zealand and accord them the respect they deserved. He went as far as abandoning his prepared speech notes in Auckland to suggest to the government that it had a lot of work to do to improve the plight of Māori and rectify their marginalisation in their own country. He spoke of the links between the indigenous peoples of South Africa and New Zealand and their shared experience of 'pain of conquest, dispossession and oppression'.[35] Despite the deliberately pointed nature of his comments, Auckland's (and the country's) most widely read daily newspaper, the *New Zealand Herald*, did not report them. Māori media, on the other hand, gave them full coverage.

Arson at Takahue

With Māori–government relations severely strained, the government's actions in the week following the national hui to quell a protest in Te Hiku o te Ika backfired badly, leaving permanent scars and divisions in the small community at the centre of the protest.[36] Members of a hapū from Takahue in the Far North had taken over an old school site which they wanted returned to them.[37] Goaded into action by the national news media trumpeting the refusal of Māori to move off the site, the government once again consulted with one of its now-disgraced Māori advisors from the same region. On the same day, the media also broke the news of a report to Parliament by the Auditor-General which severely criticised the government's fiscal envelope policy.[38] The next day, 21 September, the government instructed the police to remove the Takahue protestors from the school site. The police did so and the school was burnt to the ground.

The media and Parliament went into their second frenzy concerning Māori in 1995. The Prime Minister used the incident to vent his fury on Māori activists who had been visiting the site when the fire was lit. Both he and the national media were very quick to blame the protestors at Takahue for the fire[39] although the protestors were equally adamant that they had nothing to do with it.[40] The local Kaitāia newspaper, the *Northland Age*, and Māori radio stations throughout the country were the only news media to broadcast the protestors' statement that two of their party had seen a member of the police squad setting the school alight. The *Northland Age*, however, dismissed the statement, saying that the police had scotched the claim. Iwi leaders from the area were divided, some placing complete blame for the loss of the school on the protestors while others blamed the government and its advisor and their determination to maintain unquestioned control of Māori.

When all the smoke surrounding the incident finally cleared several months and several court cases later, no one was charged with arson.[41] Those arrested at the site were simply convicted of relatively minor offences and discharged or given suspended sentences.[42] But what both the government and its advisor for the Far North had not taken into account was the well-documented level of animosity that has existed between Māori and certain individual members of the police force in the Far North for many years.[43] At the end of day, the protestors' report on the person they had seen setting the school alight that day was never disproven.

... And at Taumaranui

Although the Takahue incident was a disaster from all points of view, one Minister managed to use another torching of a government building as a catalyst to start repairing Māori–government relations. Ngāti Hauaroa of Taumaranui in the central North Island had been locked in an increasingly bitter battle with the police over attempts to build a police station on a wāhi tapu[44] and the Department of Conservation over the management of their lands, forests and river. These disputes had been running for many years. Three weeks before the Takahue fire, a Department of Conservation office in Taumaranui was torched. The national news media did not report it until the Takahue incident and it slipped by with very little comment.

The government had been warned about the increasing and potentially explosive situations involving the department and Māori throughout the country in a report from a Māori member of the New Zealand Conservation Authority in June 1995.[45] The report outlined a broad spectrum of issues which needed urgent attention and laid the responsibility for the existing level of conflict between Māori and the Department squarely on the shoulders of the Director-General of Conservation.[46] The department's biggest problem was that it administers almost one-third of the land in New Zealand, almost all of which is under claim by Māori. The department's refusal to allow Māori to participate in the management of those lands, or to protect their wāhi tapu (sacred sites), or to collect their customary food and other flora and fauna from them had incensed Māori for many years. The department's attitude in these matters was largely dictated by the very strong environmentalist lobby, the more powerful of which had lobbied successfully against any Māori involvement anywhere on the lands administered by the Department.[47] As a result Māori staff employed to address Māori issues were marginalised and used mainly as a buffer between the Department and angry Māori communities, rather than working to ensure the implementation of section 4 of the Conservation Act 1987, which requires the Department to 'give effect to the principles of the Treaty of Waitangi'.

While the Minister of Māori Affairs took the report seriously, the Minister of Conservation, at the request of his Director-General, dismissed it out of hand. As a result the Māori members of Parliament tabled the report in the House in September and demanded answers of the Minister of Conservation to a long list of questions. On the instructions of his officials the Minister fobbed off most of the questions but Māori throughout the country backed the report, demanding that something be done. Whanganui Māori in particular made direct representations to the Minister.

Minister of Conservation steps in on Whanganui problems
The Minister finally intervened in the Whanganui matter after the torching of the department's office, bypassing his Director-General and sending his most senior Māori official and his public relations manager to try to sort the situation out. Many months and many meetings later, both Whanganui Māori and the department's senior Māori official were able to report

they were making progress. Yet all they had done was jointly draw up a document acknowledging each other's position and status as Treaty partners, stating what each side's position was (even though they were very different from each other), and making solemn undertakings to keep working through the issues with good faith on both sides. Despite scepticism on the part of some Māori leaders, Whanganui Māori reported being satisfied that the government had demonstrated a willingness to drop its high-handed tactics and start talking to them as equals.

Ngāi Tahu claims settlement negotiations recommence in the face of damaging litigation

The Whanganui talks were one of the very few bright spots in Māori–government relations in 1995–96, yet they received almost no media coverage. A reconciliation which allowed the government to recommence negotiations with the South Island tribe, Ngāi Tahu, on the settlement of their multi-billion dollar claim was given more coverage. That involved making Ngāi Tahu a $10 million payment on the condition that they withdraw very damaging proceedings against the government from the courts. Ngāi Tahu had taken several cases against the Crown in recent years and eventually won most,[48] and with an election looming in October 1996 the government was entering damage control mode.

Negotiations abandoned in Te Hiku o te Ika

As part of its run up to the election, the government was determined to prove it could negotiate at least a couple of major settlements. By June 1996, however, it had had to abandon negotiations in Te Hiku o te Ika for the Muriwhenua claims because of challenges to the mandates of the two claim negotiators. In an election year the government could not afford the backlash from pushing through yet another settlement with negotiators with no mandate. Furthermore

Takahue is part of the Muriwhenua claim and any attempts to revisit it as part of a settlement would almost certainly have re-opened wounds in that community. The government had been extremely sensitive about being seen to buckle to Māori pressure of any kind, especially given the Prime Minister's hardline attitude. As a result the Minister of Conservation's progress in Whanganui was not repeated in Te Hiku o te Ika until 2008.[49]

---

1 MLR, June 1996, p. 1.
2 Waitangi Tribunal, 1996, *Taranaki Report: Kaupapa Tuatahi: Te Muru me te Raupatu* (Wai 143), Wellington, GP Publications, pp. 13, 310.
3 Waitangi Tribunal, *Taranaki Report*, p. 6.
4 Waitangi Tribunal, *Taranaki Report*, pp. 314–5.
5 Waitangi Tribunal, *Taranaki Report*, p. 1.
6 Waitangi Tribunal, *Taranaki Report*, p. 2.
7 Waitangi Tribunal, *Taranaki Report*, p. 3.
8 Waitangi Tribunal, *Taranaki Report*, p. 5. Both the Māori terms tino rangatiratanga and mana motuhake are frequently translated as 'Māori sovereignty', although this is a translation that the Tribunal has eschewed in its reports. The Chief Judge of the Māori Land Court and Chairman of the Waitangi Tribunal, Taihākurei Durie, has argued that the word 'sovereignty' is not a helpful word in respect of either the Crown or Māori. He considers 'state responsibility' and 'aboriginal autonomy' respectively to be more appropriate today. (Waitangi Day Address, 6 February 1996, reported in MLR, February 1996, p. 8). However, as a judicial body and a creature of statute, the Tribunal is appointed by and answerable to the Crown, which, since 1840, has vehemently denied and forbidden any acknowledgement of the existence of Māori sovereignty. Māori, however, have always held fast to the belief that they never ceded mana or Māori sovereignty to the British Crown and retain it to this day despite the extensive and overwhelming drive of the British Crown to eradicate all vestiges of its existence.
9 Waitangi Tribunal, *Taranaki Report*, p. 6.
10 Waitangi Tribunal, *Taranaki Report*, pp. 6, 7–8.
11 Waitangi Tribunal, *Taranaki Report*, p. 9.
12 Waitangi Tribunal, *Taranaki Report*, pp. 10, 12, 13.
13 Waitangi Tribunal, *Taranaki Report*, pp. 13, 14.
14 Waitangi Tribunal, *Taranaki Report*, p. 307.
15 Waitangi Tribunal, *Taranaki Report*, pp. 308, 309, 310, 311.
16 Waitangi Tribunal, *Taranaki Report*, p. 312.
17 D V Williams, 2005, 'Myths, National Origins, Common Law and the Waitangi Tribunal', *Murdoch University Electronic Journal of Law*, vol. 11 no. 4, http://www.murdoch.edu.au/elaw/issues/v11n4/williams114nf.html, para 21; Giselle Byrnes, 2004, *The Waitangi Tribunal and New Zealand History*, Melbourne, Oxford University Press, p. 150.
18 Waitangi Tribunal, *Taranaki Report*, pp. 314–5.
19 Minister of Māori Affairs, 1996, 'Tribunal Interim Report on Taranaki Claims Welcomed', 14 June 1996, http://www.beehive.govt.nz/release/tribunal+interim +report+taranaki+claims+welcomed

20 See for example Minister of Treaty Negotiations Doug Graham's statement that it was not the intention of the government that Māori should agree with the parameters set by government (Graham, *Trick or Treaty*, p. 59).

21 Jobs Research Trust, 1995, 'Diary', *The Jobs Letter* no. 25, http://www.jobsletter. org.nz/jbl02501.htm; Audrey Young, 1995, 'Bolger Adamant on Maori Claims: Sovereignty Issue a Distraction Away From Treaty Discussions says PM', *New Zealand Herald*, 19 September 1995, p. 1.

22 Such as Sir Kenneth Keith, 1995, 'The Roles of the Tribunal, the Courts and the Legislature' in Geoff McLay (ed.), 1995, *Treaty Settlements: The Unfinished Business*, Wellington, New Zealand Institute of Advanced Legal Studies and Victoria University of Wellington Law Review, p. 47: 'In the present world, ... no state is fully sovereign in its external relations and ... no politician or government or parliament has real internal sovereignty.' See also Palmer, 'Where to from Here?', p. 153: 'Once upon a time, we thought the New Zealand Government was sovereign. We hardly think that now.'

23 Shenagh Gleeson, 1995, 'Backing for PM on Sovereignty', *New Zealand Herald*, 15 May 1995, p. 7; Hone Harawira, 'Te Reo o te Kawariki', *Northland Age*, 18 May 1995, p. 3.

24 Gleeson, 1995, 'Backing For PM On Sovereignty', p. 7; Young, 1995, 'Bolger Adamant On Maori Claims', p. 1; Gifford, *Nga Korero o te Wa*, vol. 8 no. 6, 10 June 1995, pp. 7–8; Gifford, *Nga Korero o te Wa*, vol. 8 no. 10, 7 October 1995, p. 8.

25 MLR, December 1995–January 1996, p. 12.

26 Durie, *Te Mana, Te Kāwanatanga*, p. 235.

27 Hone Harawira, 'Te Reo o te Kawariki', *Northland Age*, 21 September 1995, p. 3.

28 Durie, *Te Mana, Te Kāwanatanga*, p. 235.

29 Walker, *Ka Whawhai Tonu Matou*, pp. 291–3; Hone Harawira, 'Te Reo o te Kawariki', *Northland Age*, 23 March 1995, p. 3. In this article, Harawira poses 47 questions on leadership and mandate, focusing on the Sealord negotiators, and then provides a list of eight requirements of Māori leadership.

30 See, for example, statements of three of the Sealord negotiators, Whatarangi Winiata, Robert Mahuta and Tipene O'Regan discussing leadership and endorsing these qualities – and adding several of their own (Diamond, *A Fire in Your Belly*, pp. 36, 63–8, 138). The Māori word for a tribal leader, rangatira, has been analysed as being made up of ranga, 'a shoal of fish' related to the word raranga, 'to weave' and tira, 'a group of people'. Under this analysis a rangatira is defined as a person who is able to weave the people together, like a shoal of fish, so that they all move in the same direction. Bishop Manu Bennett (quoted by Whatarangi Winiata) explains this as 'te mahi a te rangatira he whakatira i te iwi' (the work of the rangatira is binding the iwi). He adds two further qualities: 'te kai a te rangatira he kōrero' (talk is the food of chiefs), and 'te tohu o te rangatira he manaaki' (the sign of a rangatira is being able to look after others) (p. 67).

31 Sealord negotiator, Graham Latimer, is on record condoning and promoting these attributes in a leader (Noel Harrison, 2002, *Graham Latimer*, Wellington, Huia Publishers, p. 98; Jackson, 'What do Maori Want?', p. 20).

32 Harrison, *Graham Latimer*, pp. 98, 183–4.

33 Quoted in Stone, 'Reflections: A House Divided Against Itself', p. 84.

34 See also the discussion in Chapter 2, 'Attempts to repeat Waikato-Tainui in Te Hiku o te Ika create uproar'.

35 1996, 'Popular Guest', *Mana* no. 11, Summer 1996, p. 6.

36 1995, 'Support Rolls in for Takahue Rebuilding', *Northland Age*, 26 September 1995, p. 1.

37 1995, 'This is for Takahue – Maori and Pakeha', *Northland Age*, 4 April 1995, p. 1.

38 MLR, September 1995, p. 8.

39 Hone Harawira, 'Te Reo o te Kawariki', *Northland Age*, 28 September 1995, p. 3; Adam Gifford, 1995, 'Fires at Takahue: The Corruption of the Occupation Strategy' originally published to NATIVE-L, a now-defunct mailing list; republished at http://groups.yahoo.com/group/worlds-indigenous-people/message/8053, accessed 2010.

40 1995, 'Support Rolls in for Takahue Rebuilding', *Northland Age*, 26 September 1995, p. 1.; Gifford, *Nga Korero o te Wa*, vol. 9 no. 3, 23 March 1996, p. 6.

41 Gifford, *Nga Korero o te Wa*, vol. 9 no. 1, 27 January 1996, p. 6.

42 1996, 'Two singled out for suspended sentences', *Northland Age*, 11 April 1996, p. 3.

43 1995, 'From Cries of Traitor to Applause', *Northland Age*, 12 October 1995, p. 1; 1998, 'East Coast Youth "Abused by Police"', *Northland Age*, 22 January 1998, p. 1; 1998, 'Provocation and Harrassment', *Northland Age*, 29 January 1998, p. 2; 1998, 'The Audacity of It', *Northland Age*, 3 February 1998, p. 2; Letter from Karikari Trust to Hon. Richard Prebble, 19 March 1998. The police officer had numerous official complaints laid against him by members of the local Māori community. He finally resigned from the New Zealand Police early in 1999 (1999, 'Gary Baty's Leaving – But He's Staying', *Northland Age*, 26 January 1999, p. 3).

44 Kerry Stewart, 1995, 'Tension Remains High On Waahi Tapu Site', *New Zealand Herald*, Auckland, 23 February 1995, p. 9.

45 Margaret Mutu, 1995, *Report to the Minister of Māori Affairs on the New Zealand Conservation Authority*, Wellington, New Zealand Conservation Authority.

46 Mutu, *Report on the New Zealand Conservation Authority*, p. 3. The Director-General, Bill Mansfield, finally quit the Department of Conservation in May 1997 (Hunt, Graeme, 'Weight of Evidence', *New Zealand Listener* vol. 198 no. 3390, April 30 – May 6 2005, http://www.listener.co.nz/issue/3390/features/3907/weight_of_evidence.html;jsessionid=DCC5CCC0F1FDF49A223DF7D72A55A1A1).

47 Mutu, *Report on the New Zealand Conservation Authority*, pp. 6–9, 10.

48 MLR, March 1995, p. 1; MLR, September 1995, p. 3; MLR, October 1995, p. 6; MLR, March 1996, p. 2; MLR, May 1996 pp. 5, 7; MLR, October 1996, p. 7; MLR, September 1996, p. 8.

49 See chapter 15. Ngāti Kahu signed an Agreement in Principle with the Crown in 2008 which set out the agreement to establish a statutory board to take over the management of all lands currently administered by the Department of Conservation. The board would be chaired by Ngāti Kahu and conduct all its business in accordance with the tikanga of Ngāti Kahu.

CHAPTER 4:

1996–97

Māori success in the first MMP election ...
1996 was a year of major and historical changes for Māori on the political scene. The Mixed Member Proportional Representation electoral system was used in New Zealand for the first time in the October general elections and delivered fifteen members of Parliament claiming Māori descent out of a total of 120.[1] It more than doubled the number of Māori that had ever been in the house. However this was still proportionally less than the 15 percent of the population that were Māori.

The reaction from Māori was one of unrestrained delight and outpourings of hope for a better future. But there was little comment in the mainstream media, although one of the more perceptive commentators noted that it was a 'major Māori political assertion which left this supposed colonised community holding the balance of power, something which had remained beyond their grasp since the mid-1850s despite both armed and passive resistance. ... Now there are 15 rather than the traditional four Māori MPs ... [and] they are spread across all parties in Parliament. This represents a shift of revolutionary proportions.'[2]

... Encourages racist backlash
Māori success in the polls further exposed the fear of some of the non-Māori population of Māori having any say in

the affairs of the country. Public attacks on Māori increased significantly in frequency and vehemence, fuelled by an often hostile, unsympathetic and uninformed mainstream (non-Māori) news media. Māori were not unmoved by the attacks and in March a prized yachting trophy, the America's Cup, was badly damaged when a young Māori protestor attacked it.[3] In attacking a symbol of colonisation, he was highlighting the ongoing injustices borne by Māori, including increasing Māori poverty and deprivation[4] which the Waitangi Tribunal has highlighted in many of its reports. In June 1997 the reality of Māori poverty was brought starkly into focus when three Māori children were killed in fire which destroyed their home in a remote Māori settlement. Their home was a temporary shelter and the fire was caused by a candle used for lighting.[5]

The elections resulted in all five Māori electorate seats being taken by the New Zealand First Party. This was a major swing away from the Labour Party, which Māori had supported for over sixty years. MPs in the Māori seats are the only ones who formally represent Māori in Parliament. The only other Māori to gain an electorate seat was the New Zealand First Party leader and later Deputy Prime Minister and Treasurer, Winston Peters. His was a general electorate seat and constituents in general electorates are overwhelmingly Pākehā. So Peters was representing a Pākehā electorate in Parliament, rather than a Māori electorate. The remaining nine MPs of Māori descent all gained list seats, seats won by parties on the party vote rather than the electorate vote. These MPs represented their parties in Parliament, rather than Māori.

No party received a clear majority. With National and Labour holding the great majority of seats between them, it fell to the third-rating New Zealand First Party to determine which party it would enter a coalition with to form a government. Māori were strongly in favour of a coalition with Labour, for although they had deserted that party during the elections, it was still far preferred over the conservative National Party, the Māori policies of which had caused so much upheaval in recent times. Given that six of the seventeen New Zealand First MPs, including the leader, were Māori, there was some confidence that the Māori wish would prevail.

In the event, Māori were stunned when New Zealand First chose to form a coalition government with the National Party.[6] However the coalition agreement appeared to address at least some major Māori concerns with National Party policies, and in particular included an undertaking to abandon the loathed fiscal envelope policy for settling Māori land claims.[7] As such there was no angry outburst, but rather a philosophical wait and see reaction. After all, there were now five Māori electorate representatives on the government benches, with an unprecedented three Māori in cabinet, one of them the Deputy Prime Minister and Treasurer. Furthermore the Māori cabinet members included a Māori Minister of Māori Affairs, who would be much more inclined to dedicate himself to making that portfolio work for Māori rather than against them as had been the case with the previous minister.

Māori MPs as fodder for racism in the media and the House

Once the government was announced, and new members started making their maiden speeches, the mainstream news media embarked on a campaign of discrediting each member of the house who was Māori, both new and old. They were baying for Māori blood and every whiff of it sent them into a frenzy. For twelve of the fifteen Māori MPs it was their first time in the House, and many of them fell easy prey to the hypercritical and strongly Eurocentric press gallery. It also ensured that they were diverted from learning and carrying out their jobs as MPs.

It started with the very experienced leader of New Zealand First, Winston Peters, soon after the elections in October 1996, for a disturbance in a nightclub.[8] In November, it was the deputy leader, Tau Henare, for speaking out of turn during the coalition negotiations.[9] From January to July 1997 it was Tuku Morgan for his role in the establishment of a new and struggling Māori television station.[10] In February, Winston Peters again, this time for bumping into another MP a little harder than it may be considered necessary,[11] Tau Henare for wearing wrap-around sun glasses in public and Donna Awatere for unpaid parking fines from several years ago.[12] In March, it was Tuariki Delamere for problems with his children.[13] Tariana Turia came in for a sustained blasting for daring to articulate Māori aspirations of tino rangatiratanga and self-determination in her maiden speech and referring to non-Māori as tauiwi[14], or foreigners.[15] The backgrounds of both Alamein Koopu and Ron Marks were too humble and Dover Samuels had problems with his people at home.[16] In May, it was Tutekawa Wyllie for not declaring $1,350 in election expenditure (while others under investigation were not named).[17] By breaking an unwritten rule between Māori MPs about not publicly attacking each other, Sandra Lee managed to attract prominent media coverage, which only served to display her own lack of understanding of Māori protocol and politics.[18] By mid-1997, the only Māori MP to be spared public ridicule by the media was the only Māori in the National Party caucus, Georgina te Heuheu. A lawyer by training, te Heuheu was a member of the Waitangi Tribunal until she entered Parliament and, presumably, posed no perceived threat to the Pākehā hegemony in Parliament that the media were so desperate to preserve. That hegemony is maintained through institutionalised racism which had always ensured that Māori were totally marginalised and largely irrelevant in Parliament.[19]

Attacks on the pilot Aotearoa Television Network and Tuku Morgan

The racist nature of the media attacks on Māori MPs after the 1996 general election descended to the ridiculous with one particular MP, Tukuroirangi Morgan, a New Zealand First MP and himself a journalist, steadfastly refused to compromise the Māori right to be Māori both in and outside Parliament. His perceived arrogance towards the Pākehā domination of the House and the country turned his ex-colleagues into a virtual lynch mob against him. They identified his past role in a new and struggling Māori television station, Aotearoa Television Network, and, with the backing of the Labour Party and particularly its leader, Helen Clark, successfully hounded the station out of existence.[20] For weeks the media created headlines out of the fact that Morgan had paid $89 for an item of underwear while working for the station.[21] The government asked the Serious Fraud Office to investigate and the media frenzy finally fell silent when they returned a decision in July 1997 that Morgan had done nothing illegal.[22] In May he auctioned the item of underwear off to help raise money to assist a young cancer sufferer.

The setting-up of a Māori television station had come about as the result of a hard-fought battle between Māori and the Crown to force the Crown to protect the Māori language. It started in 1984 when Professor Whatarangi Winiata led the New Zealand Māori Council challenge against the broadcasting authorities by setting up Aotearoa Broadcasting System (ABS) to apply for a warrant to run the new third television channel.[23] The parlous record of state broadcasters in respect of the Māori language contributed to what both the High Court and the Privy Council were later to describe as the perilous state of the Māori language.[24] Māori had determined that only initiatives driven and controlled by Māori were likely to revitalise the language, particularly in broadcasting. The ABS application was unsuccessful, having been undermined by the state broadcaster, the Broadcasting Corporation of New Zealand,[25] but a 1986 Waitangi Tribunal report found that the Māori language is a taonga and that the Crown had breached the Treaty by not protecting it.[26] One of the Tribunal's recommendations was that broadcasting policy should recognise that the Treaty obliges the Crown to recognise and protect the Māori language. This was subsequently endorsed by the High Court and the Privy Council.[27] Crown reluctance to facilitate Māori use of television to promote Māori language resulted in litigation being pursued aggressively.[28] By May 1997, the fourteenth legal action relating to broadcasting had been filed, highlighting Māori exasperation with the Crown in this area.[29]

The Privy Council ruling meant that the Crown had a legal obligation to fund Māori into television broadcasting.[30] The matter should have been very straightforward but, as one of Aotearoa Television's managers put it, the government had 'paid lip service to its supposed commitment to Māori television and then simply walked away.'[31] Government funding provided for the pilot Aotearoa Television was grossly inadequate,[32] there were neither time nor resources to develop a policy,[33] and even though the network produced far more than the government contracted them for and its programmes were high quality,[34] the funding was eventually withdrawn, causing the station to fail.[35]

The vehement attacks on Aotearoa Television in the media and in the House, which contributed directly to its downfall, drew accusations that this was simply Māori-bashing. It appeared to have more to do with a Pākehā backlash against increasing Māori success in the Waitangi Tribunal and the courts, and emerging Māori strength in Parliament, than with the quality of Aotearoa Television's programmes.[36] Some saw it as Labour retaliating against Māori for deserting them in the Māori seats, and the Māori leaders of New Zealand First for their decision to go with National rather than Labour into government.[37] The vehemence and sheer determination behind the attacks highlighted for Māori how far Pākehā were prepared to go to keep Māori under their control and subject to their racist whim. Māori MPs were an open and easy target for the racism. They had dared to enter the strongly Eurocentric forum of the New Zealand Parliament and such a visible Māori presence was not at all welcome. But it was Tuku Morgan who took the brunt of that backlash because, unlike most others, he stood up to the racist bullying and refused to cower under the onslaught.

And what of the media coverage of scandals in high places in the Pākehā community?

By comparison, events such as the jailing of the Auditor-General Jeff Chapman for fraud;[38] District Court judge, Martin Beattie, being charged with fraud[39] while a more junior judge in the same court, Robert Hesketh, who accepted Beattie's advice, pleaded guilty to the same offence;[40] a third judge, Ross Malcolm Elliott, being charged with child molestation;[41] a multi-million dollar bungle by a government department trying unsuccessfully to eradicate a moth threatening ornamental trees in a wealthy Auckland suburb;[42] the dismissal of Charles Sturt as the head of the Serious Fraud Office;[43] the resignation of Bill Mansfield as the Director-General of Conservation two years after the viewing platform at Cave Creek collapsed claiming fourteen lives;[44] and an MP spending NZ$29,000 on taxi fares[45] were all relegated to the inner pages of the major daily newspapers while Māori members of Parliament were attacked on the front pages. Television and radio were little better.

Some victories in the courts and the Waitangi Tribunal

Yet while the news media was openly antagonistic toward Māori, the Waitangi Tribunal and the courts continued to deliver decisions and findings in support of them. In December 1996 in the long-running dispute over the allocation of fishing quota to Māori as a result of the fisheries 'settlement', the Privy

Council ruled that the courts could not decide on matters of Māori social structure and overturned a Court of Appeal decision which had declared recently formed urban Māori corporate bodies to have the same status as traditional iwi.[46] In February 1997, the District Court upheld the customary rights of Māori to fish their ancestral fishing grounds in rivers without having to obtain a licence to do so.[47] In March, the long-awaited report on the Muriwhenua land claims was released by the Waitangi Tribunal. It signalled a whole new approach to the consideration of land transactions between Māori and Pākehā in the nineteenth century and had major implications for land claims throughout the rest of the country.

The *Muriwhenua Land Report* breaks new ground by considering Māori understandings of land transactions

The *Muriwhenua Land Report* of 1997 found that through a myriad of dishonourable and illegal acts, the Crown had deprived Māori of the five iwi of Te Hiku o te Ika of nearly all their lands before 1865. The report was the first to consider the Māori interpretation of early land transactions between Māori and English missionaries and Crown agents. The Crown had always assumed and argued vehemently before the Tribunal that the transactions were English-custom land sales which extinguished the Māori title to them. The claimants argued equally vehemently that the notion of 'land sale' did not exist in Māori culture at the time and that the transactions were Māori-custom tuku whenua, which gave usufructuary but not proprietary rights to the land. The weight of evidence produced by both parties strongly favoured the claimants and the Tribunal found accordingly, concluding that Māori title to large portions of their lands had never been extinguished.[48]

However, the Tribunal went further and examined the social and economic circumstances of the five iwi which resulted from this landlessness. They reported that Māori of the region were reduced to 'penury, powerlessness and eventually state dependence'[49] and that 'the Maori people in Muriwhenua became, and still are, a people at risk.'[50] It also said in respect of the transactions '[f]iduciary responsibilities and Maori understandings were ignored in favour of a policy of total extinguishment of native title ... Maori became confined to the least fertile or the most remote parts of the Muriwhenua territory. They became excluded from a stake in the economic order for which they had bargained and for which, in terms of their customs, they had given generously.'[51]

The Tribunal concluded that there had been clear breaches by the Crown of the principles of the Treaty, including those of protection, honourable conduct, fair process and recognition, and that 'The people were marginalised on marginal lands, insufficient for traditional subsistence and inadequate for agrarian economy. The social and economic consequences for the Muriwhenua [iwi] have been profound, with burgeoning impacts in terms of physical deprivation, poverty, social dislocation as families dismembered in search of work elsewhere, and loss of status during long years of petition and protest when Muriwhenua leaders were made as supplicants to Government bureaucrats.'[52] The Tribunal reported that recommendations should be made as soon as possible to give the tribes relief and that, for the first time since they were empowered to do so in 1988, they would use their powers to order the return of Crown forests and State enterprise lands.[53]

A legal commentator considered the report to be 'extraordinary' for several reasons.[54] First, the Tribunal upheld the claimant argument that the government failed to properly purchase more than 300,000 acres of land in transactions up until 1865. Second, the Tribunal questioned the very notion of tenure, and the onus which that places on Māori to prove that Māori title has not been extinguished over Crown lands. And finally, the Tribunal signalled that it was ready for the first time to use its considerable power to make binding recommendations.

The government's only reaction, delivered by the Minister in Charge of Treaty of Waitangi Negotiations, was to strongly and angrily condemn the Tribunal for daring to say it might use its power to make binding recommendations[55] and to warn Muriwhenua Māori that they should put aside any hope of being delivered justice as a result of their successful claims.[56] That aside, its reaction was very similar to that for the 1996 *Taranaki Report*: muted, urging everyone to read the report but not subsidising its publication so that the $100 price tag would ensure that only a few people, and mainly the legal fraternity, would read it.

In the meantime the government was desperate to get Muriwhenua claimants to settle without getting orders from the Tribunal. This had less to do with the $100 million in compensation and approximately 50,000 acres of land which the Tribunal could order to be returned to the iwi, and more to do with the precedent it would set for other, much larger, Crown forests elsewhere, and particularly in the central North Island, where the compensation alone had been estimated at several billions of dollars. That would completely blow apart the ridiculously low $1 billion budgeted to settle all Māori claims.

Yet the government refused to provide either funding or resources to assist the iwi to prepare for entering into negotiations. Then in June the three children died in the fire in Te Hiku o te Ika and the conditions of poverty in the area were put on display for the whole country to see.[57] The government was severely criticised for allowing such conditions to continue to exist but remained unmoved. The iwi of Te Hiku o te Ika announced that they were returning to the Tribunal for binding recommendations and would be demanding that urgent steps be taken to alleviate the Māori poverty in the region.

A bright spot – Philip Tataurangi wins the Australian PGA Championship

On 17 November 1996, Ngāti Kahungunu's Phil Tataurangi won the Australian Professional Golfers' Association Championship in Sydney. He turned professional in 1993 and qualified for the United States PGA Tour. At twenty-three, he was the youngest player on the Tour in 1994. He has played on the USPGA Tour since 1997.[58]

---

1 1996, 'Maori Political Muscle – *at last*', *Mana* no. 14, Summer 1996–97, pp. 38–9.

2 Tom Brooking, 1996, 'The Year that Broke the Mould: MMP the Highlight of a Year of Triumph and Disappointment', *New Zealand Herald*, 31 December 1996, p. D2.

3 Harris, *Hīkoi*, p. 127; Suzanne McFadden, 1997, 'Chanting as Cup Smashed', *New Zealand Herald*, 15 March 1997, p. A1.

4 Roger Wakefield, 1997, 'Cup "Symbol of Everything Accused Hated"', *New Zealand Herald*, 15 March 1997, A3.

5 1997, 'Grief and Anger at Matauri Bay', *Northland Age*, 24 June 1997, p. 1; Gifford, *Nga Korero o te Wa*, vol. 10 no. 6, 28 June 1997, p. 4.

6 Gifford, *Nga Korero o te Wa*, vol. 9 no. 10, 26 October 1996, p. 5; Gifford, *Nga Korero o te Wa*, vol. 9 no. 11, 23 November 1996, pp. 5–6; Gifford, *Nga Korero o te Wa*, vol. 9 no. 12, 21 December 1996, pp. 5–6.

7 Gifford, *Nga Korero o te Wa*, vol. 9 no. 12, 21 December 1996, p. 5.

8 Audrey Young, 1996, 'PM "Grumpy" as Peters Skips Talks: Restaurant Incident "Not Responsible"', *New Zealand Herald*, 31 October 1996, p. A1.

9 1996, 'Henare Shoots from the Lip', *New Zealand Herald*, 19 November 1996, p. A12.

10 The *New Zealand Herald* published no fewer than fifty articles over this period attacking Morgan, and on several occasions as many as five articles appeared in a single edition of the newspaper. See, for example, 6 and 18 February 1997.

11 Twelve articles appeared in the *New Zealand Herald* between 7 and 26 March 1997.

12 Bernard Orsman, 1997, 'MP Relative Incurred Car Fines', *New Zealand Herald*, 20 February 1997, p. A3.

13 Tony Wall, 1997, 'Drug Trespass Notice Sent to Minister's Son', *New Zealand Herald*, 22 March 1997, p. A1.

14 'Tauiwi' is the word Māori use to describe non-Māori: those who arrived here long after Māori arrived.

15 Patricia Herbert, 1997, 'Maori "spoon-fed like imbeciles"', *New Zealand Herald*, 27 February 1997, p. A5.

16 Gifford, *Nga Korero o te Wa*, vol. 9 no. 12, 21 December 1996, p. 4; Gifford, *Nga Korero o te Wa*, vol. 10 no. 6, 28 June 1997, p. 6.

17 Gifford, *Nga Korero o te Wa*, vol. 10 no. 3, 27 March 1997, p. 5; Gifford, *Nga Korero o te Wa*, vol. 10 no. 5, p. 7.

18 Gifford, *Nga Korero o te Wa*, vol. 10 no. 2, p. 2; Gifford, *Nga Korero o te Wa*, vol. 10 no. 6, 28 June 1997, p. 6; Gifford, *Nga Korero o te Wa*, vol. 10 no. 7, 31 July 1997, p. 6; Gifford, *Nga Korero o te Wa*, vol. 10 no. 8, 30 August 1997, p. 5.

19 Walker, *Ka Whawhai Tonu Matou*, pp. 144–6.
20 Derek Burns, 1997, *Public Money, Private Lives: Aotearoa Television – the Inside Story*, Auckland, Reed, p. 9.
21 See footnote 10 above.
22 Derek Burns, 1997, 'The Serious Fraud Office Report', in Burns, *Public Money, Private Lives*, p. 235.
23 Durie, *Te Mana, Te Kāwanatanga*, p. 71; Andrew Robb, 1993, 'Going to the Top', *Mana* no. 2, April–May 1993, p. 58.
24 Durie, *Te Mana, Te Kāwanatanga*, p. 70.
25 Durie, *Te Mana, Te Kāwanatanga*, p. 71; Robb, 'Going to the Top', p. 58.
26 Waitangi Tribunal, *Report of the Waitangi Tribunal on the Te Reo Māori Claim*, p. 9.
27 MLR, January 1994, p. 5; Andrew Robb, 1995, 'No Need to Lose Heart', *Mana* no. 5, February–March 1995, pp. 51–2.
28 Durie, *Te Mana, Te Kāwanatanga*, p. 71; Robb, 'Going to the Top', *Mana* no. 2, April/May 1993, pp. 58–61.
29 Durie, *Te Mana, Te Kāwanatanga*, p. 74.
30 Burns, *Public Money, Private Lives*, p. 7.
31 Burns, *Public Money, Private Lives*, p. 11.
32 In the 1996/7 fiscal year, the government provided $8 million to set up and run Māori Television, which, apart from purchasing equipment and facilities, covered the commissioning or producing of nineteen hours of original programming a week. In the same year, Television New Zealand, the state broadcaster, received $4.6 million to produce just two hours and fifty minutes of Māori television programmes a week. If Māori Television had been funded at the same level it would have received $28.65 million for the year (Burns, *Public Money, Private Lives*, p. 8.)
33 Jackson, 'What do Maori Want?', p. 20; Debra Reweti, 2006, 'Māori and Broadcasting', in Malcolm Mulholland (ed.), *State of the Māori Nation: Twenty-first Century Issues in Aotearoa*, Auckland, Reed, p. 184.
34 Reweti, 'Māori and Broadcasting', p. 184.
35 Burns, *Public Money, Private Lives*, p. 7.
36 Durie, *Te Mana, Te Kāwanatanga*, p. 73.
37 Burns, *Public Money, Private Lives*, p. 9.
38 Warren Gamble, 1997(b), 'Chapman "guilty" on 10 Charges', *New Zealand Herald*, 1 March 1997, p. A3; 1997, 'Chapman Gets Six Months', *Evening Post*, 14 March 1997, p. 1; Brian Easton, 1997, 'Accounting for Difference: How Should we Judge Jeff Chapman?', *New Zealand Listener*, 3 May 1997, http://www.eastonbh.ac.nz/?p=31
39 'White Collar Crime', http://www.crime.co.nz/c-f-cat.aspx?cat=461
40 'White Collar Crime', http://www.crime.co.nz/c-f-cat.aspx?cat=461
41 Warren Gamble, 1997(c), 'Defendant in Child Sex Case is a Judge', *New Zealand Herald*, 8 March 1997, p. A3.
42 Edward Rooney, 1997, 'Chief Admits Mistakes in Battle to Kill Moths', *Sunday Star Times*, 12 January 1997, p. A4; Scion, 1998, 'Every Moth Matters – the Eradication of the White-spotted Tussock Moth', *Forest Health News* no. 72, March 1998, http://www.nzffa.org.nz/images/design/Pests/Tussock-moth/tussock-mothFHNews72.html
43 Rob Drent, 1997, 'Public View of SFO All Wrong, Say Staff', *Sunday Star Times*, 16 March 1997, p. 5.
44 Warren Gamble, 1997(a), 'Mansfield Denies Being Pushed Out', *New Zealand Herald*, 18 January 1997, p. A3; Graeme Hunt, 1996, *Scandal at Cave Creek: A shocking failure in public accountability*, Auckland, Waddington, in association with the *National Business Review*.
45 Rodney Hide, 1997, 'Another MP Bites the Dust as Taxi Meter Ticks Over', *National Business Review*, 11 April 1997, p. 26.
46 MLR, December 1996–January 1997, pp. 2–4.

47 MLR, February 1997, pp. 3–5.
48 Waitangi Tribunal, 1997, *Muriwhenua Land Report* (Wai 45), Wellington, GP Publications, p. 410, http://www.waitangi-tribunal.govt.nz/reports/
49 Waitangi Tribunal, *Muriwhenua Land Report*, p. 1.
50 Waitangi Tribunal, *Muriwhenua Land Report*, p. 8.
51 Waitangi Tribunal, *Muriwhenua Land Report*, p. 5.
52 Waitangi Tribunal, *Muriwhenua Land Report*, p. 404.
53 Waitangi Tribunal, *Muriwhenua Land Report*, p. 404.
54 MLR, March 1997, p. 6.
55 The Tribunal has been under threat to have its powers to make binding recommendations removed by successive governments since 1990 (Hamer, 'A Quarter-century of the Waitangi Tribunal', p. 7 and footnote 22 in particular for specific threats by Minister Doug Graham and then Minister Margaret Wilson).
56 Gifford, *Nga Korero o te Wa*, vol. 10 no. 3, 27 March 1997, p. 8.
57 1997, 'Grief and Anger at Mataturi Bay', *Northland Age*, 24 June 1997, p. 1; Gifford, *Nga Korero o te Wa*, vol. 10 no. 6, 28 June 1997, p. 4.
58 Phil Tataurangi's official website is http://www.philtataurangi.com/main.cfm?id=13

Dame Te Ātairangikaahu (Tainui) with Nelson Mandela. In the background by the door is Sir Hepi te Heuheu. (Mana/Tai Moana)

Tukuroirangi (Tuku) Morgan (at right) and whānau (from left), Kawariki, Reikura, Carolyn and Riria. (Mana)

*Taipā, Far North, part of the successful Ngāti Kahu and Muriwhenua Treaty of
Waitangi claims against the Crown. (Margaret Mutu)*

*Te Oneroa a Tōhē (Ninety Mile Beach) taken from Whangatauatia, Ahipara, part of
the successful Muriwhenua Treaty of Waitangi claims against the Crown. (Mana/
Siobhan Herbert)*

Dame Miraka Szaszy (Ngāti Kurī), one of the kuia who played a leading role in the Muriwhenua claims and fought to outlaw discrimination against indigenous peoples through the drafting of the United Nations' Declaration on the Rights of Indigenous Peoples. (Mana/ Sally Tagg)

Professor Pat Hohepa (Te Māhurehure, Ngāpuhi), who was instrumental in the establishment of the Waitangi Tribunal in 1975. (Gil Hanly)

Hon. Matiu Rata (Ngāti Kurī), Minister of Māori Affairs 1972–75. (Gil Hanly)

Tuaiwa (Eva) Rickard (Tainui Awhiro). (Gil Hanly)

Hon. Tau Henare (Ngāti Hine). (Mana)

*Chief Judge, then Justice Joe Williams (Ngāti Pūkenga), Chairman of the Waitangi Tribunal 1999–2008. (Jeremy Rose/*Scoop Review of Books*)*

Waihoroi Shortland (Ngāpuhi) plays Hairoka (Shylock) the Jewish moneylender in Te Tangata Whai Rawa o Wēniti. *(Mana/Kirsty Griffin)*

Sir Robert Mahuta (Tainui). (Mana)

Tariana Turia (Ngāti Apa/Wairiki, Ngā Rauru, Tūwharetoa) beside the Whanganui River. (Courtesy of the Māori Party)

Hīkoi of Hope – the march against poverty organised by the Anglican Church. (Courtesy of the St John's Theological College Library)

Selwyn Murupaenga (Ngāti Kurī), associate producer, and Don Selwyn (Ngāti Kurī, Te Aupōuri, Ngāti Kahu), executive producer/director of Te Tangata Whai Rawa o Wēniti, *the Maori-language version of* The Merchant of Venice. *(Mana/Ruth Kaupua)*

Metiria Turei (Rangitāne, Ngāti Kahungunu ki Wairarapa, Te Āti Haunui-a-Pāpārangi). (Courtesy of the Green Party)

Tapu Misa (Sāmoa), columnist for the New Zealand Herald. (Tapu Misa)

Whangarā, location of the film Whale Rider. (New Zealand Herald)

At the launching of Māori Television: (from left) Wayne Walden (Ngāti Kahu),
Chairperson of Māori Television, Dr Huirangi Waikerepuru (Ngāti Ruanui), who took
the Māori language claims to the Waitangi Tribunal, and Joe Hawke (Ngāti Whātua).
(Gil Hanly)

Paikea, the whale rider, on the meeting
house at Whangarā marae, Te Tairāwhiti.
(New Zealand Herald)

Māori Television exterior. (Courtesy of Māori TV)

Judge Caren Fox (Ngāti Porou), Deputy Chairperson of the Waitangi Tribunal, who reprimanded the Prime Minister for attacking a judge. (Mana)

Bic Runga. (Mana)

CHAPTER 5:

1997–98

Great sadness at the passing of leaders

Sir Hepi te Heuheu

The second half of 1997 was a time of great sadness for Māoridom as some of its finest leaders passed away. Sir Hepi te Heuheu of the central North Island Ngāti Tūwharetoa people was one of a rapidly dwindling number of traditional ariki, having been installed in the office after his father's death in 1944.[1] In 1956 he became chairman of the Tūwharetoa Trust Board, a position he held until his death.[2] He followed the family tradition of holding steadfastly to tino rangatiratanga, Māori autonomy and independence. In 1985 he led a delegation to the Prime Minister, David Lange, seeking changes to the state-owned enterprises legislation to protect Māori Treaty rights. The Waitangi Tribunal did likewise in 1986 at the beginning of the Muriwhenua claims hearings. It resulted in a new clause, which became section 9 of the Act: '[n]othing in this Act shall permit the Crown to act in a manner that is inconsistent with the principles of the Treaty of Waitangi.'[3] Later the New Zealand Māori Council was able to call on this section in the Court of Appeal in the famous Lands case, to prevent the sale of state-owned enterprise lands without protecting Māori claims to those lands.[4]

Although he was a conservative within the Pākehā political spectrum, Sir Hepi commanded great respect among Māori, having the mana and ability to draw everyone together. In

1989, in response to increasing calls from iwi to establish an autonomous national Māori organisation to represent their interests, he called iwi together from across the country to a hui at Taupō. With the Tainui leader, Dame Te Ātairangikaahu, and the head of the Rātana faith, Te Reo Hura, he then convened a subsequent hui that set up the National Māori Congress in 1990.[5] Initially, all major iwi affiliated to the Congress subscribed to its philosophy of whakakotahitanga (unification of the iwi), tino rangatiratanga (tribal sovereignty), and mana motuhake (discrete power, authority and control).[6] Over a thousand people attended each of its hui and there were several significant achievements.[7] However divisions between iwi started manifesting over the deliberately divisive fisheries settlement and then the Crown's carve up of railways lands. In the event, iwi were too impoverished to be able to provide the level of finance needed to sustain the Congress's work. Its last formal meeting was held in 1996 at Hopuhopu, where all Māori candidates for Parliament were scrutinised.[8]

It was in the last few years of his life, in January and then in September 1995, and then in April 1996, that Sir Hepi convened three national hui at Hīrangi to discuss government proposals to settle Treaty of Waitangi claims, the detested fiscal envelope policy. Once again, each was attended by well over a thousand people. In his opening address, Sir Hepi stated that Māori were no longer content to react to proposals unilaterally formulated by government, and that until the country had a constitution that allowed Māori to determine policies for Māori, there would be continuing disquiet and an ongoing sense of injustice.[9] It was at these hui that Māori self-determination and sovereignty were debated at length and a large number of proposals about how constitutional change could take place were considered. Despite his conservatism, Sir Hepi carried the uncompromising message from the hui to the government and withstood the Prime Minister's criticism and insults with calm dignity.[10] His funeral ceremonies in

August 1997 brought thousands of Māori from all parts of the country.[11] Non-Māori government representatives also attended.

Tuaiwa (Eva) Rickard

At the opposite end of the Pākehā political spectrum was Tuaiwa (Eva) Rickard, who passed away in December 1997. Eva had campaigned fearlessly against the confiscation of lands from Māori and led many public protests against different governments and their anti-Māori policies.[12] Her effectiveness was demonstrated with the return of her own hapū's lands at Raglan after a ten-year battle. During the Second World War, the New Zealand government destroyed Te Kopua, Eva's birthplace, to make way for a military airfield, and the Māori landowners were evicted.[13] After the war the land was not returned to its Māori owners, but instead was turned into a golf course. In 1978 Eva and nineteen others were arrested for trespassing on the Raglan golf course. Television images of her arrest were a defining moment in the struggle.[14] After the land was returned it became a focus for local job training and employment programmes, as well as a focus for the Māori sovereignty movement.[15] Eva was a strong supporter of Māori women and younger Māori and spent much time in her later years actively encouraging and mentoring a large number of potential leaders.[16]

Matiu Rata

Eva was also a forthright critic of Māori who sold out to the government on various issues, compromising the tino rangatiratanga not only of their own hapū and iwi, but also of other Māori. She reserved her harshest criticism for the Māori men who negotiated the national settlement that extinguished Māori fishing rights, the now infamous Sealord Deal.[17] The negotiators included the Minister of Māori Affairs from 1972 to 1975, Matiu Rata, who passed away tragically in July 1997 as a result of injuries sustained in a car accident. He had been responsible for introducing the legislation which set up the Waitangi Tribunal in 1975.[18] He and his advisor, Dr Patrick Hohepa, had sought to give effect to Māori self-determination, setting the Tribunal up as a 'people's forum' through which Māori could be listened to. It was to provide a restorative and cathartic affect.[19] Although the Tribunal was slow getting started, since 1982 it has been unsurpassed in its ability to ensure that Māori receive at least some measure of justice for their ill-treatment at the hands of successive governments since 1840.

Fisheries allocation has now been in the courts for five years

In his later years, Matiu Rata led the Muriwhenua claims of the five iwi of Te Hiku o te Ika to the Waitangi Tribunal. The claims resulted in the Sealord Deal.[20] Although this brought him into bitter conflict with his own and several other iwi he never lost hope that the deal would eventually bring benefits to all Māori.[21] Yet by 1998, the final settlement and distribution of the proceeds of the deal had been tied up in the courts for more than five years. Māori had little confidence in the courts being able to resolve the multiplicity of issues the deal had spawned, given that the judges were invariably non-Māori.[22] There was also mounting criticism about the amount of money being spent on litigation and the fact that lawyers, rather than Māori, were benefiting from the settlement.

For example, during the 1997–98 period the High Court was asked to determine the meaning of the word 'iwi'. Māori academics and other experts from around the country were brought in to give expert evidence. The dispute arose because of what is euphemistically called 'the urban migration', the massive dislocation of Māori from their traditional territories to the cities, especially following the Second World War, in the wake of the loss of their lands and economic bases.[23]

This inevitably led to dire poverty and the 'migration' was an attempt to escape it. Governments deliberately encouraged Māori to move to the cities during and after the War in order to provide factory workers and menial labourers in the cities, especially in Auckland and Wellington.[24] This, combined with the policies of assimilation vigorously pursued by successive governments since the 1840s,[25] had ensured that many Māori no longer actively participated in their traditional social structures. The proceeds of the Sealord deal were to be distributed to Māori, and the Treaty of Waitangi Fisheries Commission, tasked with allocating the settlement, had interpreted that to mean iwi, which can mean either a traditional tribal structure where descent from one particular ancestor determines membership, or people in general. The Commission had interpreted iwi to mean traditional tribal groupings.

Some urban non-traditional groupings filed court proceedings after a decision was made to allocate only to traditional iwi. In April 1996 the Court of Appeal ruled that urban Māori interests must be taken into account.[26] In January 1997 that decision was quashed by the Privy Council, which ruled that the Court of Appeal should not have defined the word 'iwi'. The matter of defining the word 'iwi' and determining whether urban Māori are iwi was referred back to the High Court.

Treaty land claims settlements – Whakatōhea fails, Ngāi Tahu reaches agreement

Negotiations to settle the Whakatōhea lands claims on the East Coast were conducted with somewhat indecent haste before the 1996 general elections, and fell through when the iwi later rejected it.[27] The much larger Ngāi Tahu land claims in turn reached agreement stage in September 1997, although opposition to the agreement slowed progress towards ratifying and finalising it.

The Ngāi Tahu negotiators agreed to settle the iwi's approximately $20 billion claims against the Crown for losses involving approximately 34.5 million acres of land – approximately 80 percent of the South Island[28] – for $170 million in cash plus the return of various parcels of land, several islands, lakebeds, greenstone deposits and statutory recognition of the iwi in conservation, food gathering and areas of cultural, historic and spiritual significance.[29] It is the longest-running claim against the Crown, with Ngāi Tahu having first lodged a petition in 1849. In announcing the agreement the iwi's chief negotiator, Sir Tipene O'Regan, noted that the offer could not deliver justice for their grievances, but rather 'we will no longer be a deeply disadvantaged people who have lost their land, their assets and culture.' A poll of registered iwi members showed strong support for the proposed settlement even though the largest hapū strongly opposed it.[30]

Customary fisheries negotiations fail

Settlement of the long-running customary fisheries disputes did not fare so well.[31] For three years, negotiators appointed by Māori had been trying to reach agreement with the government on regulations for Māori customary fishing. In December the negotiators resigned, citing frustration at the government's refusal to abide by its own legislation in drawing up the regulations and obstructive tactics being used by officials. The Minister of Fisheries, John Luxton, seized the opportunity to attack Māori customary fishing rights and attempted to bring in draconian regulations essentially curtailing all Māori fishing rights.[32] He was supported in his attack by several right-wing amateur fishing enthusiasts. Individual Māori were targeted by the Ministry of Fisheries wanting to make examples of Māori customary fishermen.[33]

Māori reaction was predictably swift and angry. The Minister was warned that any attempt to curtail Māori customary fishing rights would simply lead to widespread civil disobedience by Māori. They were already very angry that the Sealord Deal had removed their commercial fishing rights, and that the same deal had reduced the remaining non-commercial rights to regulations. Any further reduction in their rights simply would not be tolerated.[34]

For the first time, the presence of three Māori in cabinet had a significant effect on the outcome. As a result the Minister of Fisheries was unable to introduce his preferred regulations and was restricted to only minor amendments to current legislation. A national hui of representatives of all tribes was convened. It clearly instructed the Minister that Māori would determine what Māori customary fishing regulations would be, and any regulations which did not have Māori support would not be accepted. The Prime Minister instructed the Minister to sort the mess out properly and bring in regulations which had Māori support.[35]

Refusing to accept the position the Māori negotiators had developed after their own extensive consultation with iwi, the Minister then embarked on his own consultation round with Māori throughout the country. The overwhelming response in hui was to simply confirm what the Māori negotiators had already told him. However, he also consulted widely with non-Māori in an attempt to bring pressure on Māori to give up their rights. Although he was instructed to complete the job by April 1998, the results of the consultation round had still not been announced by late June.

In the meantime the media had carried various reports of coastal hapū and iwi, around the North Island in particular, imposing their own traditional management methods over their sea territories by banning commercial fishing until the stocks were sufficiently recovered. Every ban had been imposed because of severe depletion of the hapū or iwi's traditional fish stocks. Compliance with the bans was difficult to monitor and it is not known how effective they were. Apart from the Minister of Fisheries saying that these rāhui had no legal standing (because they were not mentioned in any legislation) but conceding that they are not illegal, there was remarkably little public opposition to them. Some iwi reported considerable support, particularly amongst local communities. Various letters to editors praised Māori for taking charge where government ministers, under pressure from the fishing industry, had been unable to restrict commercial fishing activities and hence prevent continued depletion.

1 Alex Frame, 2007, 'Te Heuheu Tukino VII 1919–1997', in *Dictionary of New Zealand Biography*, http://www.dnzb.govt.nz/
2 Frame, 'Te Heuheu Tukino VII 1919–1997'.
3 1997, 'He Maimai Aroha: Hepi te Heuheu ', *Mana* no. 18, October–November 1997, p. 6.
4 The famous Lands case (*New Zealand Maori Council v Attorney-General* [1987] 1 NZLR 641). See footnote 20 of chapter 2.
5 Frame, 'Te Heuheu Tukino VII 1919–1997'.
6 Walker, *Ka Whawhai Tonu Matou*, p. 294.
7 See references throughout Durie, *Te Mana, Te Kāwanatanga* to the work of the Congress in respect of broadcasting, fisheries, forests, government employment policies, iwi governance (and the Rūnanga-a-Iwi Bill), a Māori body politic, Māori candidates for Parliament and water rights (see pp. 273–4 of Index).
8 Durie, *Te Mana, Te Kāwanatanga*, pp. 102–3.
9 Frame, 'Te Heuheu Tukino VII 1919–1997'.
10 See chapter 2.
11 Frame, 'Te Heuheu Tukino VII 1919–1997'; 1997, 'He Maimai Aroha', *Mana* no. 18, October-November 1997, p. 6.
12 1995, 'Eva Rickard: Still has a Job to do', *Mana* no. 9, Winter 1995, pp. 24–5.
13 New Zealand History online, 2008(a), 'Eva Rickard', http://www.nzhistory.net.nz/people/eva-rickard; 1995, 'Eva Rickard: Still has a job to do', pp. 24–5.
14 New Zealand History online, 'Eva Rickard'.
15 Wikipedia contributors, 'Eva Rickard', http://en.wikipedia.org/wiki/Eva_Rickard accessed 2009.
16 Wikipedia contributors, 'Eva Rickard'.
17 See chapter 2.
18 New Zealand History online, 2008(b), 'Matiu Rata', http://www.nzhistory.net.nz/people/matiu-rata
19 E T Durie, 2010, 'Treaty Claims and Self-Determination', Manu-Ao lecture series, 3 March 2010, http://www.manu-ao.ac.nz/
20 Mutu, 'Recovering Fagin's Ill-gotten Gains', pp. 192–5.
21 Durie, *Te Mana, Te Kāwanatanga*, p. 167.
22 Durie, *Te Mana, Te Kāwanatanga*, p. 171.
23 Mason Durie, 2005, *Ngā Tai Matatū*, Melbourne, Oxford University Press, pp. 20–4.
24 Walker, *Ka Whawhai Tonu Matou*, pp. 197–9; Durie, *Ngā Tai Matatū*, p. 21.
25 Walker, *Ka Whawhai Tonu Matou*, pp. 146–8, 151–2, 172; Durie, *Te Mana, Te Kāwanatanga*, pp. 54–5; Durie, *Ngā Tai Matatū*, pp. 191–4.
26 MLR, May 1996, pp. 1, 5–7; Durie, *Te Mana, Te Kāwanatanga*, pp. 165–6.

27 Walker, *Ka Whawhai Tonu Matou*, pp. 308–9; Durie, *Te Mana, Te Kāwanatanga*, pp.198–9.

28 Although Ngāi Tahu lost 34.5 million acres, they claimed only 3.4 million acres or one tenth of what was lost because that was what they had been promised as reserves (Te Rūnanga o Ngāi Tahu, 2009, 'About Ngāi Tahu – The Claim History', http://www.ngaitahu.iwi.nz/About-Ngai-Tahu/Settlement/Claim-History.php).

29 Te Rūnanga o Ngāi Tahu, 2009, 'About Ngāi Tahu – The Settlement', http://www.ngaitahu.iwi.nz/About-Ngai-Tahu/Settlement/Claim-History.php; MLR, October 1997, pp. 6–8; MLR, November 1997, pp. 8–10; MLR, December 1997–January 1998, pp. 11–12; Durie, *Te Mana, Te Kāwanatanga*, pp. 200–3; Walker, *Ka Whawhai Tonu Matou*, pp. 307–8.

30 Durie, *Te Mana, Te Kāwanatanga*, p. 203.

31 Margaret Mutu, 1998, 'Māori Customary Fishing Rights', in L Pihama and C W Smith (eds), *Economics, Politics, and Colonisation Volume Three: Fisheries and Commodifying Iwi*, Auckland, International Research Institute for Māori and Indigenous Education University of Auckland, pp. 58–64; Durie, *Te Mana, Te Kāwanatanga*, p. 62.

32 Mutu, 'Māori Customary Fishing Rights', p. 64.

33 Durie, *Ngā Tai Matatū*, p. 129. See for example MLR, November 1997, pp. 4–5; MLR, April 1998, p. 2.

34 Mutu, 'Māori Customary Fishing Rights', p. 64.

35 Mutu, 'Māori Customary Fishing Rights', p. 64.

CHAPTER 6:

1998–99

Collapse of National-New Zealand First coalition weakens Māori input into government

Politically the second half of 1998 was very disappointing for Māori. In 1996 New Zealand First had captured all five Māori seats in Parliament and formed a coalition government with the National Party. Cabinet included three Māori ministers, all from New Zealand First, with the leader of New Zealand First, Winston Peters, as Deputy Prime Minister. However disputes within the New Zealand First leadership severely weakened their position in government. National had survived a leadership coup earlier in 1998, but the replacement of Prime Minister Jim Bolger with Jenny Shipley signalled much less commitment to the coalition. In August Shipley sacked Peters from Cabinet and the coalition dissolved.[1] Peters had sacked the deputy leader of New Zealand First, Tau Henare, in July but Henare continued as the Minister of Māori Affairs after the collapse of the coalition. The sacking led fairly rapidly to a split within the New Zealand First caucus. Once the coalition government dissolved leaving National as a minority government, the split in New Zealand First was formalised. It lost seven of its MPs, including four of the five Māori seat MPs. Two of the Māori MPs remained in cabinet initially as independents. By October Tau Henare had set up a new Mauri Pacific Party, with five of the defecting New Zealand First MPs.[2]

National's previous two Ministers of Māori Affairs had had little understanding of Māori, with the most recent, John Luxton, being openly antagonistic toward Māori, and derisive and dismissive of Māori aspirations for their own future. Tau Henare was a welcome change, not only because he is Māori, but also because he understood and empathised with the constant struggle Māori have had against their European colonisers and oppressors. As a result he was not afraid to point out the anomalies which permeate New Zealand society in its unequal treatment of Māori and Pākehā, and the racism against Māori which is deeply embedded in the structures of almost all government and public institutions throughout the country.[3] He fought with only moderate success to capture a disproportionately small part of the 1999 budget for Māori but ensured that funding was allocated to areas of immediate practical concern to Māori, such as the building and restoration of their marae, the restoration and enhancement of the Māori language, and the development of Māori education, housing and health. He has also publicly supported debate taking place on the issue of constitutional change where the National Party, and in particular its Minister of Treaty of Waitangi Negotiations, Doug Graham,[4] had dismissed any consideration of the issue.

Henare's outspoken support of Māoridom continued to bring down the wrath of Parliament and the Pākehā media on him. Headlines flashed his latest choice of colourful words used to illustrate a point, attacking him on his use of the English language rather than considering the issue he was raising.[5] The constant attack and denigration had begun to take its toll and undermine Māori confidence in him. With a general election due in October 1999 he and his fledgling party faced an uphill battle to remain in Parliament, let alone in government.

The Hīkoi of Hope – a huge protest march against poverty
While Māori were losing ground on the government benches, the extent of Māori poverty throughout the country continued to grow. In September the Anglican Church, with support from other churches, trade unions and Māori, organised a protest march named the Hīkoi of Hope.[6] Two groups set out simultaneously from the very far north and the very far south of the country. During the month-long march over 38,000 people joined the march, focusing the nation's attention on the massive cuts successive governments had made to social service agencies and tertiary student funding and the fact that New Zealand had the fastest-growing gap between rich and poor of any OECD country.[7] Burgeoning student debt was then well over four billion dollars,[8] with the result that Māori enrolment in universities had been reducing over the past two years after having slowly but steadily increased over the past decade.[9]

The two groups on the march converged on Parliament grounds on 1 October, with five thousand marchers confronting parliamentarians. Attempts by some government ministers to deny the existence of poverty in New Zealand brought swift and angry reactions during the march. The government had published its report *Progress Towards Closing the Social and Economic Gaps Between Māori and non-Māori*[10] just three months earlier in July. That report had confirmed the existence of increasing gaps between Māori and non-Māori in terms of every social and economic indicator. The Hīkoi of Hope delivered a strong message to the government that the key to addressing Māori poverty lay in changing the constitution so that Māori can have a fair share of power as a full partner under the Treaty of Waitangi.[11] While the Prime Minister attempted to dismiss the notion, many commentators, both Māori and non-Māori, publicly encouraged debate on the issue. One of the leaders of the Hīkoi and long-time Māori advocate,

Professor Whatarangi Winiata, warned that unless changes were made some Māori would be too impatient to wait any longer and they would be prepared to die for the cause.[12]

Politicians bicker after floods ravage impoverished Māori communities

Then, in January 1999, three mainly Māori communities in the Far North that were amongst some of the most impoverished and neglected communities in the country watched helplessly as torrential rain brought down surrounding hillsides and tonnes of mud, rock and trees swept away their homes.[13] For decades Māori had complained of the lack of services they receive from local government not only in the form of roads, water and power supply, but also protection against natural disasters.[14] As usual with any such disasters, it was the local marae which came to the rescue of the homeless and functioned as the disaster headquarters. As local Māori were trying to move quickly to clean up and reconstruct the community, local and central government bickered over who should do what, whether or not the army should be sent in to help and who was going to pay. Politicians visited and left behind promises which were at best partially fulfilled. Help for the communities in the form of food, clothing and household goods flooded in from around the country while the politicians continued to argue. The government finally allocated $135,000 for rehabilitation work,[15] enough money to build just one house. $2 million was allocated to rebuild the school on a new site.[16] But the marae received an insulting $10,000 grant to cover its costs for using all its meager resources to organise the disaster recovery. The local authority complained bitterly when central government directed them to contribute towards rebuilding the community.[17] Local Māori simply got on with rebuilding their community as best they could with what they were given or could find. The handling of disasters such as this demonstrate how deeply entrenched racism is in New Zealand.

The Waitangi Tribunal defies the government and …

1) … Uses its powers to make binding recommendations

Efforts to restore the economic bases of Māori continued through the Courts and the Waitangi Tribunal. In July 1998, after the government refused to settle a long-running claim concerning the Tūrangi township in the central North Island, the Tribunal used its powers to order not only the return of land but also the amount of compensation to be paid.[18] Although it had had this power since 1988, this was the first time it had been used. For several years the government had been threatening to remove the Tribunal's powers to make orders if it ever used them.[19] In the event, Ngāti Tūrangitukua and the Crown negotiated a settlement within the ninety-day period allowed before the Tribunal's decision would have become binding, and a Deed of Settlement was signed in September.

2) … Finds that Māori own rivers

The Waitangi Tribunal also issued two long-awaited reports relating to the Rangitaiki, Wheao and Whirinaki Rivers of Te Ika Whenua in the Bay of Plenty[20] and Whanganui River[21] in September 1998 and June 1999. Disputes over the ownership of the rivers, and their abuse which had resulted in severe pollution and environmental degradation, had been drawn out for over 100 years. Finally the Tribunal found that Māori do own the rivers, saying in the *Whanganui Report*: '[i]t is neither a privilege nor racist that a people should be able to retain what they have possessed. Property rights go to the heart of any just legal system.'[22] The Tribunal recommended that the Crown recognise and protect Māori rights in respect of these rivers. Minister in Charge of Treaty of Waitangi Negotiations, Sir Douglas Graham, once again reacted angrily to a Tribunal report saying 'The government does not accept that Māori have an interest akin to ownership in rivers.'[23]

3) ... Condemns the Crown for denying Māori access to the radio spectrum

In June 1999 the Tribunal issued *The Radio Spectrum Management and Development Final Report*, finding that Māori have a right to a fair and equitable share in the radio spectrum especially where the Crown has an obligation to promote and protect Māori language and culture.[24] The government had planned to auction parts of the radio spectrum to major international telecommunications and broadcasting companies. The Tribunal said that the Crown had failed to respond to repeated warnings from Māori, the courts and the Privy Council that denying Māori access to a significant role in radio, television and communications would be extremely damaging for the Māori language. The Crown is obliged under the Treaty of Waitangi and its own legislation to protect the Māori language.[25]

Tainui successfully injuncts the Crown over Electrocorp

Māori continued to have to take the government to the High Court to prevent it from selling off assets over which they had claims. In March 1999 Tainui successfully sought an injunction preventing the Crown splitting up the assets of the nation's largest electricity producer, the state enterprise Electricity Corporation of New Zealand, and putting its assets into several new state-owned enterprises.[26] The Tainui Trust Board, which has outstanding claims on the Waikato River, sought firm legal assurances from the Crown that those claims would not be affected by the split. When those were not forthcoming to their satisfaction Tainui sought to restrain the Crown until it had made the undertakings. Within hours of the injunction being granted, the Crown agreed to give the assurances Tainui had sought.[27]

And the fisheries allocation debacle continues …

However the allocation of fisheries assets resulting from the Sealord deal had become bogged down in litigation as Māori fought Māori in the courts.[28] In August 1998 the High Court ruled in favour of the Treaty of Waitangi Fisheries Commission in its decision to allocate the proceeds of the settlement to traditional iwi bodies and not to the modern city-based corporate bodies set up to assist dislocated Māori living in the cities.[29] The urban Māori corporates and other groups not recognised as iwi appealed this decision. They then successfully sought an injunction against the Treaty of Waitangi Fisheries Commission when they attempted to make their long-awaited recommendations on allocation to the Minister of Fisheries. They argued that the High Court had not considered the Waitangi Tribunal's 1998 *Te Whānau o Waipareira Report*, which had found that Waipareira Trust, one of the urban Māori corporate bodies, had a status no less than that of an iwi.[30]

Many Māori who were angry with the Sealord deal from the outset continued to observe that a large portion of the benefits of the so-called settlement had gone on lawyers and consultants, and that many iwi were still not in the business of fishing even though that was the primary aim of the settlement.[31] And in the meantime the Crown continued to sit back and observe the legal carnage, distancing itself from the conflict.[32] For although it quite consciously caused the strife among Māori by rushing through legislation to divest itself of the responsibility of having to sort out how Māori were to be compensated in practical terms through the settlement, it could not be held legally accountable for it unless Māori were prepared to move to overturn the original Sealord deal.

1 Wikipedia contributors, 2009, 'Tau Henare', http://en.wikipedia.org/wiki/Tau_ Henare accessed 2009.
2 Wikipedia contributors, 2009, 'Tau Henare'.
3 Wena Harawira and Nevak Ilolahia, 1997, 'What Makes Tau Tick?', Mana no. 15, Autumn 1997, p. 28.
4 Carol Archie, 1995, 'Doug Graham', in Māori Sovereignty: The Pakeha Perspective, Auckland, Hodder Moa Beckett, p. 121.
5 Gifford, Nga Korero o te Wa, vol. 10 no. 8, 30 August 1997, p. 5.
6 Wairaka.net, 1998, 'Media Statement for Hīkoi of Hope Follow-up Delegation Visit to Parliament', 9 December 1998, http://www.wairaka.net/ubinz/Hikoi/; 1998, 'The Hīkoi of Hope', Mana no. 24, October–November 1998, pp. 22–3.
7 Statistics New Zealand, 1998, New Zealand Now: Income, Wellington, Statistics New Zealand.
8 Controller and Auditor-General, 2000, 'Part 3.6: Student Loan Debt', in Report of the Results of the 1999-2000 Central Government Audits, Wellington, Office of the Controller and Auditor-General, http://www.oag.govt.nz/central-govt/3rd-report/docs/part3-6.pdf. As at October 2010 the New Zealand University Students' Association estimates that student debt is greater than $11 billion, http://www.students.org.nz/
9 Ministry of Education, 2005, 'Māori Students in Formal Tertiary Education by Subsector 1994-2004', in Māori in Tertiary Education, Wellington, Ministry of Education, http://www.educationcounts.govt.nz/publications/maori_ education/maori_in_tertiary_education
10 Te Puni Kōkiri, 1998, Progress Towards Closing the Social and Economic Gaps between Māori and non-Māori: a Report to the Minister of Māori Affairs, Wellington, Ministry of Māori Affairs.
11 Whatarangi Winiata, 1998, 'Reducing the Socio-economic Disparities in Housing, Employment, Health and Education', in Ian Ritchie (ed.), 1998 Hīkoi of Hope website, http://www.wairaka.net/ubinz/Hikoi/; 1999, 'Politics: A Call for Change', Mana no. 26, February–March 1999, pp. 46–7.
12 Winiata, 'Reducing the Socio-economic Disparities'; 1999, 'A Call for Change', pp. 46–7.
13 1999, 'Whaddya Reckon About This Lot, Augie', Northland Age, 26 January 1999, p. 1; 1999, 'He Pitopito Korero: Pakaru Pangaru', Mana no. 26, February–March 1999, p. 17; Jeff Foote, Maria Hepi, Marara Rogers-Koroheke and Hone Taimona, 2005, Urban Water Decision Making Project: Learning from the Stories of Nga Puna Wai o Hokianga, Environmental Science and Research Ltd, http://www. ocvs.govt.nz/documents/work-programme/building-good-practice/good-practice-in-action/whirinaki-water-project-evaluation-report.pdf
14 Margaret Mutu, 1991, Rating and Valuation of Māori Land in Te Taitokerau, Auckland, Department of Māori Studies, University of Auckland.
15 1999, 'Pakaru Pangaru', p. 17.
16 1999, 'Pakaru Pangaru', p. 17.
17 Foote, Hepi, Rogers-Koroheke and Taimona, Urban Water Decision Making Project, p. 15.
18 Waitangi Tribunal, 1998(a), The Turangi Township Remedies Report (Wai 84), Wellington, GP Publications, http://www.waitangi-tribunal.govt.nz/reports/
19 MLR, August 1998, pp. 2–3; Hamer, 'A Quarter-century of the Waitangi Tribunal', p. 7.
20 Waitangi Tribunal, 1998(b), Te Ika Whenua Rivers Report (Wai 212), Wellington, GP Publications, http://www.waitangi-tribunal.govt.nz/reports/
21 Waitangi Tribunal, 1999(d), The Whanganui River Report (Wai 167), Wellington, GP Publications, http://www.waitangi-tribunal.govt.nz/reports/
22 MLR, June 1999, p. 9.
23 MLR, December 1998/January 1999, p. 12.
24 MLR, June 1999, p. 11.
25 MLR, January 1994, p. 5; Robb, 'No Need to Lose Heart', p. 51.

26 MLR, April 1999, pp. 8–10.
27 MLR, April 1999, p. 10.
28 MLR, December 1996/January 1997, pp. 2–4; MLR, August 1997, pp. 3–5; MLR, October 1997, pp. 2–3; MLR, November 1997, pp. 2–4; MLR, December 1997/January 1998, pp. 6–7.
29 MLR, August 1998, pp. 3–8; 1998, 'The Judge Opts for Iwi', *Mana* no. 23, August–September 1998, pp. 51–4.
30 MLR, August 1998, p. 8.
31 Mutu, 'Recovering Fagin's Ill-gotten Gains', pp. 94–5.
32 Mutu, 'Recovering Fagin's Ill-gotten Gains', p. 95.

CHAPTER 7

1999–2000

Māori return to Labour – for now …

In 1996 Māori deserted the Labour Party and gave all the Māori seats to the Māori-led New Zealand First Party. In 1999 they returned them: all six seats returned to Labour, thus ensuring a Labour-led government. The basic error New Zealand First made was to enter a coalition with National against the clearly expressed wishes of Māori. Māori were starting to become a political force in New Zealand[1] and governments were having to learn quickly to shed the deeply-ingrained habit of ignoring and dismissing Māori issues. With the gap between Māori and non-Māori widening for every socio-economic indicator,[2] Māori looked to Labour to restore some semblance of justice. On election night in November 1999 the new Prime Minister, Helen Clark, thanked Māori for returning all the Māori electorates to Labour. Māori then waited to see what Labour would return to Māori.

Dover Samuels, Minister of Māori Affairs for a short six months

Initially it seemed that the Prime Minister was serious about Māori issues. Three Associate Ministers were appointed to assist the Minister of Māori Affairs, Dover Samuels. It soon became obvious, however, that the Minister was a political liability. First he gave the Prime Minister bad advice on how to conduct Waitangi Day, with the result that she snubbed

Ngāpuhi, the country's biggest iwi, by not going to Waitangi.[3] Then he became embroiled in an employment dispute with his press secretary. When he became prey to what were eventually unproven allegations of sexual impropriety from the right-wing Association of Consumers and Taxpayers (ACT) Party in June 2000, the Prime Minister removed his warrant. Soon after several convictions for violence and theft which Samuels had not declared to the Labour Party came to light. Having watched the Minister of Māori Affairs in the previous government spending more time fending off right-wing attacks than doing his job, Māori were not unsympathetic to the Prime Minister's decision. Dover Samuels was replaced by the first-term MP Parekura Horomia, a career bureaucrat with a strong preference for maintaining a low public profile who could be relied on to support his political masters.

Can the PM's Cabinet Committee on Closing the Gaps really bring government departments to account for Māori deprivation and poverty?

The Prime Minister had indicated her lack of confidence in Dover Samuels long before she removed his warrant. In January 2000 she set up the Cabinet Committee on Closing the Gaps (between Māori and non-Māori) and decided to chair it herself.[4] Samuels admitted that he was unable to make headway with many heads of government departments and that they were less likely to disregard the Prime Minister. He was reported as saying that government agencies had an entrenched culture of ignoring Māori issues and Ministers of Māori Affairs.[5] The Prime Minister started referring to herself as the *de facto* Minister of Māori Affairs.[6] One of the first decisions of the cabinet committee was to give the Ministry for Māori Development greater powers to conduct accountability audits on all government agencies. Negative reactions from the Opposition benches indicated that the Ministry was going to continue having difficulty accessing information from other government agencies that resented having to account for what they were or, more likely, were not doing for Māori.[7]

PM's choice for Hauraki electorate easy target for right-wing ACT Party

The usual opposition tactic for ensuring that Māori needs are not addressed is to keep up personal attacks on Māori members of the House. After the 1999 election the main target was John Tamihere, the flamboyant member for the new Hauraki electorate. Helen Clark had backed his selection as the Labour candidate for the seat, rejecting the Māori selection. Prior to the election Tamihere had been the chief executive officer of an urban Māori corporation, the Waipareira Trust, which operates from West Auckland.

The right-wing opposition party ACT, using information fed to it by disgruntled Māori in West Auckland, forced an inquiry into the Trust's use of public funds. Tamihere's inexperience in the House showed in the early stages of the inquiry as he named and attacked members of the Waipareira Trust whom he accused of leaking information to ACT.[8] Their vehement denials forced Tamihere to apologise.[9] Although the Trust was cleared of specific allegations, ACT continued to needle Mr Tamihere about its operations and his own conduct.[10]

Rest of the Māori in Parliament keep their heads down

Given Parliament's and the media's recent history of attacking Māori members personally, it is not surprising that the fourteen other Māori who entered or were returned to Parliament in November 1999 maintained a low profile both in the House and the media. Despite this, some, such as Tariana Turia, continued with their outspoken support of Māori being able to determine what is best for them. However, given the strongly

Eurocentric nature of the New Zealand Parliament, the job of achieving the necessary attitudinal changes needed both in and outside the House if any real progress for Māori was to be achieved would fall largely to non-Māori MPs and Ministers.

Police shoot young Māori student – was it racially motivated?

It was therefore a welcome change for the Prime Minister to acknowledge the racism against Māori which is deeply ingrained in the New Zealand Police after the shooting of a Māori university student on 30 April 2000. Māori had repeatedly raised this issue over many decades but had always been ignored. On this occasion, Steven Wallace was smashing windows in a street in Waitara with a golf club and a baseball bat. Rather than apprehending him and taking him into custody, Senior Constable Keith Abbott shot him four times, fatally wounding him.[11] Those on the scene who attempted to help Wallace gave different accounts of what happened from those of the police. The Māori community of Waitara, whose post-colonial history has been referred to by the Waitangi Tribunal as a 'never-ending war' with the Crown,[12] were outraged, seeing this as yet another tragic episode in their one hundred and fifty year battle for justice. Questions asking why Wallace had been killed went unanswered. Calls for Abbott to be charged with murder were ignored. The Race Relations Conciliator received a number of calls asking him to intervene because the Māori people of Waitara believed it was a racist shooting and the 'result of long-term antagonism between Māori youth and the police in Waitara and Taranaki' rather than an accident.[13] He visited Waitara and several other Taranaki Māori communities in May and July 2000. By mid-July, the preliminary report into the shooting had still not been released.[14]

A new Treaty Minister, a slightly different approach – but no real change

The new Minister in Charge of Treaty of Waitangi Negotiations, Margaret Wilson, was a first-time MP and close ally of the Prime Minister. It had been hoped that Labour would abandon National's loathed fiscal envelope policy.[15] Disappointingly Wilson retained it. She did, however, take a slightly different approach to negotiations. In her first six months in office she met with claimant groups in their own territories. She was also prepared to listen to all claimants, regardless of representation disputes, and to work closely with the different social groupings of whānau, hapū and iwi, a welcome change from the previous government's reliance on its preferred negotiators. This angered the small elite group of Māori who had stalked the halls of Parliament for decades and succeeded in negotiating deals and settlements without consulting with those they claimed to represent. Many of the deals had turned sour, and ensured that claimants would re-litigate them. The different approach by the new Minister aimed to bypass the elite group that had commandeered settlements in the past. In mid-2000 it remained to be seen whether she had the political capability to outsmart those very experienced operators and return the benefits of settlements to those most in need of them. It also remained to be seen whether her different approach signalled any real change in the attitude of the Crown, or whether she was simply undertaking a sorely needed public relations exercise in order to achieve the same ends as the previous government.

In June 2000 the Minister issued her statement of principles for settling claims.[16] It indicated that areas of serious concern for Māori would remain in the settlement process. These were particularly in respect of her statement that lands administered by the Department of Conservation (almost a third of the country) would not be readily available for settlement and that the Crown would continue to assert that it had title to natural resources[17] (which includes water, rivers and lakes, petroleum, minerals, geothermal resources and the foreshore and seabed). She also intended to review the Treaty of Waitangi Act,[18] the legislation which determines the operation of the Waitangi Tribunal. It was widely believed that she would use the review to attempt to remove the Tribunal's powers to make binding recommendations. If she did, her principle of repairing and re-establishing the shattered relationship between Māori and Crown would fail. In the event the Waitangi Tribunal's power remained intact. The Minister, who was also the Attorney-General, was replaced in 2005 following her disastrous handling of the the foreshore and seabed matter.[19]

Ngāi Tahu settlement seems OK

Settlements entered into by the previous government continued to be problematic, although the $170 million Ngāi Tahu settlement had been able to return benefits for that iwi. Their chief negotiator, Sir Tipene O'Regan, took graceful retirement as the next generation moved in to administer and maximise the tribe's benefits from the settlement. Apart from the grievances of one hapū and a few minor upsets as the tribe's administration determined the best combination of skills and experience needed to take the tribe into the new millenium, proceeds from the settlements appear to have been able to set Ngāi Tahu well on the path to social, economic and cultural recovery.[20]

Tainui – not so good

Tainui, on the other hand, who also received a $170 million settlement, suffered serious setbacks. Although they had been able to make a large number of charitable disbursements to their beneficiaries, they were making huge losses on several high-risk investments.[21] Internal discord had simmered for several years, as hapū that were disenfranchised by the settlement warned of impending disaster. Tainui's chief negotiator, Sir Robert Mahuta, who had stepped down once the settlement was completed, was brought back in 2000, five years after the settlement, when the settlement 'went off the tracks'.[22] He became embroiled in very public slanging matches, but refused to stand down in spite of ill health, remaining to shepherd through the eventual recovery of Tainui's settlement. Even the highly regarded Kīngitanga (the ruling elite of Tainui of whom Sir Robert is a member) came under attack. As with almost all of the problematic settlements, those who derived the greatest benefit appeared to be a select handful of well-paid consultants and lawyers. Calls on the government to intervene were, as always, ignored, despite their obvious involvement in creating the chaos in the first place.

And the fisheries allocation debacle grinds on ...

The allocation of fisheries assets from the Sealord Deal continued to be held up in the courts throughout 1999 and 2000.[23] Although 76 percent of traditional iwi, representing 63 percent of all Māori, had supported the allocation model proposed by the Treaty of Waitangi Fisheries Commission, urban Māori corporations and other groups not recognised as iwi continued to use the courts to delay the allocation. In May a group of twenty-five iwi released an independent report from the New Zealand Institute for Economic Research which showed that Māori were losing over $1 million per month as a result of the delays. They were calling for the government to legislate to allow the immediate allocation of the assets.

As does the radio spectrum row ...

Māori continued to battle the government to stop them allocating parts of the radio spectrum without providing for the Māori interest in them. In June 1999 the Waitangi Tribunal upheld the claim by Māori to the radio waves.[24] In March 2000 the government agreed to sell to Māori, at a

5 percent discount, a parcel of the 3G spectrum (needed for the application of new generation cellphones and data transfer technology). They continued to refuse to allocate to Māori any of the 2G spectrum needed for mobile telephone services, claiming it had all been allocated. The New Zealand Māori Council lost its cases against the Crown in the High Court and the Court of Appeal over the allocations of the radio spectrum and took the matter back to the Privy Council.[25]

At long last, a constitutional debate opens – only to be closed down immediately

Māori had maintained for some time now that the only way we would be treated fairly in our own country was if there were constitutional changes. The previous government forbade any discussion on this issue. In April 2000 the new government and the Institute for Policy Studies at Victoria University, Wellington hosted a conference entitled 'Building a Constitution'.[26] New Zealand has no written constitution. The only document which qualifies for that status is Te Tiriti o Waitangi, the original and authoritative Māori version of the Treaty of Waitangi. Although the conference was by invitation only, and was attended mainly by parliamentarians, the judiciary, the legal profession and academics, several of Māoridom's strongest advocates for the entrenchment of the Treaty in a constitution attended. They included Judge Joe Williams, of Ngāti Pūkenga, the then Chief Judge of the Māori Land Court,[27] Annette Sykes of Ngāti Pikiao, a lawyer who had been a strong and outspoken advocate of Māori rights for many years,[28] Moana Jackson, Ngāti Kahungunu, a lawyer who heads the Māori Legal Services and is also a strong advocate of Māori rights,[29] Justice Edward Taihākurei Durie, of Ngāti Kauwhata and Rangitāne, then Chairman of the Waitangi Tribunal and a High Court Judge,[30] Professor Whatarangi Winiata, Ngāti Raukawa, professor of accountancy at Victoria University of Wellington and the head of Te Whare Wānanga o Raukawa in Ōtaki,[31] Denese Henare, Ngāpuhi, a lawyer and Law Commissioner,[32] Caren Wickliffe, Ngāti Porou, a Senior Lecturer in Law at the University of Waikato,[33] and Professor Mason Durie, Ngāti Kauwhata and Rangitāne, the head of the School of Māori Studies at Massey University.[34] Each presented carefully considered and practical proposals for advancing debate on the constitution indicating that the Treaty was essential and that Pākehā domination and oppression of Māori must cease. A very wide range of views was presented, and, predictably, there was no consensus. There was, however, support for the establishment of two constitutional commissions, one for Māori and one for non-Māori. Following the conference the Prime Minister declared that she did not consider there was any compelling demand to do anything and there would be no further discussion.[35] Hopes of Labour making some progress towards official recognition of the true status of Māori in Aotearoa/New Zealand were dashed.

1 Durie, *Te Mana, Te Kāwanatanga*, p. 73.
2 Te Puni Kōkiri, 1998, *Progress Towards Closing the Social and Economic Gaps between Māori and non-Māori: a Report to the Minister of Māori Affairs*, Wellington, Ministry of Māori Affairs.
3 Television New Zealand, 4 July 2000.
4 Jobs Research Trust, 2000, 'The Jobs Budget 2000', *The Jobs Letter* no. 126, 23 June 2000, http://www.jobsletter.org.nz/jbl12610.htm
5 NZPA, 2002(b), 'Clark Making Right Noises Says Samuels', *nzherald.co.nz* , 2 June 2002. This had already been officially reported in respect of the Department of Conservation in 1995 (Mutu, *Report on the New Zealand Conservation Authority*, p. 10).
6 Television New Zealand, 4 July 2000.
7 Audrey Young, 2000(a), 'PM Insists on Full-Value Maori Policy', *New Zealand Herald*, 29 February 2000, p. A3.
8 Eugene Bingham, 2000(a), 'Angry Tamihere Names "thieves"', *New Zealand Herald*, 29 March 2000, p. A2 .
9 Eugene Bingham, 2000(b), 'Tamihere Sorry for Thief, Addict Gibe', *New Zealand Herald*, 6 April 2000, p. A5 ; Vanessa Bidois, 2000(a), 'Tears Flow as MP Says Sorry for Drugs Slur', *New Zealand Herald*, 15 May 2000, p. A3 .
10 Kevin Norquay of NZPA, 2000, 'Tamihere Promises to Expose Cost of Claims', *New Zealand Herald*, 12 May 2000, p. A5; 2000, 'MPs Drop Investigation into Waipareira Trust', *New Zealand Herald*, 7 June 2000, p. A5.

11 Peace Movement Aotearoa, 2000(a), *The Shooting of Steven Wallace*, http://www.converge.org.nz/pma/steven.htm#articles

12 Waitangi Tribunal, *Taranaki Report* (see chapter 3).

13 Peace Movement Aotearoa, 2000(b), 'Relationships in Taranaki', http://www.converge.org.nz/pma/steven.htm#articles

14 Peace Movement Aotearoa, *The Shooting of Steven Wallace*.

15 Although part of the coalition agreement between National and New Zealand First in the previous government was that the 'fiscal envelope' policy be abandoned, in practice nothing changed and the policy remained intact.

16 MLR, July 2000, p. 10.

17 MLR, July 2000, p. 10.

18 MLR, July 2000, p. 10.

19 See chapter 10.

20 Te Rūnanga o Ngāi Tahu Annual Report 2000.

21 Walker, *Ka Whawhai Tonu Matou*, p. 305.

22 Diamond, *A Fire in Your Belly*, p. 138.

23 MLR, April 1999, p. 7.

24 Waitangi Tribunal, 1999(b), *Radio Spectrum Management and Development Final Report* (Wai 776), Wellington, GP Publications, http://www.waitangi-tribunal. govt.nz/reports/. See also chapter 6.

25 Durie, *Ngā Tai Matatū*, pp. 244–5; MLR, June 2000, pp. 5–6; MLR, August 2000, p. 4.

26 Colin James (ed.), 2000, *Building the Constitution*, Wellington, Institute of Policy Studies, Victoria University of Wellington.

27 Judge Williams delivered one of the opening speeches, entitled 'Building the Constitution Conference' (see James (ed.), *Building the Constitution*, pp. 44–7).

28 Annette Sykes' paper was entitled 'Te Tiriti o Waitangi: A Vision of Respect of Civilisations and Cultures' (see James (ed.), *Building the Constitution*, pp. 144–52).

29 Moana Jackson's paper was entitled 'Where Does Sovereignty Lie?' (see James (ed.), *Building the Constitution*, pp. 196–200).

30 Justice Durie's paper was entitled 'The Treaty in the Constitution' (see James (ed.), *Building the Constitution*, pp. 201–4).

31 Professor Winiata's paper was entitled 'How Can or Should the Treaty be Reflected in Institutional Design?' (see James (ed.), *Building the Constitution*, pp. 205–6).

32 Denese Henare's paper was entitled 'Can or Should the Treaty be Replaced?' (see James (ed.), *Building the Constitution*, pp. 207–13).

33 Caren Wickliffe's paper was entitled 'Multiculturalism and the Constitution – Lessons from Another Country: Fiji' (see James (ed.), *Building the Constitution*, pp. 244–58).

34 Professor Durie's paper was entitled 'A Framework for Considering Constitutional Change and the Position of Māori in Aotearoa' (see James (ed.), *Building the Constitution*, pp. 414–25). It contained a proposal for two constitutional commissions: the Māori Constitutional Commission would ensure that debate took place amongst Māori to reach the Māori position or positions and then distil these to serve as a basis for discussions with the other commission, the Constitutional Commission (p. 423).

35 John Armstrong, 2000, 'Slow Shove to Point of no Return', *New Zealand Herald*, 15 April 2000, p. A15.

CHAPTER 8:

2000–01

Postcolonial Traumatic Stress Disorder, Māori poverty and violent offending

As more high-profile cases of Māori not coping in New Zealand society have been brought to the nation's attention, Māori leaders started to make a much more concerted effort to steer debate toward consideration of not only the underlying causes but also the acceptance of Māori-defined remedies and solutions. Several Māori parents and caregivers have been convicted in the past year for the severe abuse and murder of young children. Three more children and then an adult lost their lives in house fires in the Far North in April and June 2001. These fires, like those that claimed the lives of three children in a fire in the same region in 1997, were a direct result of continuing poverty and deprivation. Young Māori offenders are increasingly being convicted for brutal rapes, murders and home invasions. And the rate of Māori youth suicide is one of the highest in the world and increasing at an alarming rate.[1]

In a hard-hitting speech to the New Zealand Psychological Society Conference in August, Tariana Turia, the Associate Minister of Corrections, Health, Housing, Māori Affairs, Social Services and Employment, confronted these issues directly.[2] Predictably, the speech brought the wrath of mainstream New Zealand media down on her. In asking New Zealand psychologists to consider, analyze, and find remedies for the effects of postcolonial traumatic stress disorder on Māori, she pointed out that she saw the connections between home invasions and the invasion of the home lands of indigenous people by a people from another land. 'What I have difficulty in reconciling,' she said, 'is how "home invasions" [elicit] such outpourings of concern for the victims and an intense despising of the invaders while the invasion of the "home lands" of Māori does not engender the same level of emotion and concern for the Māori victims.'[3]

... And the Prime Minister bans the H-word – Holocaust ...

However, the section of Turia's speech that riveted the media for weeks afterward was the Minister's reference to the holocaust that indigenous people, including Māori, had suffered as a result of colonial contact and behavior. 'I understand that much of the research done in this area focused on the trauma suffered by Jewish survivors of the holocaust of World War II,' she said. 'I understand that the same has been done with Vietnam veterans. ... The Treaty of Waitangi Tribunal ... made a reference [to the holocaust suffered by Māori] in its *Taranaki Report* of 1996.'[4]

Overnight the media declared that the word 'holocaust' was the sole preserve of Jewish people, misquoted Turia,[5] and launched an attack on her[6] that in its viciousness surpassed even the attacks on Tuku Morgan in 1997. Dr Danny Keenan of Massey University and of Taranaki descent described the response as 'little short of incredible'.[7] In his article published in the *New Zealand Herald* he explained that many indigenous peoples who have suffered centuries of dispossession, genocide and horrific histories of loss at the hands of colonisers have used the word holocaust to describe their experiences. So have other non-Jewish peoples. The use of the word in Britain and the United States has provoked 'prolonged and quite bitter academic argument' although many academics have argued that the word does not belong exclusively to the Jewish people.[8]

The Prime Minister nevertheless attempted to censor Turia by issuing an edict banning the use of the word 'holocaust'.[9] The edict had to be toned down to *advice* in the face of a massive backlash from Māori, including other Māori members of Parliament, in support of Turia. In turn, Turia apologised to the Jewish community if her comments had caused them offence. She drew unexpected support from some non-Māori quarters including a retiring member of the conservative National Party, Simon Upton, who commented 'New Zealanders who react with horror that she should have described it as a holocaust are being a bit precious – or indulging in collective amnesia'.[10]

... So other Māori MPs duck for cover – except for Dover and Sandra ...

Following the sustained attack on Tariana Turia, other Māori members of Parliament kept a low profile. The two exceptions were Dover Samuels, who was still in the media spotlight in his fight against the Prime Minister for forcing his resignation in June 2000, and Sandra Lee, who lost leadership of her own party, Mana Motuhake, in June 2001.[11]

... But the government still abandons the 'Closing the Gaps' policy

Tariana Turia had long championed the strengthening and provision of resources for the basic social groupings within Māori society – the whānau, the hapū and the iwi. The previous, conservative National government had developed a policy that aimed to close the gaps between Māori and non-Maori following the release of the very damaging report *Progress Towards Closing the Social and Economic Gaps between Māori and non-Māori: a Report to the Minister of*

Māori Affairs in 1998.[12] The present government carried on the policy, allocating funding in its 2000 budget for social services and employment initiatives specifically targeted at Māori and Pacific Island communities. The government undertook to scrutinise mainstream departmental budgets to ensure that funding meant for Māori actually delivered for Māori. The Prime Minister indicated that 'the evidence is that it has not been'.[13]

The government immediately came under fire from right-wing politicians demanding that the government stop providing special funding targeted specifically for Māori.[14] Bowing to that pressure, the Prime Minister abandoned the policy in December 2000, noting the advice of her Māori caucus members that Māori do not wish to close the gaps between themselves and Pākehā if it means becoming the same as Pākehā.

Prime Minister under fire from Māori

For many years Māori had called for control of their own destinies, along with the necessary resources to do so. The Prime Minister came under fire from the traditionally supportive Rātana church when she made her annual visit late in January 2001. They put her on notice that unless her government performed and delivered to Māori it would lose Māori support at the next election in 2002. She was also severely criticised for refusing to attend Waitangi Day celebrations at Waitangi and for ordering the Governor General not to attend.[15] Tariana Turia and Minister of Māori Affairs, Parekura Horomia, defied her and attended.

In an attempt to dampen Māori criticism, the 'closing-the-gaps' policy was replaced by the 'capacity-building' policy,[16] which allowed for funding to be given to local Māori groups and organisations to develop their own programmes. However, given the scarcity of administrative expertise in many of these groups, unless the Ministry of Māori Development provided a lot of personnel on the ground to assist and train people on the job, and to help contract the appropriate expertise, this policy would also fail.

Lack of governance and administrative expertise causing concern but no media scrutiny ...

It was becoming increasingly obvious that the lack of administrative experience and expertise in Māori communities, particularly in commercial matters, was a matter of serious concern.[17] In many cases progress in development is severely hampered where communities are not able to accept outside advice. The beneficiaries of many Māori trusts (including the Crown Forestry Rental Trust, which receives millions of dollars every year on behalf of Māori) have repeatedly accused their boards of corruption and mismanagement. Most of those organisations have received less media scrutiny than is perhaps warranted, given the extent of Māori anger about them, but the same cannot be said of Tainui, which has been subjected to intense media scrutiny and criticism over the past year.

... Except for Tainui

As a result of some unwise investments, Tainui had sustained losses totaling approximately \$35 million of their Treaty of Waitangi settlement of \$170 million, which they received in 1995. By mid-2001, the country's largest daily newspaper had been conducting a campaign against Tainui for over a year, attacking them for the handling of their settlement, naming individual members of the governing body, and openly fueling animosity and disputes between members. The *New Zealand Herald* website[18] lists more than eighty articles attacking Tainui, prominently published in the news sections in 2000–01, despite the fact that the compensation money is not public money but private money belonging to the iwi. Even the death of the chief negotiator, Sir Robert Mahuta, who had battled first the government and then his own people over Tainui's losses, did not stop the newspaper's onslaught.

Sir Robert Mahuta

On 1 February 2001, Sir Robert Mahuta passed away. He was Waikato-Tainui's chief negotiator for the $170 million package of money and land transferred to Tainui by the Crown in 1995 as settlement for the 1.2 million acres (486,502 hectares) of Waikato lands confiscated in 1863.[19] It was a deal Sir Robert knew was both unjust and unfair. He was a member of the kāhui ariki, or paramount Tainui family, and was adopted at four weeks of age by Koroki, the fifth of the Tainui kings. He grew up at Waahi Pā near Huntly. He spent his younger adult years working in the Huntly coal mines, serving in the army and being posted to Malaysia, working as a wharfie, a freezing worker and a labourer on building sites before turning to education. He completed an MA in Anthropology at the University of Auckland, was appointed the director of the Centre for Māori Studies and Research at the University of Waikato and was working towards a PhD at Oxford University in England when problems at Waahi with the Huntly Power Station drew him back home. After he had negotiated the 1995 Waikato-Tainui settlement he withdrew from tribal business to concentrate on setting up an endowed college at Hopuhopu based on the Oxford University model. When high-risk investments of the Tainui settlement funds resulted in large financial losses he was brought back in 2000 to remedy the situation. In the face of strong criticism and failing health, he steered the Tainui settlement back to recovery. He was buried outside the main doors of his endowed college.[20]

Much more respectful coverage of Pākehā commercial disasters

By comparison with the *Herald*'s treatment of Tainui, attempts to locate critical comment on that same newspaper's website about the $600 million losses of Air New Zealand,[21] the $54 million debt of ENZA (which took over from the New Zealand Apple and Pear Marketing Board),[22] Qantas New Zealand debts of $88 million,[23] Brierley losses of $4.5 billion over the past ten years,[24] and the collapses of many publicly listed companies with far higher losses and debts than Tainui typically produced only passing mentions in the business pages until the company actually failed.[25] On rare occasions the chairman of the board was named, but the anonymity and personal privacy of the rest of the directors was carefully protected and respected.

Successful Māori settlements overlooked by the media

Tainui may have publicly faltered in the handling of its settlements, but other iwi that had received settlements had fared better. Many refused to discuss their progress with mainstream media, and although a couple had been prepared to talk about their achievements they received only fleeting mention.[26] Ngāi Tahu, for example, had continued to invest its settlement conservatively and wisely. The $170 million settlement received in 1998 was by 2001 valued at over $366 million, and Ngāi Tahu was once again the largest landowner in its ancestral homeland, the South Island. [27] In Rotorua, Ngāti Whakaue's settlement of $5.2 million was then valued at $17 million.[28] In Auckland, Ngāti Whātua of Ōrākei had received a total of $8 million plus some housing since 1987. Their assets were then valued at more than $60 million.[29]

Treaty of Waitangi Fisheries Commission commercially successful but the fisheries allocation debacle continues …

In terms of profit margins and growing the asset, by far the most successful settlement was the $170 million Sealord fisheries settlement reached in 1992. The Treaty of Waitangi Fisheries Commission: Te Ohu Kaimoana exercised control over more than 40 percent of the country's fishing quota. It had assets valued at $457 million dollars (net assets).[30] However, the assets and funds that made up the settlement were not given to Māori but to a Crown-appointed commission, the Treaty of Waitangi Fisheries Commission: Te Ohu Kaimoana, whose task was to allocate the assets and funding to recognised iwi. It had yet to make any allocation, having been dogged by litigation, which saw many millions of dollars of the Commission's (and hence iwi) money spent on lawyers. Essentially the Crown still controlled the proceeds of the settlement. Iwi were in 2001 demanding that Parliament legislate the allocation as they watched the benefits from profits that should be theirs being spent on ridiculously high fees for commissioners and an ever-increasing cadre of lawyers. Regular press releases were issued by the Treaty Tribes Coalition, which represented more than thirty iwi in the allocation debate, detailing the extent of the losses calculated for each iwi's region while the proceeds remained tied up in the Commission.[31]

Waitangi Tribunal celebrates its twenty-fifth birthday but still struggles with government indifference to its funding, findings and recommendations

Almost all settlements had come about as a result of claims presented to the Waitangi Tribunal. In October 2000 the Tribunal celebrated its twenty-fifth birthday. Despite ever-decreasing funding to keep it operating, it had registered 869 claims, and published thirty-seven major reports and a further thirty-one minor reports.[32] Many of these reports deal with several claims at once, and 140 claims had been dealt with fully or in part. Yet fewer than twenty of these claims had been settled, and no claimant group had received all the land and compensation they were entitled to.[33] While the tribunal had built an impressive record and rewritten the history of the country, its work would count for little unless there was the political will to implement its recommendations. Although Māori leaders had pointed out repeatedly that the settlement of these claims was fundamental to the treatment of the crippling postcolonial traumatic stress disorder being suffered in those communities, in far too many cases governments have refused to accept the tribunal's recommendations. As a result, along with the length of time it takes to process a claim through the Tribunal (usually many years) and some questionable appointments to the Tribunal of members who are openly antagonistic to claimants,[34] Māori were starting to lose faith in the Tribunal's ability to deliver the justice they so desperately sought.

Despite this, the Tribunal had provided many positive and valuable outcomes for Māori. Most importantly, they had upheld the overwhelming majority of claims they had heard from Māori.[35] This in itself provided a certain measure of relief given that most claims are many generations old and had always either been dismissed, ignored or grossly under-compensated by governments and bureaucrats in the past.[36] Then, for the first time, there has been an official record of the history of claimant grievances, which includes the histories as recounted by the claimants and are not solely the Eurocentric view of Pākehā historians and bureaucrats intent on either obfuscating or avoiding reference to the damage done to Māori by British immigration. The Tribunal had also largely removed Māori protest from the streets and away from the view of the public,[37] as the Labour government had intended in 1975,[38] although flagging confidence in the Tribunal's ability to effect any real change could alter this. And it had provided a forum in which Māori could openly air their grievances about the breaches of the Treaty and their human rights that were expressed by way of protest in the 1970s.[39]

But the Tribunal came under sustained attack from Pākehā for the support it had given Māori. Some Pākehā found it extremely painful to have to come to terms with their past in this country and strongly resisted having to do so. They went as far as making personal threats against the Tribunal.[40]

Successive governments continued to show distain and disrespect for the Tribunal's reports and recommendations, despite the fact that it is a judicial body. They ensured that it has always been severely under-resourced and unable to carry out its inquiries in a timely manner.[41] They also kept it under constant threat of losing one of the few powers it has: the power to make binding recommendations. Ministers in Charge of Treaty of Waitangi Negotiations in both National- and Labour-led governments are on record as threatening to remove these powers if the Tribunal ever used them.[42]

Settlements
Pākaitore
Settlements reported in 2000–01 included the high-profile Pākaitore, or Moutoa Gardens, area in Whanganui. Māori, and some non-Māori, from throughout the country had poured into Whanganui in 1995 in support of the iwi of the area who had taken back a small area of their traditional lands.[43] After a long standoff, the iwi eventually withdrew in the hope of settling the matter some other way.[44] Tariana Turia was a very prominent member of that protest. In February 2001 she also featured prominently as the Whanganui District Council finally gave up its 'ownership' of the gardens. Although the land was not returned to Whanganui Māori, a committee made up of themselves plus representatives of the Crown and the District Council now administers it.

Pouakani, Ngāti Ruanui, Te Uri o Hau
Other settlements were reported: Pouakani in the central North Island achieved the return of 250 acres (100 hectares) of conservation land, a 4749 acre (1922 hectare) farm, joint management of their sacred mountain, Tītīraupenga, and payment of $2.65 million to the descendants of the original owners of a 100,000 acre (49,514 hectare) block.[45] Ngāti Ruanui in north Taranaki received $41 million, 25 acres of

land and recognition of their fishing rights—a settlement that generated strong protests including High Court action.[46] The settlement of the claims of Te Uri o Hau of Northland was particularly alarming: it covered fifteen claims, fourteen marae, and the loss of several hundred thousand hectares of land, but returned only $8.5 million, some commercial properties valued at $7.1 million, less than 74 acres of land and recognition of their fishing rights.[47]

Māori opposition to genetic engineering

In the battle being fought by Māori on many fronts to protect the country's natural resources, the fight against the use of human genes in animals has been particularly bitter. An application by the New Zealand Pastoral Agricultural Research Institute to the Environmental Risk Management Authority for permission to carry out this genetic engineering was strongly opposed by Māori. The authority decided to override Māori concerns and gave permission for the work to be carried out on the ancestral lands of Ngāti Wairere in the Waikato district, rejecting the advice of their own Māori expert and their own Māori advisory body.[48] When both of those joined Ngāti Wairere in taking a case against it to the High Court,[49] the authority threatened to disestablish the advisory committee. The chairman of the committee subsequently resigned, and the committee withdrew from the case. The case to the High Court was lost, although ERMA did come in for some criticism in the decision.[50]

A breakthrough in local government – Māori representation on Bay of Plenty Regional Council

Although Māori have a strong legislative mandate through the Resource Management Act for the protection of their lands, culture and resources at a local level, enforcing those provisions has proved extremely difficult when there are few or no Māori elected to local government. In the Bay of Plenty,

Māori lobbied successfully to have their own representation in local government. A bill put before Parliament provided for the creation of a Māori constituency in that region and allowed Māori to vote for their own representative on the Bay of Plenty Regional Council.[51] The bill did in fact become law (the Bay of Plenty Regional Council (Maori Constituency Empowering) Act 2001) and set an important precedent for the rest of the country.[52]

1 Philippa Howden-Chapman, Simon Hales, Ralph Chapman and Ilmo Keskimaki, 2005, *The Impact of Economic Recession on Youth Suicide: Report 4: Social Explanations for Suicide in New Zealand*, Wellington, Ministry of Health.

2 MLR, August 2000, p. 9.

3 MLR, August 2000, p. 9.

4 MLR, August 2000, p. 10.

5 New Zealand Press Council, 2001, *Case Number 815: John Gamby Against the New Zealand Herald*, http://www.presscouncil.org.nz/display_ruling. php?casenumber=815

6 Danny Keenan, 2000, '*Dialogue: Whose Holocaust? That is Still a Good Question*', *New Zealand Herald*, 7 September 2000, p. A13; Ranginui Walker, 2002, 'Māori News is Bad News', in Judy McGregor and Margie Comrie (eds), *What's News: Reclaiming Journalism in New Zealand*, Palmerston North, Dunmore Press, pp. 229-30.

7 Keenan, 'Whose Holocaust?'.

8 Keenan, 'Whose Holocaust?'.

9 Keenan, 'Whose Holocaust?'; Wikipedia contributors, 'Taranaki', http:// en.wikipedia.org/wiki/Taranaki accessed 2009; Audrey Young, 2000(b), 'Turia Accepts Edict on Holocaust Term', *New Zealand Herald*, 7 September 2000, p. A5.

10 MLR, December 2000/January 2001, p. 11.

11 Archive of Executive Government, 'Hon Sandra Lee', http://www.executive.govt. nz/minister/lee/

12 Te Puni Kōkiri, *Progress Towards Closing the Social and Economic Gaps*.

13 Jobs Research Trust, 'The Jobs Budget 2000'.

14 Jobs Research Trust, 'The Jobs Budget 2000'.

15 Ministry for Culture and Heritage, 2009, 'Waitangi Day in the 21st Century', http:// www.nzhistory.net.nz/politics/treaty/waitangi-day/21st-century-waitangi-day

16 Dover Samuels, 2000, 'Capacity Building Boost for Māori Affairs', press release, 15 June 2000, http://www.executive.govt.nz/budget2000/gaps-samuels.htm

17 Wena Harawira, 1997, 'You Can Blow it All', *Mana* no. 15, Autumn 1997, pp. 72-4.

18 See http://www.nzherald.co.nz/

19 Graham, *Trick or Treaty*, pp. 76-7; MLR, December 1994-January 1995, pp. 12-13; MLR, May 1995, p. 9; Diamond, *A Fire in Your Belly*, p. 138; chapter 2.

20 Diamond, *A Fire in Your Belly*, pp.113-46; 2001, 'He Maimai Aroha: Bob Mahuta', *Mana* no. 38, February-March 2001, pp. 6-7; James Ritchie, 2001, 'Robert Te Kotahi a Koroki Mahuta', *Mana* no. 39, April-May 2001, pp. 70-1.

21 The *Herald* finally made critical comment about the company when Air New Zealand announced a loss of $1.425 billion and an $885 million government bailout on 13 September 2001.

22 Philippa Stevenson, 2001, 'Apple Growers Biting Back at ENZA Dispute', *New Zealand Herald*, 2 July 2001, p. D4.

23 Simon Hendery, 2001, 'Qantas NZ Takeover an Option to Boost Aussie's Share', *New Zealand Herald*, 6 April 2001, p. C1. This article does not mention the size of the debt, only that it is 'sizeable'.

24 Dita de Boni, 2001, 'BIL Chief Looks on Brighter Side', *New Zealand Herald*, 19 March 2001, p. D1.

25 Eugene Bingham, 2001, 'The Grounding of Qantas NZ: a Blow That Came in the Dark', *New Zealand Herald*, 28 April 2001, pp. B6–7.

26 Angela Gregory, 2001, 'Treaty Settlement Success Stories: How They Did It', *New Zealand Herald*, 10 January 2001, p. A13.

27 Te Rūnanga o Ngāi Tahu Annual Report 2000.

28 Gregory, 'Treaty Settlement Success Stories'.

29 Secretary, Ngāti Whātua ki Ōrākei Trust Board, personal communication.

30 Treaty of Waitangi Fisheries Commission, 2002, *Statement of Financial Position of the Treaty of Waitangi Fisheries Commission Group, Annual Report to Parliament for the year end 30 September 2002*, p. 36, http://teohu.maori.nz/te_ohu/archive/reports/Treaty%20of%20Waitangi%20Annual%20Report%202003.pdf

31 See, for example, Vanessa Bidois, 2000(b), 'Troubled Waters Loom for Maori Fisheries', *New Zealand Herald*, 4 July 2000, p. A11.

32 Director of the Waitangi Tribunal, personal communication.

33 Mutu, 'Recovering Fagin's Ill-gotten Gains'.

34 The most notable example is former Labour cabinet minister Michael Bassett, a member of the Tribunal from 1994 to 2004. He faced several challenges during his time on the Tribunal because of alleged bias.

35 Claims that have not been upheld include claims by Pākehā (for example, the Tozer claim and the Guard Family claim) which have been held to be frivolous and vexatious. The Tribunal can only consider claims from Māori (MLR, October 2000, p. 2).

36 For example, in the *Muriwhenua Land Report* the Tribunal noted that Muriwhenua Māori had suffered 'loss of status during the long years of petition and protest' (p. 404).

37 Hamer, 'A Quarter-century of the Waitangi Tribunal', p. 6.

38 W H Oliver, 1991, *Claims to the Waitangi Tribunal*, Wellington, Department of Justice, pp. 9–10.

39 Hamer, 'A Quarter-century of the Waitangi Tribunal', p. 12. Harris, *Hīkoi*.

40 Hamer, 'A Quarter-century of the Waitangi Tribunal', p. 7.

41 Hamer, 'A Quarter-century of the Waitangi Tribunal', p. 10; MLR, November 2000, p. 10.

42 Hamer, 'A Quarter-century of the Waitangi Tribunal', footnote 22.

43 Snedden, *Pakeha and the Treaty*, p. 105.

44 1995, 'He Pitopito Korero: Not Over Yet', *Mana* no. 9, Winter 1995, p. 9.

45 MLR, September 2000, p. 7.

46 MLR, May 2001, pp. 6–8.

47 MLR, December 2000/January 2001, pp. 9–10.

48 MLR, August 2000, p. 5; Maui Solomon, 2000, 'Te Marae Atea: An affront from ERMA', *Mana* no. 35, August–September 2000, pp. 52–3.

49 MLR, August 2000, p. 9.

50 MLR, April 2001, pp. 2–6.

51 2001, 'Maori Seats on BOP Council Could be a Reality by October', *nzherald.co.nz*, 10 May 2001.

52 Ann Sullivan, 2003, 'Māori Representation in Local Government', in Janine Haywood (ed.), *Local Government and the Treaty of Waitangi*, Melbourne, Oxford University Press, pp. 150–3; Maureen Waaka, 2006, 'Local Government', in Malcolm Mulholland (ed.), *State of the Māori Nation: Twenty-first Century Issues in Aotearoa*, Auckland, Reed, pp. 219–25.

CHAPTER 9:

2001–02

Supporting Māori sovereignty is politically unsafe
In a year dominated by the approaching general election, Māori watched the government, like the Māori Members of Parliament, steer away from any public debate on Māori issues. In recent years, Māori MPs had come under sustained attack from the conservative opposition and the mainstream media whenever they had attempted to articulate Māori aspirations for greater control over their lives. Calls from non-Māori lending support to those aspirations generally received little or no media coverage. So when Pākehā groups at Waitangi on Waitangi Day in February 2002, including the Green Party, publicly stated their support for Māori sovereignty, it went unreported in mainstream media. Several days later it was partially reported when the Greens' leader signaled a softening of the stance on Māori sovereignty because 'many people find the term very frightening'.[1]

Local councils, not Māori, left to decide if Māori representation allowed
Yet even Te Puni Kōkiri, the Ministry for Māori Development, as part of the local government reforms, was advocating restructuring local government to ensure that Māori had greater control over their own affairs. The Local Government Act 2002 provided for separate Māori seats for the Bay of Plenty Regional Council, and enabled other councils to follow

suit if they wished to. But even if councils were prepared to break from the electoral system that favours the election of middle-class, middle-aged Pākehā males to office[2] in order to have Māori representation in local government, that could be contested by a local poll.[3] In 1986 the Royal Commission on the Electoral System had noted that the First Past the Post electoral system, since abandoned for parliamentary representation but still used in local government, was unfair, inequitable and unrepresentative of the general populace.[4] One of its many recommendations for fairness and equity was that democratic participation should afford due respect to, and recognition and inclusion of, the indigenous population, that is, Māori.[5] Yet the 2002 Act barely acknowledges that, and, once again, it is left to overwhelmingly Pākehā councils and voting populations to decide whether Māori should represent themselves. This electoral system continues to deny effective Māori representation,[6] even in areas where the majority of the population is Māori.[7]

Māori views on Māori sovereignty ... in the New Zealand Herald!

In the final weeks before the July 2002 election, as right-wing parties were attacking the Treaty of Waitangi and promoting a cut-off date for all Māori claims against the Crown, the largest mainstream newspaper ran a story on Māori views of Māori sovereignty.[8] It had to admit that a significant number of Māori it interviewed wanted Māori sovereignty recognised, yet the article concentrated on reporting Māori giving reasons for why it should not be recognised.

Mainstream media Māori bashing

Mainstream media coverage of Māori issues continued to be a matter of concern on several occasions in 2001–02. Claims that the media were Māori bashing surfaced on several occasions. One prominent example was a television documentary on the so-called 'Treaty industry'.[9] The large number of people who work to bring Māori Treaty of Waitangi claims before the Waitangi Tribunal, or to settle them in negotiation with the government of the day, are referred to by right-wing politicians as making up the 'Treaty industry'.[10] The impression given is that these people receive large payments for doing this work. While that is correct for many of the (usually Pākehā) professionals contracted to assist Māori claimants, the Māori whose claims they are almost always work voluntarily or with minimal remuneration. Yet it is Māori that right-wing politicians and the television documentary were targeting.

The programme interviewed a disgruntled historian[11] and two disaffected former employees of the Crown Forestry Rental Trust.[12] The Trust is a body that administers many millions of dollars of rental monies paid on Crown-owned forests, and allocates some of its income towards assisting Māori to prepare, present and negotiate claims against the Crown to those forests.[13] Most of this money goes to historians, lawyers, accountants and other professional advisors. The Trust had been under investigation by the Māori Affairs select committee.[14] The television programme was apparently designed to air concerns about the slow pace and possible corruption in the Treaty claims process but instead sensationalised an alleged 'Māori mafia', none of whom were named, running the Trust to its advantage.[15] It then attempted to blame Māori for the parlous state of the settlements.

So why is the Treaty claims settlement process so chronically slow?

Of the 908 claims registered with the Waitangi Tribunal over the past twenty-six years, fewer than 20 have resulted in any land being returned to the claimants or compensation being paid out. Furthermore, not a single claimant group has received all the land and compensation they are entitled to.[16] In 2001–02 the Labour-led coalition government partially settled just one claim: that of Ngāti Tama, in the Taranaki region, where the Tribunal reported Māori had suffered a holocaust in its 1996 report.[17] Ngāti Tama lost more than 104,000 acres. The settlement returned just 4,620 acres and $14.5 million.[18] The three other settlements achieved under the Labour-led government had been similarly mean-spirited.

Yet the 'Treaty industry' television programme made no mention of the real reasons for the chronically slow and inadequate Treaty claims settlement process. The main reason was that every government that had been in power over the past decade had refused to take any Māori advice on the need to radically reformulate its unfair, unjust and racist settlement policy.[19] Then there was the ongoing underfunding of the Waitangi Tribunal.[20] There was also the pivotal role of the 'experts' in the industry, the lawyers, historians and government bureaucrats many of whom seem to actively prolong the process. Most of these people are Pākehā[21] who 'can charge apparently exorbitant fees.'[22] However, instead of commenting on these issues, the programme raised 'already disproved allegations about impropriety by some Māori lawyers.'[23] Despite its lack of funding, the Waitangi Tribunal intervened to try to speed up its hearings and reporting process, fast-tracking the Gisborne district hearings through in seven months in contrast to others which have taken more than four years.[24]

Kidnapping of Baby Kahurautete Durie

The media coverage of the kidnapping of the eight-month-old daughter of a lawyer and a High Court judge, both of whom are Māori, caused further consternation. The fact that the child had been adopted from within the couple's extended family according to widely practiced Māori custom was frowned on by mainstream media as being 'not regarded as formal adoption in New Zealand law'.[25] Several newspapers tried to imply that it was Māori who were somehow to blame for the

(From left) Gloria Herbert, Chairperson, Te Rūnanga o Te Rarawa (who organised the Hands Across the Beach event in 2004), Professor Pat Hohepa (Te Māhurehure, Ngāpuhi) and Titewhai Harawira (Ngāpuhi). (Gil Hanly)

The Hands Across the Beach protest on Te Oneroa a Tōhē (Ninety Mile Beach) in the Far North in February 2004. (Shiobhan Herbert/Mana)

Over 1,000 people joined hands on Te Oneroa a Tōhē (Ninety Mile Beach) in the Far North in February 2004 to protest the government's foreshore and seabed legislation. (Gil Hanly)

Ngāti Kahu on the Foreshore and Seabed Hīkoi in Kaitāia, Far North, 23 April 2004. (Courtesy of Hone Harawira)

Gil Hanly, photographer. (Courtesy of Hone Harawira)

Annette Sykes (Ngāti Pikiao), legal expert and lawyer for many arrested for defending Māori rights, in Rotorua, 1 May 2004. (Courtesy of Hone Harawira)

The Foreshore and Seabed Hīkoi, the harbour bridge in Auckland, 27 April 2004. (Gil Hanly)

The Foreshore and Seabed Hīkoi on Queen St, Auckland, 27 April 2004. (Gil Hanly)

The Foreshore and Seabed Hīkoi leaves Te Puea marae, Māngere, Auckland, 28 April 2004. (Gil Hanly)

The Foreshore and Seabed Hīkoi was very good-natured, and there were no arrests over its two-week duration. (Courtesy of Hone Harawira)

Ken Mair (Whanganui), activist and community worker, in Whanganui, 3 May 2004. (Courtesy of Hone Harawira)

Hone Harawira and Moana Jackson outside Te Papa in Wellington, 5 May 2004. (Gil Hanly)

Ngāti Kahu in Wellington, 5 May 2004. (Gil Hanly)

Moana Jackson and Dr Pita Sharples (Ngāti Kahungunu) in the Foreshore and Seabed Hīkoi in Wellington, 5 May 2004. (Mana)

Dr Pita Sharples leading the Hīkoi to Parliament, 5 May 2004. (Mana)

kidnapping, despite Māori protestations to the contrary.[26] Yet when the baby was found and the kidnapper arrested and sent to jail for eleven years, there was very little discussion of the fact that he was Pākehā and that his sole motivation for the kidnapping was money.[27]

World Trade Center bombing – Māori perspectives

Māori views of the bombing of the World Trade Center in New York on 11 September were also ignored until the initial furore started to die down. While they were appalled at the incident, they were not surprised.[28] Māori elders from around the country, many of them ex-servicemen, were interviewed by Māori radio stations shortly after the bombing. All expressed views that the United States could not expect to keep attacking and making war on other nations and not expect some form of retaliation. It was several days before similar views started to surface in the mainstream media, and the Green Party went on record as opposing New Zealand troops being sent to Afghanistan.[29]

New Zealand Herald turns its sights on Māori Television

In the 2000–01 reporting period, the country's largest newspaper ran a campaign against Tainui. Then in 2001–02 it was the turn of Māori television with the *New Zealand Herald* listing no fewer that eighty articles over that year on its website (the same number listed for Tainui the previous year). Criticism of Māori television had been going on for more than six years as mainstream media, backed by government officials, ignored Court of Appeal rulings and battled to keep Māori out of the industry. When the chairman of the channel's board attacked the media for Māori bashing in April, they retaliated by closely scrutinising all the workings of the channel. When they discovered that the Chief Executive Officer, who was Canadian, had falsified his qualifications, the number of articles per day attacking Māori television peaked. The day after the board sacked the CEO, ten articles, including an editorial, ran in the *New Zealand Herald*. They were rather stunned, however, when the CEO was denied bail and subsequently jailed for six months,[30] a punishment that legal experts saw as fitting the crime. Then the *Herald* was silenced completely by the appointment in May of an interim CEO who was one of the very few Māori millionaires and a very experienced businessman. He refused to speak to any mainstream media and in interviews with Māori media said he was not interested in anything that the mainstream media had to say.

Tariana Turia not afraid to take on mainstream media

The one Māori MP prepared to take on the mainstream media, Tariana Turia, did so in March, referring to the media as 'hysterical, hostile and ill-informed' over her reference to a Māori holocaust in 2000. She predicted that the media would attack her during campaigning for the 2002 general elections.[31] Her prediction appeared to have been enough to stop them doing so. Turia travelled around the country attending many Māori gatherings, including those organised in different tribal regions for ministers of the Crown to meet Māori in their own territories. Although the media attended such events, they were not interested in what Māori were saying at them. Requests of the Prime Minister at these hui to be more outspoken in support of Māori drew the response that when she said such things to the media they never reported them. In the main she considered that the media was only looking for incidents that would allow them to report Māori negatively.[32]

Te Tangata Whai Rawa o Wēniti: The Māori *Merchant of Venice*, a stunning performance

Yet there were also the occasional bright patches. In February, the film of the Māori language version of Shakespeare's *The Merchant of Venice* played to rapturous audiences throughout the country. Despite the historic and cultural importance of the piece, in particular because of the endangered state of the Māori language, it received minimal media coverage. Yet a four-star rating and an excellent review from a Pākehā film critic appeared in the *New Zealand Herald*.[33] Later in 2002 it won the coveted Audience Award at the Louis Vuitton Hawaii Film Festival.[34] Massey University later conferred an honorary doctorate on the producer, Don Selwyn, for his many years of stage, television and film work and his training and mentoring of young talent.[35]

MAI FM tops the ratings

And then in April, an iwi radio station topped the ratings to become Auckland's most preferred radio station.[36] Ngāti Whātua's MAI FM caters for Māori and Pacific Island youth and features rap music, rhythm and blues, jazz, hip hop, and more recently, New Zealand-produced music. While its popularity had displaced mainstream radio stations in the popularity polls, it followed naturally from the fact that in the twenty-five years and under population in Auckland, 20 percent are Pacific Islanders and 16 percent are Māori. That, and the fact that a survey of MAI FM listeners indicated that they did not watch television because it did not reflect them. Likewise mainstream advertising.

Prime Minister apologises to Chinese and to Samoans – but not to Māori

Although the Prime Minister claimed to be supportive of Māori, her apologies to non-Māori sectors of the New Zealand society drew some bitter responses from Māori. In February she apologised to the Chinese community for the government forcing them to pay a poll tax of £10 to enter the country from 1881, increasing it to £100 in 1896, and not repealing it until 1944.[37] Then in June she apologised to the Samoan community for the New Zealand government's role in the 1918 Spanish flu epidemic in Samoa and the gunning down of Mau movement supporters calling for self-government by peaceful means in Apia in 1929. Samoa was under New Zealand rule during these incidents. In 1918 the New Zealand administration in Apia took no action to quarantine a ship that had previously docked in Auckland while the 1918 Spanish flu epidemic was raging there. Instead, it allowed passengers with the flu to disembark in Apia, thus introducing the epidemic into Samoa. Up to 8500 or 22 percent of Samoans died as a result.[38] Then, on Black Saturday, 29 December 1929, after many years of unrest as a result of the oppression and persecution of Samoans by the New Zealand administration, unarmed supporters of the Mau movement were fired on by the New Zealand police with rifles and a machine gun. Eight people were killed.[39]

Although both these apologies were long overdue, an apology to Māori is far longer overdue. While some individual iwi had received formal apologies on the condition that they have been prepared to settle and effectively extinguish all their historical Treaty of Waitangi claims, Māori had yet to receive any overall, unconditional apology for their ongoing ill-treatment at the hands of successive colonial governments and the numerous breaches of the Treaty of Waitangi perpetrated against them.

And there's heaps to apologise for

Māori commentators noted that while the Prime Minister was apologising to others, Māori on the East Coast were protesting to stop their lands being sold to American developers;[40] Māori elders in Northland were being arrested for attempting to defend their wāhi tapu;[41] the police in Whāngārei were being repeatedly criticised by the courts for their treatment of Māori youth;[42] the Chief Justice sent a Waitara policeman to the High Court to defend a charge of murdering Steven Wallace;[43] Raglan police were criticised by a District Court judge for chasing two Māori onto a marae and scuffling with them inside the sacred meeting house;[44] and a conviction for not giving a name and address to a policeman was overturned by the High Court when it ruled that it is not an offence to answer a policeman in Māori, one of the two official languages of New Zealand.[45]

The government had long been aware that Māori receive unfair treatment. Apart from the many damning reports of the Waitangi Tribunal and its own *Closing the Gaps* reports highlighting the huge and growing disparities between Māori and non-Māori achievement, its report on the tertiary education sector had resulted in tertiary institutions being warned that unless the recruitment, retention and completion rates for Māori improved markedly, they would be stripped of some of their government funding. Yet the local government reforms did almost nothing to address the lack of roading, water supply, electricity, housing and basic living standards for many rural Māori communities. Apologies and remedies for all of these and many other indignities still suffered by Māori are long overdue.

Attacks on Māori make MPs of Māori descent reluctant to publicly support their own

It is doubtful that the answer to Māori difficulties lies within the existing parliamentary system. In June the Prime Minister announced that the country would go to a general election four months early, at the end of July. The main election issues for Māori were Treaty settlements, education and housing. Genetic modification was also an issue, with Māori largely opposed to it. The apparent lack of performance of many MPs who claim Māori descent was another issue. One commentator noted that of the sixteen Māori members in the last Parliament, less than half of them could be relied on to advocate for Māori[46] and only one, Tariana Turia, was prepared to fight publicly in support of Māori issues. The poor performance was not unexpected given the severe attacks from both the media

and conservative opposition parties on any outspoken Māori
MPs and the fact that party loyalties had effectively prevented
Māori MPs acting as a single bloc.

July general election sees a record twenty MPs of Māori descent in Parliament

Yet the July 2002 elections saw a record number of twenty
MPs who claimed Māori descent in a Parliament of 120
members, eleven representing their own electorates and the
rest as list members for their parties. But none of these were
independents. All seven Māori electorate seats remained
with Labour, with the Labour Māori caucus at a record ten
members in the full Labour caucus of fifty-two. Yet despite
the strong Māori numbers, the Māori caucus indicated shortly
after the elections that it was requesting just three Ministerial
appointments inside cabinet and three outside cabinet in what
would become a Labour-led minority government.

Of the remaining parties, the traditional mainstream
conservative party, National, returned only twenty-seven
members, with their vote dissipated amongst right-wing
minor parties. Only two of their members were Māori. Of the
three other right-wing parties represented in the house, New
Zealand First gained thirteen seats, while ACT and United
Future each gained nine. The New Zealand First Party was
led by a Māori, the charismatic Winston Peters, and despite
a general impression that he was Māori bashing, six of his
thirteen members were Māori. ACT had one Māori member
while United Future had none. The left-leaning Green Party
gained only eight seats, one of which went to a Māori. The
Progressive Coalition had two members, neither of whom
were Māori. Labour entered negotiations with both the
Greens and United Future about the composition of the next
government.

1 Audrey Young, 2002(a), 'Greens move to defend Maori sovereignty stand', *New Zealand Herald*, 9 February 2002, p. A7.
2 Sullivan, 'Māori Representation in Local Government', p. 137.
3 MLR, April 2002, p. 7.
4 Sullivan, 'Māori Representation in Local Government', p. 135.
5 Sullivan, 'Māori Representation in Local Government', p. 137.
6 Sullivan, 'Māori Representation in Local Government', p. 144.
7 Te Puni Kōkiri, 2006, *Te Kotahitanga o te Whakahaere Rawa: Māori and Council Engagement Under the Resource Management Act 1991*, Wellington, Te Puni Kōkiri, p. 20. 55 percent of the Wairoa District Council's population is Māori, but this is not reflected in the council's elected membership.
8 Simon Collins, 2002, 'One Man's Poll: Maori in the New Millenium', *New Zealand Herald*, 9 July, 2002, p. A9.
9 Television New Zealand, *Assignment*, 2 May 2002.
10 Audrey Young, 2002(b), 'NZ First Will Campaign on Treaty, Race Issues', *New Zealand Herald*, 19 April 2002, p. A6; NZPA, 2002(c), 'ACT Wants End of Year Deadline for Lodging Treaty Claims', *nzherald.co.nz*, 3 July 2002.
11 Michael Bassett, 2002, 'Halt the Treaty Gravy Train', *Dominion*, 6 February 2002, p. 12.
12 Moana Jackson, 2002, 'The English text', *Mana*, June–July 2002, p. 51.
13 See the website of the Crown Forestry Rental Trust, http://www.cfrt.org.nz/about/
14 Māori Affairs Select Committee, 2002, 'Inquiry into the Crown Forestry Rental Trust', press release, 19 September 2002, http://www.scoop.co.nz/stories/PA0209/S00337.htm
15 Fran O'Sullivan, 2002, 'Forest Action Begins – Touch Wood', *New Zealand Herald*, 6 May 2002, p. D2.
16 Mutu, 'Recovering Fagin's Ill-gotten Gains', p. 203.
17 Waitangi Tribunal, *Taranaki Report*, p. 312.
18 Mutu, 'Recovering Fagin's Ill-gotten Gains', p. 203.
19 See chapter 2 on the fiscal envelope.
20 Hamer, 'A Quarter-century of the Waitangi Tribunal', p. 10; MLR, November 2000, p. 10.
21 Jackson, 'The English text'; Tapu Misa, 2002(b), 'Parliamentary Colour in Quantity, but Quality in Doubt', *New Zealand Herald*, 31 July 2002, p. A13.
22 Jackson, 'The English text'.
23 Jackson, 'The English text'.
24 Hamer, 'A Quarter-century of the Waitangi Tribunal', pp. 12–14.
25 Greg Wycherley, 2002, and Richard Knight, 'Whangai Adoption a Grey Area', *New Zealand Herald*, 17 April 2002, p. A3.
26 Angela Gregory, 2002, 'Treaty Experts Sceptical Over Kahu Kidnap Link', *New Zealand Herald*, 17 April 2002, p. A3.
27 Paula Oliver, 2002, 'Details of Kahu Kidnap Revealed', *New Zealand Herald*, 25 May 2002, p. A2.
28 Moana Jackson, 2001, 'Terror and Democracy', *Mana* no. 42, October–November 2001, p. 50.
29 Scott MacLeod and Reuters, 2001, 'Global Chorus for Peace', *New Zealand Herald*, 1 October 2001, p. A4.
30 2002, 'He Pitopito Korero: John Davy', *Mana* no. 46, June–July 2002, p. 12.
31 John Armstrong, 2002, 'PM's Tip to Turia: "Bite your lip"', *New Zealand Herald*, 11 March 2002, p. A7.
32 Helen Clark, personal communication.
33 Peter Calder, 2002, 'Te Tangata Whai Rawa o Weneti', *New Zealand Herald*, 16 February 2002, p. E6.
34 2002, 'Chatterbox: Picking up Good Vibes, and Bryan', *nzherald.co.nz*, 16 November 2002.
35 'He Pitopito Korero: Don Selwyn', p. 12.

36 Louisa Cleave, 2002, 'Mai FM Steals Newstalk ZB's Mantle as No.1', *New Zealand Herald*, 18 April 2002, p. A1.
37 Margaret Mutu, 2009(a), 'Media and Literature: Depictions of Māori and Chinese', in Manying Ip (ed.), *The Dragon and the Taniwha: Māori and Chinese in New Zealand*, Auckland, Auckland University Press, p. 247.
38 Tapu Misa, 2002(a), 'The Spoiling of Samoa', *New Zealand Herald*, 1 June 2002, p. B5; Michael Field, 1991, *Mau: Samoa's Struggle for Freedom*, Auckland, Polynesian Press.
39 Misa, 'The Spoiling of Samoa'; Field, *Mau*.
40 2002, 'Protestors Occupy Young Nick's Head', *nzherald.co.nz*, 15 July 2002.
41 Bridget Carter, 2002, 'Jail Activists Vow to Battle On', *New Zealand Herald*, 5 June 2002, p. A2.
42 Daniel Jackson, 2001(a), 'Lawyers to Watch Whangarei Police', *New Zealand Herald*, 18 October 2001, p. A5; Daniel Jackson, 2001(b), 'Top Officer Will Investigate Whangarei police', *New Zealand Herald*, 19 October 2001, p. A5; Daniel Jackson and Scott MacLeod, 2001, 'Judge Says Women Forced to Confess', *New Zealand Herald*, 27 October 2001, p. A3; Tony Wall, 2001(a), 'Strong Arm of the Law Put in the Dock', *New Zealand Herald*, 3 November 2001, p. A1; Tony Wall, 2001(b), 'Police defy judge's rebuke', *New Zealand Herald*, 4 November 2001, p. A1.
43 2002, 'Chief Justice Sends Steven Wallace Case Back to Court', *nzherald.co.nz*, 14 June 2002.
44 NZPA, 2002(a), 'Judge Rebukes Police Over Marae Fracas', *New Zealand Herald*, 12 February 2002, p. A7.
45 MLR, March 2002, p. 7.
46 Misa, 'Parliamentary Colour in Quantity, but Quality in Doubt'.

CHAPTER 10:

2002–03 – The Year the Crown Declared War over the Foreshore and Seabed

Record number of Māori MPs but only two in cabinet …

The July 2002 general election delivered twenty MPs who identified as Māori out of a House of 120 members. Ten of them were in the Labour caucus of fifty-two which led the coalition government. All seven of the Māori seats went to Labour. Māori therefore expected to see at least three Māori cabinet ministers, with the same number or more becoming ministers outside cabinet. It was indicative of things to come that only two Māori cabinet ministers were appointed, along with another two outside cabinet. One of the ministers outside cabinet was Tariana Turia, who returned to the House with a very substantial 7,536 majority in the new Taihauāuru seat. Turia had developed the reputation of being the only MP in the House prepared to speak out fearlessly on behalf and in support of Māori, no matter how strident the media and opposition attacks on her became. Many Māori hoped she would be included in cabinet as she had certainly earned such an appointment. Her appointment as a minister outside cabinet sent a clear message that the Labour caucus was still uncomfortable with Māori who consistently support their own people.

... And only two outspoken in their support of Māori

However Turia was no longer the only Māori MP able to articulate Māori aspirations accurately, clearly and consistently.[1] Metiria Turei, a first-time list MP in the Green Party,[2] showed considerable potential. Her maiden speech caused a predictable backlash. In it she spoke at length about racism. 'I grew up in a working-class Māori family, and we were poor ... Like many Māori, I grew up with this sharing as a fundamental expression of my Māori self. But I also grew up in a racist society, where the expression of Māori values is considered a failure to cope in a modern society. The notion that a Western-styled, two parent family unit is the only cornerstone of a decent society is an example. That notion is a racist one ... To be a Māori in this society is to be revolutionary by mere existence. My politicization, my subversiveness, was grounded in my living my life as a Māori. My personal political journey has led me to the reasonable conclusion that the present State has no legitimacy, and that it must ultimately be transformed into a system that implements Te Tiriti o Waitangi ... in my own journey of empowerment, politicization, and subversiveness, I have found myself a member of the establishment, but not now, nor ever, its advocate.'[3] In January 2003 she told the *New Zealand Herald* 'I really hate the hate mail. I get it any time I say anything about Māori at all, of any description.'[4] Although the mainstream media ignored most of her press releases, her party did not appear to be censoring them.[5]

National Party attacking Māori from every possible angle

Georgina te Heuheu of the conservative National Party, on the other hand, had found herself increasingly having to contradict her party leader. After the party failed miserably in the general election, the National leader abandoned any pretence of supporting Māori aspirations and set out to attack any policy or programme aimed at improving Māori circumstances. As lawyer and commentator Moana Jackson put it, '… in Parliament the idea of parliamentary privilege seems to have become the privilege to demean Māori people, Māori initiatives, and Māori rights.'[6] The National Party leader called for the abolition of the seven Māori seats in Parliament; demanded that the government legislate to vest the foreshores and seabed in the Crown, effectively confiscating those areas from Māori; argued that Māori should be given no special consideration in any matter and that all New Zealanders are the same (thus wilfully disregarding all socio-economic indicators which contradict this); attacked the government for setting aside money in the budget for a Treaty of Waitangi education programme; attacked the Waitangi Tribunal for saying that Māori have an interest in the country's oil and gas resources; and promised to stop Māori making claims under the Treaty of Waitangi and to remove those aspects of the Resource Management Act and Local Government Act which protect Māori relationships with their ancestral lands.[7] His racist outbursts had not improved National's showing in the opinion polls.

Māori objections to replacement of Privy Council ignored
In April 2002 the government indicated that it intended to introduce legislation setting up a new Supreme Court which would replace the London-based Privy Council. More than 90 percent of Māori who made submissions to the Select Committee hearings in 2003 opposed the proposed legislation.[8] The select committee report noted that for Māori submitters 'Constitutional rearrangement including the Treaty of Waitangi was considered a prerequisite for the establishment of a Supreme Court … Consultation with Māori and the status of the Treaty of Waitangi, along with the wider context of reform of constitutional arrangements were the main additional issues raised in submissions from many Māori.'[9] Submissions often noted that the present judicial system discriminates against Māori with Māori being convicted and

imprisoned at a far greater rate than non-Māori. The Privy Council is perceived as independent of New Zealand and not tainted with the same racism that exists in the New Zealand courts. Many felt that a Supreme Court made up entirely of New Zealand judges would continue to discriminate against Māori. The comments on racism and discrimination were not mentioned in the Select Committee's report.

Media attacks on Māori Television finally halted

In May 2002 a very successful Māori businessman, Wayne Walden, was appointed to the Māori Television Service as the acting Chief Executive Officer to guide its setting up.[10] He managed to stop media attacks on the Service and its personnel by refusing to speak to mainstream journalists. The media appeared to lose interest completely after having attacked the Service continually over the previous twelve months. By January the budget allocated by government to set up the service had increased from $6 million to $13 million with hardly a murmur of dissent. Legislation formally setting the service in place was eventually passed in May 2003 after years of strenuous efforts to stop it.[11] The Opposition eventually supported the legislation and its passing into law went unmentioned in the mainstream media.[12]

Bullyboy tactics employed in the continuing fisheries allocation debacle

The allocation of fisheries quota by the Treaty of Waitangi Fisheries Commission continued to be bogged down in disputes between Māori. Eleven years after the so-called 'settlement' the allocation was still not complete. In December 2002, the new Commission chair tried to force an agreement[13] and the Commission ran a propaganda campaign which claimed that 91 percent of iwi representing 96 percent of Māori supported the Commission's allocation model.[14] The mainstream media believed the propaganda, praising the chairman as the saviour of warring Māori factions. Māori lawyer and commentator Annette Sykes noted, 'Television, radio and newspaper stories that report the views of someone as highly placed as the Commission chairman, Shane Jones, can combine to give those views far more authority and credence than they deserve ... we've been provided with an illusion of informed consent, when the reality is something quite different.'[15] Mainstream media subsequently ignored the fact that a large number of hapū and iwi took litigation to prevent the model being entrenched in legislation. The litigation failed and the matter was left in the hands of the Minister of Fisheries.

Local Government Act stripped of the ability to ensure Māori participation

In December 2002 the Local Government Act passed in to law.[16] Māori had hoped for some major reforms to ensure that they played a more active and meaningful role in the decision-making of local authorities, for it is at the local authority level that Māori resources are most immediately affected, where decisions are made which directly affect their ancestral lands, waterways, seas and, particularly, the sacred sites and places of special significance within them that have been ritually restricted, wāhi tapu. Although there are provisions in the Resource Management Act 1991 to recognise and provide for these matters,[17] the lack of knowledge and political will to implement the relevant sections of the Act means that Māori cultural and spiritual concerns are constantly trampled on by developers whose actions are fully condoned by consent-granting local authorities.[18] Those whānau and hapū who can afford to do so are increasingly resorting to the courts for relief. Yet the reforms which Māori sought were watered down so much during the passage of the legislation that all decisions about whether Māori should be included in decision-making were left entirely in the hands of the existing local authorities.[19] By mid-2002, only one of the 86 local authorities had made provision for Māori representation on their authority,[20] and only ten chose the Single Transferable Vote polling system[21] which would have given Māori a greater chance to be elected. The overall result appears to be a recipe for continued litigation against local authorities by Māori.

Mainstream media discrimination against Māori MPs continues

Keeping up its tradition, mainstream media persisted with its attacks on Māori MPs. In 2002–03 it was Donna Awatere-Huata's turn. When the right-wing ACT Party suspended her in Februrary 2003,[22] the media harassed her and her family for weeks, prying into their private and personal affairs. Many Māori, including MPs from other parties, spoke out against the cruel treatment by the media. By contrast the suspension of ex-Minister, Maurice Williamson, from the National Party in July 2003 made headlines for a couple of days[23] and then vanished. No mention was made of either his family or his private and personal affairs.

New Zealand Herald columnist attacks mainstream media Māori bashing

Media attacks on Māori came under attack from an unusual source this year: a columnist in the *New Zealand Herald*. Since February 2002 Tapu Misa[24] has been contributing weekly columns in the country's largest newspaper. In a column headed 'Media Perceptions of Māori Still Pretty Distorted' she noted '... misunderstanding and misinformation abound and I'm beginning to think some of it is wilful. Māori have complained for years at the way an overwhelmingly Pākehā mainstream media continue to shape and distort perceptions about them'.[25] While the newspaper continued to publish items attacking Māori, its new editor had yet to withdraw Misa's columns in the way that columns supportive of Māori have been withdrawn in the past.[26] The *Herald* continued to publish letters attacking Misa's columns, although there was also the occasional letter supporting them.

In at least seven of her columns Misa has raised the issue of racial discrimination not only against Māori, but also against Pacific Islanders (Misa is Samoan), drawing on topical issues which have demonstrated that racism is alive and well in New Zealand. Media attacks on Māori for seeking protection for their wāhi tapu or places of special significance appeared on at least four different occasions in 2002–03.[27] The Race Relations Commissioner was subjected to furious attacks for defending Māori because he had compared New Zealand's colonial history of vandalizing Māori culture and the natural environment to the Taleban's destruction of the Bamiyan Buddhas in Afganistan.[28] Misa defended the Commissioner, saying 'Joris de Bres chose to talk about the many sins of New Zealand's colonial government to help throw some light on Māori cultural issues'. However she concluded 'we are not yet ready as a society to acknowledge the ongoing effects of past wrongs'.[29]

Whale Rider attracts critical acclaim

One bright note in the year for Māori was the release of the film *Whale Rider*, based on a book written by Witi Ihimaera. It won accolades at the Sundance movie festival and awards at other festivals including Seattle, San Francisco, Maui, Toronto and Rotterdam, and enjoyed great box office success in countries such as the United States of America. It finally screened in Auckland in January and ran for several months. It is an adaptation of a well-known East Coast tradition about an ancestor who rides on a whale, and makes very poignant comments about the restrictive and inflexible nature that some adopt in respect of Māori customs. The film was produced and directed by Pākehā, which resulted in some odd distortions of the Māori world it was trying to portray.

Two Treaty settlements this year

Two settlements of Treaty of Waitangi claims against the Crown were completed in 2002–03: Ngāti Ruanui for $41 million and Ngāti Tūwharetoa ki Kawerau for $10.5 million. The money is given to the claimants so that they can buy back very small amounts of their own land from the Crown. The claims have been estimated to be worth $12 billion and $3 billion respectively.[30] As the Ngāti Ruanui Treaty Claims Settlement Bill passed into legislation, Tariana Turia warned Parliament that $41 million was only a tiny proportion of what was lost. The government also entered negotiations with four other iwi, including Ngāti Whātua o Ōrākei, whose claim covers Auckland city.

Government angry at Tribunal for its findings in favour of Māori for petroleum ...

But the government reacted angrily to decisions from the Waitangi Tribunal and the Court of Appeal which found in favour of Māori against the Crown. The Waitangi Tribunal issued its findings in May that Māori have an interest in the country's oil and gas resources and that the Crown's royalty entitlements from petroleum and its 11 percent interest in the Kupe petroleum mining license ought to be available for inclusion in settlements with affected claimants.[31] The claims were lodged by Ngā Hapū o Ngā Ruahine (of Taranaki) and Ngāti Kahungunu (of Hawkes Bay and Wairarapa) in 1999. The government immediately declared that it would ignore the recommendations that Māori interests be recognised. The Minister in Charge of Treaty Negotiations, Margaret Wilson, was also quick to squash any consideration of the Crown negotiating with Māori over royalties.[32] The Crown used the specious argument that Māori proprietary rights over the country's oil and gas resources cannot be recognised because Māori were not using those resources in 1840 when the Treaty of Waitangi was signed. But then neither was the Crown.[33] So really the argument was that the Crown did not recognise the Māori right to development and new technology. Or more accurately, despite international instruments protecting the human rights of indigenous peoples and legislation outlawing racial discrimination in this country,[34] the Crown has yet to divest itself of the notion that depriving Māori of what is rightfully theirs is as acceptable in the twenty-first century as it was during the nineteenth and twentieth centuries. It was this attitude that caused Sir Apirana Ngata to perform a haka in the House in 1937 and to cast the ultimate Māori insult at the Prime Minister of the day when mining rights were nationalised and there was no payment of royalties to Māori.[35]

... And the Court of Appeal for doing the same for the foreshore and seabed ...

One month later, on 20 June 2003, the Court of Appeal issued its decision that the Māori Land Court has the jurisdiction to investigate the title of foreshore and seabed and declare its status to be Māori customary land.[36] The Crown had wrongly assumed that it held title to all these resources, when both common law and the Treaty of Waitangi say clearly that they belong to Māori until such time as their title is properly extinguished. A legal commentator noted 'It is difficult to underestimate the importance of this decision to NZ's general legal development. In some ways, this decision is the NZ equivalent of the *Mabo* judgment of 1992.'[37]

... So Crown proposes confiscation of Māori land in the foreshore and seabed on a massive scale

Just four days later, on 24 June 2003, the government announced that it would legislate to overturn the decision of the Court of Appeal and give the ownership of all Māori interests in the New Zealand's foreshore and seabed to the Crown.[38] The government's intention to remove Māori rights in respect of such lands would amount to the largest ever confiscation of Māori property. The outcry from Māori was instantaneous, furious and uncharacteristically united.[39] The country appeared to be stunned by the level of anger expressed by Māori, who for once enjoyed the unanimous support of the ten Māori Labour caucus members along with almost all other Māori MPs in Parliament. A press release issued by Labour's Māori MPs quoted them as saying 'The land wars are over, so the consent of tangata whenua is required before customary title can be extinguished. Otherwise it is a confiscation and is likely to breach international law.'[40]

The Labour-led government reeled in the face of the onslaught, uncomfortably aware that they held all seven of the seats specifically designated for Māori in the House. Angry outbursts from Pākehā demanding that the government not bow to Māori pressure overwhelmed calls by other Pākehā to respect Māori property rights. Opposition parties went to extraordinary lengths to whip up strong anti-Māori sentiment based on imagined fears that Māori would prevent public access to the country's foreshores. It took several weeks of uninformed public debate and speculation before mainstream media started publishing any factual information relating to the issue.

Within three weeks of the government announcement Māori had convened a national hui (gathering) to discuss the issue. Over 1000 attended, many of them the mandated representatives of each of the numerous tribal groupings throughout the country. Factual information on the issues involved was available both through presentations made by experts in the field and formal written opinions. The resolutions from the gathering issued very strong warnings to both the government and all Māori MPs not to attempt to extinguish or redefine Māori customary title or rights. Representatives returned home from the meeting to inform their communities of the outcomes and to seek instructions on measures to be taken to resolve the problem. A second national gathering was to be held at the end of August. By the end of July, calls for Māori to take greater control over their own affairs and resources were becoming more widespread. The government, on the other hand, was refusing to discuss the foreshore and seabed matter with anyone other than its own caucus.

Government clashes with Māori over aquaculture

In the year leading up to the announcement on the foreshore and seabed, Māori had become increasingly strident in their criticisms of government plans to lease out areas within the coastal marine area for aquaculture purposes. In December 2002 the Waitangi Tribunal had issued findings that Māori have rights in respect of aquaculture and marine farming which the Crown had failed to take into account in its proposals to tender coastal space that arguably belongs to Māori.[41] As a result of highly exploitative commercial fishing activities, the country's natural fish stocks had become severely depleted. Shellfish farming in particular was becoming a lucrative business, although competition for use of coastal space was such that the government decided to regulate access to it for commercial purposes. The fact that this would mean that Māori would probably lose their rights to the coastal space was disregarded in official circles. After 160 years of successfully depriving Māori of almost all their natural resources, this was just another step in the same direction. Officials and the government chose to turn a blind eye to the repeated findings and warnings of the Waitangi Tribunal that the Crown cannot steal Māori resources with impunity. The decision of the Court of Appeal in respect of the foreshore and seabed caught them completely off-guard and their announcement that they intended to effectively confiscate by legislation took the country back 140 years to the last legal confiscations of Māori land. Those resulted in civil war as Māori were forced to defend their lands.

1 Tariana Turia, 2002, 'Politics: Election 2002: A Pathway of Change', *Mana* no. 46, June–July 2002, p. 41.
2 2002, 'Money-back Guarantee?', *Mana* no. 47, August–September 2002, p. 27.
3 MLR, September 2002, p. 8.
4 2003, 'Question time: Metiria Turei, Green list MP', *New Zealand Herald*, 8 January 2003, p.A8.
5 Derek Fox, 2002, 'Politics: Who'll speak up for Māori?', *Mana* no. 47, August–September 2002, p. 24.
6 Moana Jackson, 2002–3, 'Highs and Lows', *Mana* no. 49, December 2002–January 2003, p. 45.
7 National party website, http://www.national.org.nz/files/orewarotaryclub_27jan.pdf
8 Justice and Electoral Select Committee, 2003, *Report to Parliament on the Supreme Court Bill*, http://www.parliament.nz/NR/rdonlyres/710D1400-725F-47DC-8713-29F0407D9199/47916/DBSCH_SCR_2552_28191.pdf, p. 8. Of the thirty-eight submissions received from Māori, only four supported the establishment of the Supreme Court.
9 Justice and Electoral Select Committee, *Report to Parliament on the Supreme Court Bill*, p. 11.
10 Walker, 2004, *Ka Whawhai Tonu Matou*, p.373.
11 Walker, 2004, *Ka Whawhai Tonu Matou*, pp. 369–76.
12 Arotahi News Service, 2003, 'Māori TV legislation passed', Item 20, May 2003 Edition 6.
13 Irene Chapple, 2002, 'Tribes Swap Dissent For Profit', *New Zealand Herald*, 29 October 2002, p. C1.
14 Audrey Young, 2002(c), 'Fish Accord Backed by 91pc of Tribes', *New Zealand Herald*, 4 December 2002, p. A6.
15 Annette Sykes, 2003, 'Let's get it right', *Mana* no. 51, April–May 2003, p. 48.
16 MLR, April 2003, p. 7.
17 Sections 6(e), 7(a) and 8 in particular.
18 See, for example, Margaret Mutu, 2002, 'Barriers to Tangata Whenua Participation in Resource Management', in Merata Kawharu (ed.), *Whenua: Managing our Resources*, Auckland, Reed, pp. 75–95.
19 Sullivan, 'Māori Representation in Local Government', p. 144.
20 Waaka, 'Local Government', p. 225.
21 See STV legislation and background at http://www.stv.govt.nz/STV/legislation.htm
22 Government Directory online, 2003, 'ACT MP suspended', 20 February 2003, http://www.nzgovtdirectory.com/Visitors/news/Archive2003.asp
23 Audrey Young, 2003(b), 'National Caucus Suspends Williamson', *nzherald.co.nz*, 22 July 2003.
24 Tapu Misa, 1995, 'Cover Story: A Migrant Story', *Mana* no. 10, Spring 1995, pp. 14–16.
25 Tapu Misa, 2002, 'Media Perceptions of Māori Still Pretty Distorted', *nzherald.co.nz*, 27 November 2002.
26 For example columns contributed by Dr Rawiri Taonui (Rawiri Taonui, personal communication).
27 Various items in *New Zealand Herald* accessed at *nzherald.co.nz*: NZPA, 2002(d), 'Land Claim Puts Tycoon's Resort on Hold', 4 August 2002; NZPA, 2002(e), 'MP Slams Prison Costs', 4 September 2002; Anne Gibson, 2002, 'Iwi Wins Bid to Appeal on Sylvia Park', 26 November 2002; Bay of Plenty Times, 2002, 'Parties in Wahi Tapu Row Could Meet Before Christmas', 29 November 2002; NZPA, 2002(f), 'Protestors Occupy Prison Site, Warn of Taniwha Trouble', 2 December 2002; 2003, 'Row Brewing Over Urewera Pa Site', 14 April 2003.
28 NZPA, 2002(g), 'Pakeha settlers "like Taleban vandals"', *New Zealand Herald*, 4 December 2002, p. A1.

29 Tapu Misa, 2002(d), 'Let's catch racism early and hit it where it counts', *nzherald. co.nz*, 11 December 2002.
30 Mutu, 'Recovering Fagin's Ill-gotten Gains', p. 204 and footnote 67.
31 Waitangi Tribunal, 2003, *The Petroleum Report* (Wai 796), Wellington, GP Publications, http://www.waitangi-tribunal.govt.nz/reports/; MLR, June 2003, p. 11.
32 Tracy Watkins, 2003, 'Pandora's Box Warning for Oil', *Dominion Post*, 22 May 2003, p. A2.
33 Murray Hemi, 2003, 'The good oil', *Mana* no. 52, June–July 2003, p. 60.
34 The Race Relations Act 1971.
35 Tania Rangiheua, 2003, 'Time for Talk', *Mana* no. 52, June–July 2003, p. 61.
36 *Attorney-General v Ngati Apa* [2003] 3 NZLR 643 (CA).
37 MLR, May 2003, p. 1.
38 Audrey Young, 2003(a), 'Quick Move Blocks Maori Bid to Claim Rights Over Seabed', *nzherald.co.nz*, 24 June 2003.
39 Margaret Mutu, 2005(b), 'Research Ethics Associated with Treaty of Waitangi Claims and the Foreshore and Seabed Legislation', in *Tikanga Rangahau: Mātauranga Tuku Iho – The Proceedings of the Traditional Knowledge and Research Ethics Conference 2004*, Auckland, Ngā Pae o te Māramatanga: New Zealand's Māori Centre of Research Excellence, University of Auckland, p. 160.
40 2003, 'Revolt by Maori MPs over foreshore', *New Zealand Herald*, 25 June 2003, p. A1.
41 Waitangi Tribunal, 2002, *Ahu Moana. The Aquaculture and Marine Farming Report* (Wai 953), Wellington, GP Publications, http://www.waitangi-tribunal. govt.nz/reports/

CHAPTER 11

2003–04 – The Year of the Battle for the Foreshore and Seabed

Māori react very strongly to government announcement of proposed confiscation of foreshore and seabed

2003–04 was a year of massive upheaval for Māori. In June 2003 the New Zealand government announced its intention to legislate to confiscate the country's foreshore and seabed from Māori.[1] At the time there was a furious and uncharacteristically united outcry from Māori.[2] The levels of anger amongst Māori against the government on this issue increased over the next year as the government refused not only to back down but also to enter into any meaningful consultation or dialogue with those who would be directly affected, the numerous coastal whānau and hapū,[3] many of whom had had rights to their own particular areas of the coast for many hundreds of years.

Māori opposition highly organised – government steps up anti-Māori propaganda campaign – Tariana Turia resigns

Māori organised their opposition with unprecedented levels of cooperation while the government tried desperately to undermine them, issuing propaganda which warned that if Māori ownership was recognised, Māori would block off access to the country's beaches and sell them all off to the highest bidder.[4] The government's proposal,[5] then the policy[6] and finally the legislation[7] came under sustained attack as Māori used every forum, strategy and mechanism they could identify to try to have it removed. This included mounting the biggest protest march ever seen in this country.[8] They also attacked the male Māori members of the Labour government caucus, including the Minister of Māori Affairs, labeling them as traitors when they eventually supported the legislation and ignored the clear and unequivocal instructions of their constituents. Two Māori women members of government who opposed the legislation drew huge support from Māori.[9] When one of them, Tariana Turia, resigned from Parliament, forcing a by-election, voter turnout was unusually high, even though none of the main political parties stood any candidates. After setting up and co-leading the new Māori Party, Turia took 92 percent of the vote, returning triumphantly to Parliament with a new mandate.[10]

Government refuses to listen to Māori and continues pushing through legislation

But the government remained resolute and determined to pass its foreshore and seabed legislation into law well before the 2005 general election, launching attacks on Māori leaders and several judges in an attempt to deflect their criticisms.[11] Opposition parties, except for New Zealand First, opposed the legislation but made it very clear that they were not doing so to support Māori retaining their legal entitlements. The only party in Parliament that supported Māori was the Greens. And in the midst of the foreshore and seabed turmoil, highlights on the Māori calendar such as the successful launching of the long-awaited Māori Television Service in March 2004, the nomination of Keisha Castle-Hughes to win an Academy Award for her role in *Whale Rider* and then the launch of the Māori Party were all seized on by Māori to assist them in their battle to stop the government proceeding with their foreshore and seabed legislation.

Court of Appeal's decision in Marlborough case upholds Māori rights

The government decision to legislate to remove Māori rights to the foreshore and seabed was a knee-jerk reaction to the Court of Appeal's unanimous decision in the Marlborough case.[12] The decision was issued on 20 June 2003 and indicated that the Crown's assertion of its ownership of the country's foreshore and seabed was not correct and that the Māori Land Court had the jurisdiction to investigate the status of that land and determine whether it is customary Māori land. The decision upheld domestic law (The Māori Land Act), English common law (which recognises that when the English colonise another country, indigenous peoples' 'customary rights and title' to their lands remain and cannot be extinguished in times of peace without their consent), and international law (in respect of the rights of indigenous peoples). The decision brought huge, albeit very temporary relief for coastal whānau, hapū and iwi throughout the country. After 134 years of pursuing ownership of the foreshore and seabed through the courts,[13] blockages were now removed and the court could investigate Māori property rights claims, including ownership.

Foreshore and seabed legislation removes Māori rights while preserving non-Māori rights – a declaration of war

Yet four days later, in a move that showed flagrant disregard for all constitutional conventions and due process, the New Zealand government announced that it would legislate to stop all New Zealand courts considering cases already before them on the matter. The legislation would overrule the decision of the Court of Appeal and vest complete and absolute ownership in the Crown,[14] confiscating it from the whānau and hapū throughout the country who held mana whenua[15] and hence ownership of them. However the government would protect any non-Māori interests in the foreshore and seabed. So the harbour boards, port companies and an increasing number of private individuals, many of which were foreign investors and speculators, would not have their property rights removed. Such a blatantly racist approach meant that the government was effectively singling out Māori and declaring war on them. The Māori response was immediate and unanimous. There was complete opposition to and abhorrence of what the government was suggesting. But for Māori it was also simply history repeating itself. In the 1860s the government had legislated to confiscate Māori land in order to satisfy settler greed for Māori land and resources.[16] Predictably it led to the New Zealand land wars. This was no different. And the ease with which the government could flout fundamental constitutional norms, domestic, common or international law took legal scholars by surprise and brought into question the sanctity of the rule of law.[17]

Reality of Māori marginalisation – Māori MPs bow to Labour pressure and betray their constituents

However, the powerlessness and marginalisation of Māori within the New Zealand Parliament was clearly on display as their increasingly angry protests went unheeded. By August the government had published its proposal.[18] In December its policy was released.[19] In April 2004 the Foreshore and Seabed Bill was introduced into the House. In July, a parliamentary Select Committee started hearing submissions on the Bill, scheduled to report back by November. And although all ten government MPs who had declared their Māori background strenuously opposed the proposed confiscation when it was first announced,[20] Māori were stunned and mystified when all but two of them were subsequently persuaded to support it. Their support, along with the belated support of New Zealand First, would ensure its safe passage through Parliament. It was as a direct result of these betrayals that the Māori Party was set up, with a mandate that the clearly articulated wishes of the people must take precedence over the wishes of the party.[21]

Pākehā racism unashamedly displayed

After the government's announcement, it did not take long for the sinister, anti-Māori under-belly of the Pākehā population to display itself as reports of a poll indicated that most were happy to support the legislation.[22] They were happy, it seemed, for the Crown to take ownership of the foreshore and seabed regardless of the strong Māori interests already there, or the fact that the Crown had been unable to prove that it owned it in the Court of Appeal. This theft by legislation was an easy way of getting a very substantial resource for free. After all, the high standard of living enjoyed by the great majority of Pākehā New Zealanders has always depended on them being able to gain access to Māori land and resources at little or no cost, regardless of how unfair and unjust that may be for the Māori owners or the fact that most of those acquisitions were illegal. Just when Māori were hoping that the Treaty claims processes were finally signaling an end to such discrimination, it was being re-embarked upon with even greater vigor and determination.

National Party leader exploits racism – Brash's Ōrewa speech

The Opposition recognised the growing Pākehā backlash against Māori and were quick to exploit it. To his considerable political advantage, the leader of the National Party and the Opposition, Don Brash, promised, in a widely reported and controversial speech to conservative Pākehā businessmen at Ōrewa in January 2004,[23] to abolish 'special privileges' for Māori. He portrayed the Waitangi Tribunal as delivering privileges to Māori, deliberately misrepresenting its role of identifying breaches of the Treaty of Waitangi and recommending strategies for removing the prejudice caused. When Māori and the media asked him to identify the 'special privileges', it did not seem to matter that he could not do so. His ratings in the opinion polls continued to climb and he seemed to be able to ignore the fact that both history and the statistics show that it is Pākehā who enjoy substantial privileges in New Zealand, and that Māori and their Pacific Island relations are overwhelmingly New Zealand's most disadvantaged. When his spokesperson on Māori Affairs and the only Māori in the National Party caucus, Georgina te Heuheu, was unable to support her leader's attacks she was sacked and replaced by the deputy leader, who was happy to launch even harsher attacks on Māori.[24] The attacks were unashamedly and openly racist and the long-held pretence that most Pākehā New Zealanders do not harbour racist attitudes towards Māori could no longer be sustained. And so they attacked one of the country's foremost and internationally acclaimed entertainers, Bic Runga, when she told an Irish newspaper in March that New Zealand can be a racist country and that racism was a constant feature of her childhood in Christchurch.[25]

National Party Māori bashing gives government excuse to cut funding for Māori programmes

The National Party's success in attacking Māori was quickly picked up by the government, the Prime Minister announcing her own 'review' of Māori programmes.[26] In fact the government had already started withdrawing funding from Māori programmes, so the Opposition attack allowed the withdrawal to proceed more expeditiously. Most Māori programmes would have difficulty surviving without government assistance. Lack of government funding for Māori Television Services threatened to prevent it going to air. A bank loan of $13 million was organised to pay for its studios and the service went to air on 28 March 2004, enjoying good reviews from all commentators.[27] One of its very few detractors was the National Party, which promised to close it down.[28] But a poll taken in June indicated good support for the service, with non-Māori making up 65 percent of its audience.[29] The service is unashamedly supportive of Māori and often very critical of the government. It also maintains very high standards in both the quality of its service and its professionalism.

Māori Television, now finally launched, helps in the battle against foreshore and seabed legislation

Māori leaders were relying in part on the media in their battle against the government's foreshore and seabed legislation, and the Māori Television Service was a welcome addition to their resources. Since July 2003 they had been organising hui and running information campaigns to keep Māori and the general public fully informed on the issue. Within three weeks of the government's first announcement they had convened a national hui to discuss the issue. The resolutions from the 1000-strong gathering of iwi from throughout the country issued very strong warnings to both the government and all Māori MPs not to attempt to extinguish or redefine Māori customary title or rights. Representatives returned home from the meeting to inform their communities of the outcomes and to seek instructions on measures to be taken to resolve the problem. Hui were convened by iwi groups throughout the country and a second national gathering was held at the end of August.

A national Māori collective to fight the foreshore and seabed legislation – Te Ope Mana a Tai

That hui established a collective called Te Ope Mana a Tai, a name which translates approximately as 'the group which holds paramount authority for the coast and seas'. It was made up of tribal leaders, legal advisors (including judges), policy analysts, media experts and other professionals. It was headed by the iwi who had won the Court of Appeal decision and included representation from most other coastal iwi. Its mandate was to gather and disseminate information to Māori and the general public, and carry out work on behalf of Māori on this issue. The group undertook an extensive publicity campaign in an attempt to inform the country of the seriousness of the issue and to counter the misinformation being disseminated by the government that Māori would close off access to the country's beaches and sell them if their ownership was given legal recognition. Te Ope Mana a Tai also relied heavily on decisions from the many local and regional hui convened to discuss the matter and three further national hui that they convened. Other important means of keeping people informed, of strategising and of seeking support of non-Māori included a website (www.teope.co.nz), email groups, teleconferencing, public and conference presentations, university seminars and lectures, advertising through pamphlets, posters and education packages, meeting with Ministers and other MPs, supporting the national Hīkoi, Māori radio and mainstream news media. Several iwi also presented formal complaints before several United Nations committees responsible for human and indigenous peoples' rights.

Waitangi Tribunal upholds country-wide claims against foreshore and seabed policy ...

In October Te Ope Mana a Tai led a claim to the Waitangi Tribunal against the government's foreshore and seabed policy. One hundred and forty-nine claimants representing almost every coastal tribal group around the country pooled their resources and expertise to bring the claim under urgency. In March the Tribunal reported, upholding the claims and issuing very serious warnings to the government of the foolhardiness of proceeding in the manner announced in the policy. One commentator noted that the report 'is damning of the Crown framework policy, using some of the strongest language seen in a tribunal report to date.'[30]

The Tribunal noted that the government's policy contains numerous breaches of the Treaty of Waitangi, adding that 'the Government's unilateral decision to do away with these Māori property rights … could only be justified if chaos or disorder would result if there was no intervention, or if we were at war or facing some other crisis.'[31] It also strongly urged the government to act in fairness, recommending that the government go back to the drawing board and engage Māori in proper negotiations. There was no need for the government to implement any policy, the law should be allowed to take its course.

… And the government ignores the Tribunal, yet again …

Yet on the day the Tribunal released its Foreshore and Seabed report the government announced that it had already rejected the report.[32] Matters covered in the accompanying press release bore little resemblance to the content of the Report and there was speculation that the government had not even bothered to read it. The government had rejected all recent findings of the Tribunal.

… And the Prime Minister breaks even more fundamental constitutional rules and attacks a Māori judge

Many iwi had also applied to the Māori Land Court to have their cases to their own foreshore and seabed heard as soon as the Court of Appeal decision was issued. However, when it proceeded to process the case in one district in March 2004, the Prime Minister ignored constitutional convention and launched a stinging public attack on the judge hearing the case, demanding that she not hear it because she was from the same tribe as the applicants.[33] While it would be unheard of for a politician to launch a personal attack on a non-Māori judge, it seemed to be acceptable to attack a Māori judge. The judge formally reprimanded the Prime Minister in her decision.

Last resort: a 50,000-strong protest march – the Hīkoi

It was the government's ongoing refusal to listen to any Māori advice or to consider the Waitangi Tribunal's recommendations that led to the biggest and most successfully organised protest march ever witnessed in New Zealand. It was called the Hīkoi. Whānau, hapū and iwi from throughout the country, with their colorful tribal banners and flags, joined it on its way from Te Rerenga Wairua in the very Far North, starting on 22 April, and ending in Parliament grounds in Wellington on 5 May. The numbers of people who mobilised in the regions throughout the country were unprecedented. The Hīkoi itself was highly disciplined, yet good-natured, and a dignified stance was maintained throughout. Police reported experiencing no trouble and there were no arrests.[34] While many New Zealanders had become confused on the issue, the clear message of the Hīkoi was that the foreshore and seabed legislation was badly wrong and must be withdrawn from Parliament. Māori simply would not tolerate yet another Treaty breach which was so clearly illegal, immoral and unjust.

On the final day of the Hīkoi through Wellington to Parliament, the unofficial best police estimate was that there were more than 50,000 participants including the several thousand kaumātua who awaited its arrival at Parliament.[35] The government tried desperately to play down both its size and impact, claiming that there were only 15,000 participants and that it was a reaction to the leader of the Opposition's attack on Māori. However while media reports were hugely varied on the size, ranging between 10,000 and 30,000,[36] they were very clear on the message. All media reports described the march as a protest against the government's foreshore and seabed legislation. The media coverage was extensive, both locally and nationally. It also attracted significant international media attention.

Prime Minister calls marchers 'haters and wreckers' and says she prefers the company of sheep

The Prime Minister's constant criticisms of the Hīkoi over the two weeks it took to wend its way to Wellington simply fuelled the determination of the participants to deliver a clear and unequivocal message. As the numbers swelled, she referred to the participants as 'haters and wreckers', telling the media she preferred the company of a sheep to that of iwi representatives leading the march.[37] Yet even she was unable to ignore the Hīkoi. Television cameras caught her watching it from the window of her office as it completely filled Parliament grounds.[38] Many participants could not get into the grounds and remained outside on the surrounding roads and pathways to listen to the speeches of Māori leaders, including Tariana Turia, that were broadcast from inside the grounds.

1 Young, 'Quick Move Blocks Maori bid to Claim Rights Over Seabed'.
2 Mutu, 'Research Ethics Associated with Treaty of Waitangi Claims', p. 160.
3 Mutu, 'Research Ethics Associated with Treaty of Waitangi Claims', p. 163.
4 This received extensive coverage and commentary in a wide range of media including the *New Zealand Herald*, 11 August 2003, 18 August 2003, 6 September 2003, 9 December 2003; *MG Business*, 4 August 2003; *New Zealand Listener*, 9 August 2003; ZBNews interview with prime minister, 11 August 2003; Radio New Zealand interview with leader of the Opposition, 11 August 2003; *Nelson Mail*, 15 August 2003; *Horowhenua-Kapiti Chronicle*, 14 August 2003; *Dominion Post*, 16 August 2003.
5 Department of the Prime Minister and Cabinet, 2003, *The Foreshore and Seabed of New Zealand: Protecting Public Access and Customary Rights: Government Proposals for Consultation*, Wellington, New Zealand Government.
6 Office of the Deputy Prime Minister, 2003, *Foreshore and Seabed: A Framework*, Wellington, Office of the Deputy Prime Minister.
7 The Foreshore and Seabed Act 2004.
8 Mutu, 'Research Ethics Associated with Treaty of Waitangi Claims', p. 163.
9 Ruth Berry, 2004, and Ainsley Thomson, 'Government Faces Second Defection', *nzherald.co.nz*, 4 May 2004.
10 Ruth Berry, 2004(b), 'Māori Party Victors Turn Their Fire on Labour', *nzherald. co.nz*, 12 July 2004.
11 See, for example, from *nzherald.co.nz*, Ruth Berry, 2003(a), 'Maori MPs Could Revolt Over Government Foreshore Plan', 19 August 2003; Ruth Berry, 2003(c), 'Clark Rebukes Turia Over Foreshore Speech', 16 December 2003; Ruth Berry, 2003(b), 'Angry Voices Won't be Far From Foreshore Hui', 4 September 2003; Ruth Berry, 2003(d), 'Iwi Leaders Call for Foreshore Protests', 19 December 2003; Daily Post (Rotorua), 2004, 'Te Arawa Hit Back at PM's Hikoi Comments', 4 May 2004.

12 The case of 'Ngati Apa, Ngati Koata, Ngati Kuia, Ngati Rarua, Ngati Tama, Ngati
    Toa and Rangitane and Another v The Attorney-General and Others', CA173/01,
    19 June 2003, which was subsequently reported as *Attorney-General v Ngati Apa*
    [2003] 3 NZLR 643 (CA), has become known as the Malborough or the Ngāti
    Apa case.
13 Richard Boast, 2007, 'Foreshore and Seabed in New Zealand Law: A Legal-
    Historical Introduction', in C Charters and A Erueti (eds), *Māori Property Rights
    and the Foreshore and Seabed: The Last Frontier*, Wellington, Victoria University
    Press, pp. 14–29.
14 Young, 'Quick Move Blocks Maori Bid to Claim Rights Over Seabed'.
15 Mana whenua can be (very simplistically) defined as power, authority, control and
    responsibility derived from the gods for a particular area of land.
16 See, for example, the reports of the Waitangi Tribunal which inquire into
    confiscations in the 1860s: the *Taranaki Report* (1996), and Waitangi Tribunal,
    1999(a), *The Ngati Awa Raupatu Report* (Wai 46), Wellington, Legislation Direct,
    http://www.waitangi-tribunal.govt.nz/reports/
17 Kerensa Johnston and Nin Tomas, 2003, 'Who Owns the Foreshore and Seabed
    of Aotearoa', *New Zealand Law Review*, pp. 462–83; FM (Jock) Brookfield, 2003,
    'Maori Customary Title to Foreshore and Seabed', *New Zealand Law Journal*,
    August 2003, pp. 295–7; Jacinta Ruru, 2004, 'A Politically Fuelled Tsunami: The
    Foreshore/Seabed Controversy in Aotearoa me te Waipounamu/New Zealand',
    Journal of the Polynesian Society, vol. 113 no. 1, pp. 57–72; Waitangi Tribunal,
    2004, *Report on the Crown's Foreshore and Seabed Policy* (Wai 1071), Wellington,
    Legislation Direct, http://www.waitangi-tribunal.govt.nz/reports/; MLR, March
    2004, pp. 1–12; MLR, May 2004, pp. 1–6; Charters and Erueti, *Māori Property
    Rights and the Foreshore and Seabed*.
18 Department of the Prime Minister and Cabinet, *The Foreshore and Seabed of New
    Zealand*.
19 Office of the Deputy Prime Minister, *Foreshore and Seabed: A Framework*.
20 2003, 'Revolt by Maori MPs Over Foreshore'.
21 See the Māori Party website, http://www.maoriparty.org/index.php
22 2003, 'Majority Opposed to Customary Ownership', *nzherald.co.nz*, 18 August
    2003.
23 Don Brash, 2004, 'Nationhood', speech to the Orewa Rotary Club, http://www.
    scoop.co.nz/stories/PA0401/S00220.htm
24 Ruth Berry, 2004(a), 'No Surrender Vows te Heuheu as she Loses Role', *nzherald.
    co.nz*, 4 February 2004.
25 2004, *The Belfast Telegraph*, 26 March 2004.
26 2004, 'Clark to Take Another Look at Maori Policies', *nzherald.co.nz*, 24 February
    2004.
27 Walker, 2004, *Ka Whawhai Tonu Matou*, p. 402.
28 Diana McCurdy and Renee Kiriona, 2004, 'Te Reo Comes to Prime Time',
    nzherald.co.nz, 27 March 2004.
29 Jon Stokes, 2004, 'Non-Maori Fans of Maori TV', *nzherald.co.nz*, 25 June 2004.
30 MLR, March 2004, p. 1.
31 Waitangi Tribunal, *Report on the Crown's Foreshore and Seabed Policy*, p. 108.
32 Audrey Young, 2004, 'Tribunal Report Disappointing and Flawed, Says Cullen',
    nzherald.co.nz, 8 March 2004.
33 Linda Te Aho, 2010, 'Judicial Creativity' in Malcolm Mulholland and Veronica
    Tawahi (eds), *Weeping Waters: The Treaty of Waitangi and Constitutional Change*,
    Wellington, Huia Publishers, p. 122; Ruth Berry, 2004, and NZPA, 'Helen Clark
    Hits Out at Judge over East Coast Claim', *nzherald.co.nz*, 13 March 2004.
34 NZPA, 2004(a), 'Protestors Bring Capital's Traffic to Standstill', *nzherald.co.nz*,
    6 May 2004.

35 New Zealand Police, personal communication. On the instructions of the government the published police estimates were much lower.

36 NZPA, 2004(b), 'Hikoi Estimates Range From 10,000 to 30,000', *nzherald.co.nz*, 6 May 2004.

37 2004, 'Reality Check', *nzherald.co.nz*, 8 May 2004.

38 Māori Television Service, *Te Kāea*, 5 May 2004.

CHAPTER 12:

2004–06

Legislative confiscation of the foreshore and seabed continues to gnaw at Māori and the country

The Foreshore and Seabed Act 2004, passed into law on 24 November 2004 against almost unanimous opposition and protest from Māori, continued to have ongoing repercussions both nationally and internationally. Māori were the group most directly affected by the Act's provisions, yet our submissions[1] and protests[2] were ignored, with our spokespersons and leaders vilified as they sought international support against the ongoing racial discrimination practised against Māori in New Zealand.

Attorney-General admits Foreshore and Seabed Act discriminates against Māori but …

In international fora in particular, governments in New Zealand have always denied that they discriminate against Māori. Yet even the Attorney-General was forced to admit that the Foreshore and Seabed Act is discriminatory in terms of the New Zealand Bill of Rights. However, with the same arrogance and disregard that governments have always had for the property rights of Māori,[3] the Attorney-General declared that such discrimination was justified.[4] In other words, the Māori owners are legislatively forbidden from deriving benefit from their own foreshores and seabed throughout the country while others may do so. The government had been unable to prove that it owned the foreshore and seabed in the Court of Appeal. It nevertheless saw fit to abuse its powers in order to confiscate the foreshore and seabed for the benefit of non-Māori New Zealanders using legislative theft. Some iwi issued statements after its enactment stating that they did not recognise the legislation and would not allow it to be implemented in their territories.[5]

United Nations CERD criticises Foreshore and Seabed Act

The government's behaviour in respect of the foreshore and seabed was now proving embarrassing for the country. Since the legislation was passed in 2004, two reports had been issued by committees of the United Nations criticising the New Zealand government for its ongoing and active discrimination against Māori. They highlighted the urgent need to address deeply ingrained institutionalised racism. In March 2005 the United Nations Committee on the Elimination of Racial Discrimination issued a report on the compliance of the Foreshore and Seabed Act with New Zealand's obligations under the International Convention on the Elimination of All Forms of Racial Discrimination.[6] The report concluded that the Act discriminated against Māori.[7] The process for issuing the report had been instigated by Te Rūnanga o Ngāi Tahu, the Treaty Tribes Coalition and the Taranaki Māori Trust Board, which called on the committee to urge the government to withdraw the legislation. The decision of the committee included a number of critical comments, including:

- The hope that 'all actors in New Zealand will refrain from exploiting racial tensions for their own political advantage'
- Concern at the 'apparent haste with which the legislation was enacted and that insufficient consideration may have been given to alternative responses to the *Ngati Apa* decision which might have accommodated Maori

rights within a framework more acceptable to both Maori and all other New Zealanders'

- Regret that 'the processes of consultation did not appreciably narrow the differences between various parties on this issue'

- Concern at 'the scale of opposition to the legislation amongst the group most directly affected by its provisions – the Māori – and their strong perception that the legislation discriminates against them'

- The conclusion that the Act contained 'discriminatory aspects against the Māori, in particular its extinguishment of the possibility of establishing Māori customary title over the foreshore and seabed and its failure to provide a guaranteed right of redress, notwithstanding the State party's obligations under articles 5 and 6 of the Convention.'[8]

Damning report of United Nations Special Rapporteur a wake-up call for New Zealand government

In March 2006 a report critical of both the government and mainstream media was issued by the Special Rapporteur on the situation of human rights and fundamental freedoms of indigenous people, Professor Rodolfo Stavenhagen, reporting on his mission to New Zealand in November 2005.[9] It considered a large number of areas in which Māori experience difficulty and are discriminated against. While there were positive aspects to the report it urged important changes. It noted that Māori continue to be denied their right to self-determination and even collective citizenship as tribes, including the actual decision-making capacity of tribal collectives over ancestrally or culturally significant sites.[10]

On the Foreshore and Seabed Act the Special Rapporteur relied mainly on the comments of the New Zealand Human Rights Commissioner and the Attorney-General to conclude that the Act is discriminatory against Māori. '... the Act clearly extinguishes the inherent property rights of Māori to the foreshore and seabed without sufficient redress or compensation, but excludes certain properties already held in individual freehold';[11] in other words, it removes the property rights held by Māori but protects those of non-Māori. 'In the view of the Special Rapporteur, the Act can be seen as a step backwards for Māori in the progressive recognition of their rights through the Treaty Settlements Process over recent years'.[12] He recommended that the Act 'be repealed or amended by Parliament and the Crown should engage in treaty settlement negotiation with Māori that will recognise the inherent rights of Māori in the foreshore and seabed ...'.[13]

On constitutional issues, he recommended that 'a convention should be convened to design a constitutional reform in order to clearly regulate the relationship between Government and Māori people on the basis of the Treaty of Waitangi and the internationally recognised right of all people to self-determination.'[14] He went on to further recommend 'The Treaty of Waitangi should be entrenched constitutionally in a form that respects the pluralism of New Zealand society, creating positive recognition and meaningful provision for Māori as a distinct people, possessing an alternative system of knowledge, philosophy and law.'[15]

On human rights and the Waitangi Tribunal, he recommended that 'The Waitangi Tribunal should be granted legally binding and enforceable powers to adjudicate Treaty matters with the force of the law.'[16] The Tribunal does have legally binding powers over large areas of land which the Crown transferred to state-owned enterprises and also Crown Forest lands. However political pressure exerted by governments on claimants has ensured that these have not been used,[17] with the Tribunal only exercising its powers once over one small piece of land. Given that all major recommendations to the government issued by the Tribunal in recent years have been ignored, particularly those recommending the return of lands and natural resources, it is important in terms of governmental accountability that this recommendation be followed. However given also that the wealth and prosperity of non-Māori New Zealanders is dependent on them being able to freely and exclusively exploit Māori land and resources without any consideration for Māori rights in those properties, it seems very unlikely that they will willingly give up such privilege.

On Treaty settlements Professor Stavenhagen's recommendations included that 'the Crown should engage in negotiations with Māori to reach agreement on a more fair and equitable settlement policy and process.'[18] This recommendation arose from the fact that the current government settlement policy was unilaterally determined by the Crown. It is the Crown that has been proven to be the guilty party in all Treaty breaches. Yet it has used the absence of any constitutional fetter on its powers that would force it to abide by its Treaty of Waitangi and international human rights obligations to set itself up to judge and determine what settlements shall be. There have been numerous complaints that none of the Treaty settlements to date have been fair and equitable, with claimants forced to choose between very little and nothing at all. It has been calculated that settlements to date average out at less than 0.1 percent of the estimated value of lands lost.[19] Yet despite this a further five settlements have been recorded in the past year. Deeds of settlement or legislation confirming settlement were completed for the claims of Ngā Rauru, Ngāti Mutunga, Ngāti Awa, Ngāti Tūwharetoa ki Kawerau and Te Rōroa. Whether these and other Treaty claims settlements are full and final remains to be seen.

Professor Stavenhagen's recommendations included:

On education: 'More resources should be put at the disposal of Māori education at all levels, including teacher training programmes and the development of appropriate teaching materials.'[20]

On culture: 'The Māori cultural revival involving language, customs, knowledge systems, philosophy, values and arts should continue to be recognised and respected as part of the bicultural heritage of all New Zealanders through the appropriate cultural and educational channels.'[21]

On social policy: 'Social delivery services, particularly health and housing, should continue to be specifically targeted and tailored to the needs of Māori, requiring more targeted research evaluation and statistical data bases.'[22] This recommendation was aimed at reversing the reduction in funding for Māori programmes that has been implemented over the past few years.

On international indigenous rights: 'The Government of New Zealand should continue to support efforts to achieve a United Nations declaration on the rights of indigenous peoples by consensus, including the right to self-determination.'[23] At the Permanent Forum for Indigenous Peoples held in New York in May 2006, the New Zealand government opposed indigenous people having self determination and joined Canada and the United States of America to oppose the text of the draft Declaration on the Rights of Indigenous Peoples which was subsequently supported by the United Nations Human Rights Committee. The New Zealand government took this stance without any consultation with Māori. However, Māori were present at the Forum and ensured that it was informed that Māori opposed the New Zealand government stance and supported the rights of all indigenous peoples.[24]

On civil society: Finally, the Special Rapporteur made recommendations that 'Public media should be encouraged to provide a balanced, unbiased and non-racist picture of Māori in New Zealand society, and an independent commission should be established to monitor their performance and suggest remedial action.'[25] Also, 'Representatives and leaders of political parties and public organisations should refrain from using language that may incite racial or ethnic intolerance.'[26]

Māori welcome report as blueprint for reinstating Māori rights – government condemns it then ignores it

Māori welcomed the report as accurate, insightful and helpful, with several Māori academics and commentators having checked its draft for accuracy. In the months following its release the Māori Party referred to its recommendations in almost every speech they made both inside and outside Parliament. The government, which also checked its draft, predictably tried to suppress the report and then, when it was released, attacked its author and the committee he represented, and claimed falsely that both had been dismissed from the United Nations.[27] They also claimed that the report was full of errors[28] yet were unable to demonstrate what those errors were. The government announced well before the report was released that it would ignore it.

On the existence of so-called Māori privilege – 'he had not been presented with any evidence to that effect'

One of the matters noted by the Special Rapporteur was the ongoing cuts by the government to Māori funding. The government used various attacks on Māori, which gathered momentum in 2003, to justify the cuts. Particular use was made of specious claims that Māori were privileged over others, claims which the Special Rapporteur dismissed because he could find no evidence of any privilege to Māori but rather extensive evidence of deprivation and discrimination.[29] Many programmes which Māori had come to rely on for their own development were abolished while prison accommodation for inmates who are mainly Māori was substantially increased. The extent of the government's determination to deprive Māori of the benefits of public funding became clear when the Minister of Māori Affairs failed to seek any increase in the 2006 Budget for Māori Affairs.[30] And this was at a time when an increasing number of research reports into Māori wellbeing were becoming more and more strident in their criticism of government policies and treatment of Māori.[31]

Māori tertiary education institutions under attack – for being too successful

Māori funding programmes that were abolished included the Manaaki Tauira fund for Māori tertiary students and several programmes run by Māori tertiary institutions. Perhaps the most brutal attack was on one of these institutions, Te Wānanga o Aotearoa (TWOA). The aim of TWOA is to give people access to education in such a way that they not only learn, but actually enjoy their learning.[32] It targets those whom mainstream education has overlooked or discarded, and most of those are Māori.[33] It had carried out government Māori education policy to the letter and as a result was able, in a very short period, to attract more students and hence government funding than any other tertiary institution. This raised the ire of the universities in particular; they quietly but successfully lobbied to discredit TWOA and persuaded the government to launch a series of intensive audits which eventually crippled the institution. When TWOA called itself a university, the universities took umbrage and sent letters to TWOA saying they were offended.[34] Yet the universities could not acknowledge the irony in the fact that each of them call themselves whare wānanga (which TWOA is) on their websites and letterheads when they have neither the expertise nor the qualifications to do so in terms of the standards required by traditional (Māori) whare wānanga.

As a result of government harassment, TWOA took a claim to the Waitangi Tribunal which was heard in December 2005. It was the second claim they had taken, with inquiry into the first one finding that the government had breached the Treaty of Waitangi by not giving whare wānanga the same capital establishment grants as it had done for mainstream tertiary education institutions such as universities, polytechnics and colleges of education.[35] The second claim was also upheld and it was found that the Crown had sought to impose 'unilateral, poorly co-ordinated, and, from the claimants' perspective, apparently destructive' measures.[36]

Looking for the bright spots – the Māori Party

Although 2004–06 had been depressing for Māori, we could always find major national achievements worth celebrating. One was the Māori Party. It was born out of the 2004 Hīkoi, the huge protest against the foreshore and seabed legislation. The general election in September 2005 saw it win four of the seven Māori seats, taking three from the Labour Party. The same ability and expertise used to mobilise and organise Māori for the Hīkoi was used to organise Māori votes for the new Māori Party. Other parties lacked such ability and expertise and had no response to the Māori Party onslaught. As a result, for the first time in the history of the New Zealand Parliament, Māori had an independent voice and a party whose first priority was the wishes and needs of Māori.

Māori Party wipes out the Māori MP stereotype

Mainstream politicians expected Māori Party MPs to assume the roles that most Māori elected to Parliament are consigned to: either servants to the more powerful mainstream parties or largely invisible, rarely participating in anything and taking only minor peripheral roles. Much to their surprise, the four members of the Māori Party immediately took on huge and punishing workloads, responding to every bill presented to the House, travelling extensively to keep in contact with their constituents and presenting views and opinions both inside and outside Parliament that reflected Māori wishes and thinking. As required by their constituents, they conducted themselves as rangatira, with dignity and respect for others, including their political enemies. They refused to descend into the gratuitous trading of insults that demeans the New Zealand Parliament in Māori eyes. They have insisted that the Māori language's status as an official language be given meaning by using it every day in the House. It has been interesting to see other Māori speakers in the House following their example in this respect.

Michael Campbell, Ngāti Ruanui and Ngā Rauru – golf champion extraordinaire

On the sporting front, where Māori generally do well, it was with a huge sense of pride that the Māori world celebrated professional golfer Michael Campbell winning not only the US Open but also the HSBC World Match Play championship in 2005. Although Michael identifies himself strongly and proudly as Ngāti Ruanui and Ngā Rauru of Taranaki, including having his own sportswear label which features Māori patterns and designs, in most of the mainstream media he is only a New Zealander. He was the Māori Sportsman of the year and won the Halberg Supreme Award for his achievements.[37]

Robert Hewitt – miraculous survival with the help of his ancestors

Another great achievement was that of Ngāti Kahungunu's Robert Hewitt, brother of the All Black Norm Hewitt, who was lost at sea in February 2006 for four days but miraculously survived. He achieved that feat by drawing on both his Navy diver training and his knowledge derived from his Māori ancestors of the physical and spiritual aspects of the sea. Some members of the Pākehā media made no attempt to mask their racism when he talked of his use of karakia (Māori prayer). They claimed his loss at sea was a hoax.[38] The rest of the country was in awe of his achievement. It took him more than six weeks to recover from the physical trauma, including his skin splitting, severe sunburn and dehydration.[39]

Peter Loughlin, Ngāti Tūwharetoa – fashion designer par excellence

In the business world, the University of Auckland Business School honoured Ngāti Tūwharetoa's Peter Loughlin as the Outstanding Māori Business Leader for 2005 for his work in fashion design. Peter dresses some of the world's most influential and wealthy women through his House of Arushi, which is based in Dubai. Clientele include the royal families of the Kuwait, Qatar, Saudi Arabia and Oman. Every year, through his foundation scholarships, a young Māori designer is supported to travel to Dubai to work alongside Peter.[40]

---

1 The select committee hearing submissions on the Foreshore and Seabed Bill received 3946 submissions, of which approximately 94 percent opposed the bill (MLR, November 2004, p. 1).

2 Many protests were mounted around the country, including Te Rarawa's 'Hands Across the Beach' on Te Oneroa a Tōhē (Ninety Mile Beach) on 7 February 2004 (Harris, Hīkoi, pp. 147–9). The largest was the 50,000-strong Hīkoi which arrived from around the country in the grounds of Parliament on 5 May 2004. See 2004, 'Cover Story: There's a Message Here', Mana no. 58, June–July 2004, pp. 32–46; Moana Jackson, 2004, 'Marae Atea: An Enduring Memory', Mana no. 58, June–July 2004, pp. 49–50 and Harris, Hīkoi, pp. 151–5 for comment and photographs of the Hīkoi.

3 'Members of the executive and a very substantial majority of the legislature ... still treat Māori customary property rights as an inferior and dispensable form of property rights', fearing that if they do recognise these rights, then title to their landholdings will become insecure (D V Williams, 2007, 'Wi Parata is Dead, Long Live Wi Parata' in Charters and Erueti, Māori Property Rights and the Foreshore and Seabed: The Last Frontier, Wellington, Victoria University Press, p. 58).

4 See MLR, May 2004, pp. 1–6 for a summary and commentary.

5 For example, Ngāti Kahu of Te Hiku o te Ika (Far North).
6 United Nations Committee on the Elimination of Racial Discrimination, 2005, *Report on the New Zealand Foreshore and Seabed Act 2004*, Decision 1(66), 66th Session, 11th March 2005. UN Doc CERD/C/66/NZL/Dec.1.
7 MLR, March 2005, p. 7.
8 MLR, March 2005, p. 7.
9 Rodolfo Stavenhagen, 2006, *Report of the Special Rapporteur on the Situation of Human Rights and Fundamental Freedoms of Indigenous People*. Mission to New Zealand. E/CN.4/2006/78/Add.3, 13 March 2006, Geneva, United Nations Human Rights Commission.
10 Stavenhagen, *Human Rights and Fundamental Freedoms of Indigenous People*, para 42.
11 Stavenhagen, *Human Rights and Fundamental Freedoms of Indigenous People*, para 55.
12 Stavenhagen, *Human Rights and Fundamental Freedoms of Indigenous People*, para 55.
13 Stavenhagen, *Human Rights and Fundamental Freedoms of Indigenous People*, para 92.
14 Stavenhagen, *Human Rights and Fundamental Freedoms of Indigenous People*, para 84.
15 Stavenhagen, *Human Rights and Fundamental Freedoms of Indigenous People*, para 85.
16 Stavenhagen, *Human Rights and Fundamental Freedoms of Indigenous People*, para 89.
17 The Tribunal has been under threat of having its powers to make binding recommendations removed by successive governments since 1990 (Hamer, 'A Quarter-century of the Waitangi Tribunal', p. 7, and footnote 22 in particular for specific threats by Minister Doug Graham and then Minister Margaret Wilson).
18 Stavenhagen, *Human Rights and Fundamental Freedoms of Indigenous People*, para 95.
19 Mutu, 'Recovering Fagin's Ill-gotten Gains', p. 204.
20 Stavenhagen, *Human Rights and Fundamental Freedoms of Indigenous People*, para 97.
21 Stavenhagen, *Human Rights and Fundamental Freedoms of Indigenous People*, para 100.
22 Stavenhagen, *Human Rights and Fundamental Freedoms of Indigenous People*, para 101.
23 Stavenhagen, *Human Rights and Fundamental Freedoms of Indigenous People*, para 102.
24 Cat Davis, email reports on the day-to-day proceedings at the United Nations Permanent Forum for Indigenous People, New York, May 2006.
25 Stavenhagen, *Human Rights and Fundamental Freedoms of Indigenous People*, para 104.
26 Stavenhagen, *Human Rights and Fundamental Freedoms of Indigenous People*, para 105.
27 Audrey Young, 2006(a), 'UN Foreshore Report "unbalanced"', *nzherald.co.nz*, 5 April 2006; NZPA, 2006(a), 'Urban Maori? UN Envoy "stunned"', *nzherald. co.nz*, 6 April 2006; NZPA, 2006(b), 'UN Man Answers Back on Cullen Jibe', *nzherald.co.nz*, 6 April 2006.
28 NewstalkZB, 2006, and Herald online staff, 'UN Man Advises Overhaul or Scrapping of Foreshore Act', *nzherald.co.nz*, 4 April 2006.
29 Stavenhagen, *Human Rights and Fundamental Freedoms of Indigenous People*, para 54.
30 Audrey Young, 2006(b), 'Heat on Horomia Over Absence of Budget Bid', *nzherald. co.nz*, 25 May 2006.

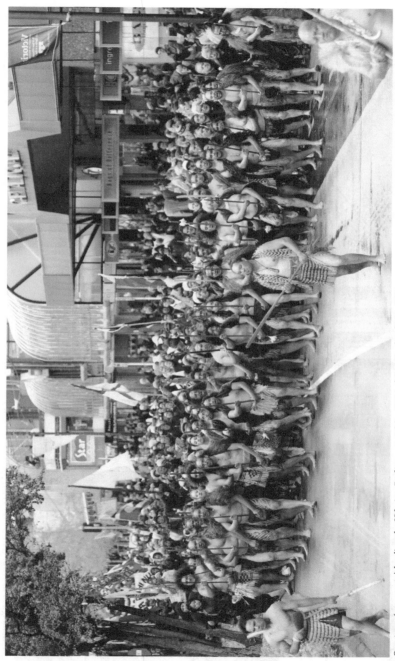

Ope taua (war party) leading the Hīkoi to Parliament, 5 May 2004. (New Zealand Herald)

Ngāti Kahungunu in Wellington, 5 May 2004. (Courtesy of Hone Harawira)

Toko Renata, Chairman of the Hauraki Māori Trust Board, who returned his QSM in disgust at the confiscation of the foreshore and seabed. (Gil Hanly)

Part of the 50,000-strong Hīkoi who made it into Parliament grounds, 5 May 2004. (Courtesy of Hone Harawira)

Tahu Pōtiki (Ngāi Tahu) and Rodolfo Stavenhagen. (New Zealand Herald)

Te Wānanga o Aotearoa – Māngere campus, Auckland. (Margaret Mutu)

Rongo Wetere (Ngāti Maniapoto), inaugural Tumuaki (Head) of Te Wānanga o Aotearoa. (Mana)

Dr Pita Sharples. (Mana/Sally Tagg)

Māori Party MPs 2005: (back, left-right) Hone Harawira, Te Ururoa Flavell (Ngāti Rangiwēwehi, Ngāpuhi), (front, left-right) Dr Pita Sharples and Tariana Turia. (New Zealand Herald)

Professor Sir Hugh Kāwharu (Ngāti Whātua). (University of Auckland)

(From left) Māori Party president, Professor Whatarangi Winiata (Ngāti Raukawa), and co-leaders, Dr Pita Sharples and Tariana Turia. (Mana)

Michael Campbell (Ngāti Ruanui, Ngāti Rauru) with the US Open Trophy. (New Zealand Herald)

Te Arikinui Dame Te Ātairangikaahu (Tainui). (Gil Hanly)

Maungakiekie (One Tree Hill) agreed for return in Ngāti Whātua ki Ōrākei's Agreement in Principle to settle their successful claims against the Crown. (Margaret Mutu)

Ngāti Whātua o Ōrākei's marae at Takaparawhau (Bastion Point). (Margaret Mutu)

Whenua rangatira (unchallenged lands) of Ngāti Whātua o Ōrākei at Ōkahu Bay, Auckland, with their papakāinga (homelands) and marae on the surrounding hills. (Margaret Mutu)

31 See, for example, Ricci Harris, Martin Tobias, Mona Jeffreys, Kiri Waldegrave, Saffron Karlsen and James Nazroo, 2006, 'Effects of Self-reported Racial Discrimination and Deprivation on Māori Health and Inequalities in New Zealand: Cross-sectional Study', *The Lancet*, vol. 367, 17 June 2006, pp. 2005–9, which concludes that 'Racism, both interpersonal and institutional, contributes to Māori health losses and leads to inequalities between Māori and Europeans in New Zealand' and 'the combination of deprivation and discrimination as measured seems to account for much of the disparity in heath outcomes assessed'; Ministry of Health and University of Otago, 2006, *Decades of Disparity III: Ethnic and Socioeconomic Inequalities in Mortality, New Zealand 1981–1999*, Wellington, Ministry of Health, which highlighted alarming and disproportionately high mortality rates for Māori; Public Health Advisory Committee, 2006, *Health is Everyone's Business*, Wellington, Public Health Advisory Committee, which concluded that being Māori or Pacific further increases the risk of death or ill-health across all socio-economic categories; the many reports of the Waitangi Tribunal; and Stavenhagen, *Human Rights and Fundamental Freedoms of Indigenous People*.

32 See the Te Wānanga o Aotearoa website, http://www.twoa.ac.nz/index. php?id=224

33 Walker, *Ka Whawhai Tonu Matou*, pp. 351–5.

34 Derek Fox, 2006(b), 'Education: Te Wananga o Aotearoa: Who's at the Helm Now?', *Mana* no. 69, April–May 2006, p. 67.

35 Waitangi Tribunal, 1999(c), *The Wananga Capital Establishment Report* (Wai 718), Wellington, GP Publications, http://www.waitangi-tribunal.govt.nz/reports/; MLR, December 2005/January 2006, p. 2.

36 MLR, December 2005/January 2006, p. 4.

37 Michael Campbell's website, http://www.cambogolf.com/profile.cfm?pageid=my-journey

38 2006, 'Claims Hewitt's Miracle Survival a "hoax" Rubbished', *nzherald.co.nz*, 12 February 2006.

39 Derek Fox, 2006(a), 'Feature: I Told Them I Wasn't Ready', *Mana* no. 69, April–May 2006, pp. 20–3.

40 Te Aratai Productions, 2006, *Darling of Dubai*, broadcast on Māori Television 3 July 2006; 1995, 'Te Rito: Peter Loughlin: Kaitātai Kākahu', *Mana* no. 10, Spring 1995, pp. 50–1.

CHAPTER 13:
2006–07

More great sadness at passing of leaders
Dame Te Ātairangikaahu

While political tension increased for Māori in 2006–07, there was also great sadness. Like our Tongan[1] and Samoan[2] relations, we lost significant leaders. In August 2006 the Tainui confederation of tribes lost their Arikinui of forty years, Dame Te Ātairangikaahu. As the hereditary leader of Tainui's Kīngitanga movement, she was their Queen. Tainui established the Kīngitanga in the 1850s in an attempt to stop the confiscation of their territories by European immigrants. They are the only tribal confederation in New Zealand to have established a British style monarchy, and although most iwi are not part of the Kīngitanga, it nevertheless enjoys widespread support and respect within Māoridom. Thus, despite Dame Te Ātairangikaahu holding no constitutional position in New Zealand law, she was often referred to as 'the Māori Queen'. She was a strong figure in Māori politics and a staunch supporter of Māori sports and culture.[3]

Emeritus Professor Sir Hugh Kāwharu

In September, Ngāti Whātua lost their paramount chief, Emeritus Professor Sir Hugh Kāwharu. He was the chair of the Ngāti Whātua o Ōrākei Māori Trust Board for more than twenty years and was the major force behind the Ngāti Whātua Treaty of Waitangi claims to the Auckland area. His determination to break though government mean-spiritedness and intransigence in order to settle the claims saw him taking on a hugely punishing workload after he retired as Professor and Head of the Department of Māori Studies at the University of Auckland in 1993. He signed an Agreement in Principle towards settlement of those claims shortly before his death.[4]

Don Selwyn

In April 2007, the veteran Māori actor and film maker and one of New Zealand's most outstanding television and film producers and directors, Don Selwyn, passed away. He was Ngāti Kurī, Te Aupōuri and Ngāti Kahu of the Far North. His greatest masterpiece was *Te Tangata Whai Rawa o Wēniti – The Māori Merchant of Venice*,[5] the film version of Shakespeare's famous play which had been translated into Māori by Pei Te Hurinui Jones in 1945.

Māori–government tensions persist; Māori protest continues but with more effective support

On the political scene, however, the racist attitudes towards Māori which continued to dominate the New Zealand Parliament resulted in ongoing and increasing tension between Māori and the government on many issues over 2006–07. Māori had once again had to resort to protest action as the government repeatedly denied us our legal rights. However, this time, coordinated protest across the country as a result of refusals to return stolen lands resulted in the government backing down and calling a temporary truce on that particular issue. For apart from strong judicial backing, particularly from the Waitangi Tribunal, and international condemnation from the United Nations,[6] the presence of the small but very effective independent Māori voice in Parliament, the Māori Party, ensured that Māori issues were no longer determined solely according to the racist whim of the major parties in the House.[7]

Treaty of Waitangi claims ongoing source of tension
The area that continued to be the major source of tension was the settlement of Treaty of Waitangi claims. British immigrants who have settled New Zealand in large numbers since the 1850s had long sought to get rid of the Treaty of Waitangi. For over a century they simply ignored it, and the courts sanctioned their behaviour.[8] But in the aftermath of World War II, international agreements outlawing racial discrimination along with highly visible and embarrassing Māori protests forced the New Zealand government into establishing the Waitangi Tribunal in 1975. Its brief is to inquire into Māori claims of breaches of the Treaty. The government of the day did not expect that the Tribunal would hear many claims, meet often or cost much.[9] However, by the 1990s the Tribunal was building an extremely bleak and ever-expanding scenario of the extensive and serious nature of the atrocities committed against Māori. In an effort to try to limit its liabilities in the area the National government announced in its policy released in 1994 that it wanted to settle the claims. It accepted responsibility for the atrocities and was prepared to compensate Māori. However money set aside for the settlements would be restricted to an arbitrarily set $1 billion and the government would avoid returning any land if it could get away with it.[10]

The loathed fiscal envelope settlement policy remains to extinguish Māori Treaty claims
Since 1994 Māori had fought against the policy. It had been drawn up unilaterally by the government with no Māori input and was deeply racist in its intent. Even in the face of ongoing strident Māori,[11] judicial[12] and international criticism,[13] neither a National- nor a Labour-led government had been prepared to either amend the policy or withdraw it and start again. As more and more claimants were being bullied into accepting pitiful settlements, it was becoming clear in 2006–07 that the primary aim of the policy was to get Māori

around the country to agree that rather than settling their Treaty of Waitangi claims, they should instead extinguish them. And furthermore, they were also effectively agreeing to a systematic extinguishment of the Treaty of Waitangi itself. In mid-2007, legislation was before Parliament to remove all references to the principles of the Treaty of Waitangi from all legislation, and it had the support of the current coalition government. And to try to minimise the international backlash, the New Zealand government joined Australia, Canada and the United States in November 2006 in opposing the adoption of the United Nations Declaration on the Rights of Indigenous Peoples. Māori had supported and worked on the Declaration for twenty years.

The Treaty of Waitangi Claims Settlement policy was designed to legislatively absolve the Crown of any and all liability and responsibility for its innumerable historical breaches of the Treaty of Waitangi and the theft of more than 90 percent of the country's lands and resources from Māori. The government did this by bullying select groups of Māori, purportedly representing 'large natural groupings' of many thousands of other Māori, into agreements that were legally binding and unchallengeable. The Crown's primary aim for the agreements was to provide:

- full and legally unchallengeable removal of legal liability for all breaches of the Treaty of Waitangi, both identified and unidentified, committed in a particular geographic area prior to 1992
- full and legally unchallengeable acceptance by the iwi of all discriminatory legislation, including the Foreshore and Seabed Act 2004, along with all assertions of Crown authority, dominance and sovereignty over Māori
- full and legally unchallengeable acceptance that iwi had relinquished all their sovereign rights and authority over identified geographic areas to the Crown.

In exchange for that agreement, the Crown was prepared to make an apology for the breaches committed prior to 1992 (but not to stop committing further breaches) and to transfer a few acres of land.[14] And while money was always mentioned as being part of settlements, if claimants wanted land returned, they had to use the money offered (and often borrow more as well) to buy the land off the Crown. The policy was, as one would expect, causing huge divisions and strife within iwi. The Crown actively and openly fostered and exploited the divisions as it moved on relentlessly to achieve maximum implementation of its policy.[15]

Of course, protection of Māori from all of these situations is guaranteed by the Treaty of Waitangi. The authoritative Māori version, known as Te Tiriti o Waitangi, promises that the Crown shall have governance over its own subjects only, that Māori sovereignty is recognised and upheld and that Māori have the rights of all British citizens.[16] Since 1987 the courts have repeatedly confirmed the influence of the Treaty.[17] It is, after all, New Zealand's founding document.[18] Had the Crown been able to control the rapacious greed of British immigrants in the nineteenth and twentieth centuries, it would not now be faced with not only remedying the wrongs but also addressing the racism that has been allowed to become deeply entrenched in the Pākehā psyche. Māori have made it very clear that delaying remedying the situation will not make it go away. And neither can legislative sleights of hand ever extinguish the Treaty of Waitangi.

Yet settlements are proceeding nevertheless
Ngāti Mutunga Settlement Act

Since mid-2006 the Crown had been dealing with twenty settlements. The Ngāti Mutunga Settlement Bill was enacted in November.[19] It provided $14.9 million for Ngāti Mutunga to buy back some of the 150,000 acres the Crown stole from them. The land alone had an estimated monetary value of

$5.19 billion,[20] making the settlement monies less than 0.3 percent of the value of the land stolen. The Settlement Act acknowledges that the settlement did not compensate Ngāti Mutunga for the atrocities committed against them.[21] These include the rape, murder and illegal incarceration of large numbers of the iwi, the government waging war on them when they refused to give their lands to British settlers, the government confiscating all of their lands and many other breaches of the Treaty of Waitangi they have suffered and continue to suffer.[22] But the Act then says that Ngāti Mutunga had forgone full compensation as its contribution to the 'development of New Zealand', and as such the settlement was full and final.[23] In the House during debate on the Bill, the Māori Party was scathing of the Crown's mean-spiritedness and referred to it repeatedly as 'the thief'. They advised Ngāti Mutunga to revisit the settlement in generations to come with a view to being properly compensated and not to accept the full and final stipulation of the Crown.[24]

Te Rōroa Claims Settlement Bill

Te Rōroa's Claims Settlement Bill came before the House in March 2007. Te Rōroa are a hapū of Ngāti Whātua who were left virtually landless. They first complained to the Crown about breaches of the Treaty 165 years ago. They had been under relentless attack from Crown officials who denied them their legal and human rights for several generations. The Waitangi Tribunal upheld all their claims in 1992, detailing countless atrocities perpetrated against them by the Crown.[25] They had been in negotiations for more than fifteen years. The settlement was for $9.5 million to be used to buy from the Crown a small portion of Te Rōroa's land, now being used commercially. Extensive wāhi tapu had been stolen from them and 2000 acres of these were returned in the settlement.[26]

In the House, the Māori Party warned that Te Rōroa had been subjected to 'a negotiations process drafted by the Crown, and the Crown alone, based on false faith and double-talk. It is a negotiations process that masquerades as being fair and reasonable in the circumstances but which, in fact, is anything but, and an empty insistence by the Crown that all settlements be full and final – an insistence that will haunt this Chamber long after it is cleared ...'[27] They went on to point out that unfair settlements imposed in 2007 such as this would be revisited by future generations. They also noted that considerably less land than what the Waitangi Tribunal had recommended was being returned to Te Rōroa. They pointed out to the House 'that an apology and a return of less than 3 percent of the claim value pepper-potted throughout the tribal homeland of Te Rōroa will simply not suffice.'[28]

Ngāti Whātua ki Ōrākei Agreement in Principle

In June 2006 Ngāti Whātua ki Ōrākei hapū signed an Agreement in Principle to settle their claims to the Auckland isthmus. It agreed to vest three volcanic cones and land around Pūrewa Creek in the hapū but stipulated that the lands were to be managed jointly by the hapū and the Auckland City Council with the Council controlling the funds. The settlement was for $8 million to be used as part payment for up to $80 million of Defence lands at Devonport, which Ngāti Whātua can buy from the Crown provided they lease it back to the Crown and the Crown pays no rent for thirty-five years.[29] The agreement came under serious threat when six other hapū with claims over the same area took the matter to the Waitangi Tribunal for an urgent hearing to prevent their claims being extinguished by such a settlement. The hearings took place in March 2007. The Office of Treaty Settlements, which manages negotiations for the Crown, came under severe criticism from the Tribunal when in addition to wrongly treating with claimants and fomenting divisions among the iwi of Auckland, it was revealed that they had withheld crucial evidence from the Tribunal during the inquiry and misled the Tribunal.[30]

Te Arawa Lakes Settlement Act

In September 2006 the Te Arawa Lakes Settlement Bill was enacted. The lakes in the central North Island, including Lake Rotorua, had been severely polluted by farm runoff and sewage disposal into the lakes. The $10 million settlement returns the lake beds to Te Arawa, leaving them to consider a clean up that it is estimated will cost $200 million even though Te Arawa is specifically not liable for the pollution.[31] This settlement extends Crown theft of Māori assets in that it claims ownership not only over the water in the lakes but also airspace above them. The term 'Crown stratum' was being used in 2007 to describe the redefined space above the lakebed.[32] In the House during the debate on this bill, the Māori Party tabled a report on Māori experiences of the Treaty of Waitangi Settlement negotiations that demonstrated strong and universal condemnation of the process by claimants.[33] Once again, the Māori Party warned that these settlements could not be full and final and would be revisited.

Central North Island forest settlements run into major problems as the Crown makes itself a beneficiary of the settlement

Attempts by the government to force through a settlement of part of the huge central North Island forestry claims relating to the Kaingaroa forest and other lands around Rotorua triggered a series of court actions. Of direct relevance to these claims was the Crown Forestry Rental Trust, which was set up in 1990 to hold forestry rental money in trust pending successful claims to forestry lands. Well over $400 million is now held by the Trust, of which almost $190 million is held for the Kaingaroa forest.[34] On top of that, the Crown Forest Assets Act provides for the transfer of Crown forest land plus compensation to Māori once their claims to the land have been upheld by the Waitangi Tribunal. Claims to the central North Island, including the Kaingaroa forest, have been before the Tribunal for some time, and the Tribunal issued its report upholding the claims in June 2007.[35]

In a truly staggering fit of arrogance and deceit the Crown managed to persuade part of the Te Arawa confederation of iwi, which is one of a very large number of claimants to the Kaingaroa forest, to settle Te Arawa's historical claims by giving over to the Crown $40.985 million in forestry rentals set aside for the Māori owners of the lands. In addition, the Crown persuaded them to use the remainder of their rental money plus another $8 million (which they have to borrow from elsewhere) to buy from the Crown the land that is rightfully theirs under the Crown Forests Assets Act 1989. The Crown stood to make a $90 million profit if it passed legislation to settle these claims along these lines. It would be able do so after having convinced the claimants to enter into an agreement that allowed the Crown to become a beneficiary of the Crown Forestry Rental Trust. At that time only those with successful claims to the land could be beneficiaries of the Trust. Those claimants also had to agree to the Crown selling the land in question to Māori: land that the Waitangi Tribunal was likely to find belonged to those and other Māori anyway. The Federation of Māori Authorities and the New Zealand Māori Council took the matter to the courts.[36] The Waitangi Tribunal issued a strongly worded report saying that it could not endorse the settlement and that it had grave concerns over the potential negative impacts on overlapping iwi.[37]

Ngāti Kahu gives up on the settlement process and repossesses its lands

However in the Far North one iwi, Ngāti Kahu, took a very different approach. They withdrew from negotiations after the Crown started to sell off part of Ngāti Kahu's Rangiputa block, currently being used by the government's farming enterprise, Landcorp. In 1997 the Tribunal had indicated that it would make binding recommendations in order to return State enterprises lands such as Rangiputa to Ngāti Kahu and other Far North iwi if negotiations with the government failed.[38] Since 1997 successive governments had threatened Ngāti Kahu that if they did seek binding recommendations under the State Owned Enterprises Act 1986, the government would repeal the Act. Once negotiations with the Crown had ceased, Ngāti Kahu moved on to the land, repossessing it. Their stance started a chain reaction as other iwi, whose lands were also being sold by Landcorp, took similar action. A protest march in the Far North town of Kaitāia in support of the repossession was the biggest the town had ever seen. In the House the Māori Party relentlessly pursued the government over the issue, calling on all iwi to follow suit and repossess their lands. After two weeks the government backed down and withdrew the lands from sale temporarily. Each of the iwi concerned pursued binding recommendations through the Waitangi Tribunal, a mechanism that allows the Tribunal to order the Crown to return state-owned enterprise land, Crown forest lands and certain other Crown lands to their Māori owners.[39]

---

1 King Taufa'ahau Tupou IV passed away in September 2006.
2 Samoa's head of state, his Majesty Malietoa Tanumafili II, passed away in May 2007.
3 MLR, August 2006, p. 1; MLR, October 2006, p. 1; Derek Fox, 2006(c), 'Cover Story: "The Lady"', Mana no. 72, October–November 2006, pp. 6–27.
4 MLR, October 2006, p. 2.
5 Māori Party, 2007(a), 'Poroporoaki: Don Selwyn', press release, 16 April 2007, http://www.scoop.co.nz/stories/PA0704/S00272.htm.
6 Stavenhagen, Human Rights and Fundamental Freedoms of Indigenous People.
7 The Māori Party, with only four MPs, continued to maintain the same punishing work schedule reported on in the previous chapter. It spoke on 164 Bills that came before the House between June 2006 and May 2007. It delivered many more speeches in the House other than these, issued no fewer than 850 press releases and still managed to travel around the country consulting widely with Māori. It was rewarded with high levels of support among Māori in various Māori polls.
8 In 1877 Chief Judge Prendergast in Wi Parata v Bishop of Wellington [1877] 3 NZ Jur (NS) 72 dismissed the Treaty of Waitangi 'as a simple nullity', a decision that prevailed for almost 100 years. In 1938 the Privy Council in Te Heuheu Tukino v Aotea District Maori Land Board [1941] AC 308 held that the Treaty can only

be recognised if it is incorporated into municipal law, a position that still exists today.

9 Oliver, *Claims to the Waitangi Tribunal*, pp. 9–10.

10 Office of Treaty Settlements, *Crown Proposals for the Settlement of Treaty of Waitangi Claims*.

11 See chapter 2.

12 Especially the Waitangi Tribunal. See for example the *Taranaki Report*, pp. 314–15.

13 See Stavenhagen, *Human Rights and Fundamental Freedoms of Indigenous People*, paras 26–7, 32–5, 42, 93–5.

14 Mutu, 'Recovering Fagin's Ill-gotten Gains', pp. 202–4.

15 Mutu, 'Recovering Fagin's Ill-gotten Gains', pp. 194–5.

16 See Appendix 1.

17 See, for example, *Huakina Development Trust v Waikato Development Authority* [1987] 2 NZLR 188; *New Zealand Maori Council v Attorney-General* [1992] 2 NZLR 576 (the State-owned Enterprises case).

18 The country named New Zealand came into formal being following the signing of Te Tiriti o Waitangi in 1840 and includes British immigrants formally invited to settle in that treaty. The original name of the country is Aotearoa (and often Te Waipounamu me Rekohu is added to distinguish the South Island and Chatham Islands), which is the name that identifies the country as Māori. It is widely used by Māori to this day.

19 MLR, February 2007, p. 6.

20 Calculated from the compensation of $34,545 per acre paid to a Pākehā who had his land confiscated for Te Rōroa's Treaty claims (Walker, *Ka Whawhai Tonu Matou*, pp. 310–11.)

21 MLR, February 2007, p. 6.

22 Waitangi Tribunal, *Taranaki Report*.

23 MLR, February 2007, p. 6.

24 Māori Party, 2007(b), 'Flavell: Ngati Mutunga', press release, 27 July 2007, http://www.scoop.co.nz/stories/PA0607/S00483.htm

25 Waitangi Tribunal, 1992(b), *The Te Roroa Report* (Wai 38), Wellington, Waitangi Tribunal, http://www.waitangi-tribunal.govt.nz/reports/

26 Office of Treaty Settlements, 2005, *Summary of the Te Roroa Deed of Settlement*, http://www.ots.govt.nz/

27 MLR, March 2007, p. 6.

28 MLR, March 2007, p. 7.

29 MLR, June 2006, p. 8.

30 Waitangi Tribunal, 2007(a), *Tāmaki Makaurau Settlement Process* (Wai 1362), Wellington, Waitangi Tribunal, p. 101, http://www.waitangi-tribunal.govt.nz/reports/

31 MLR, September 2006, p. 6.

32 Clause 10.1.1 as amended in Office of Treaty Settlements, 2006, *Deed to Amend Deed of Settlement of the Te Arawa Lakes Historical Claims and Remaining Annuity Issues*, http://www.ots.govt.nz/

33 Dion Tuuta, 2003, *Maori Experiences of the Direct Negotiations Process*, Wellington, Crown Forestry Rental Trust.

34 Crown Forestry Rental Trust, 2006, 'Forest Rental Proceeds Held in Trust at 31 March 2006', in *Notes to the Financial Statement for the Year Ended 31 March 2006*, http://www.cfrt.org.nz/doclibrary/public/thestorehouse/rta2005-2006/RentalProceeds0506.pdf

35 Waitangi Tribunal, 2008, *He Maunga Rongo: The Report on the Central North Island Claims, Stage 1* (Wai 1200), Wellington, Waitangi Tribunal, http://www.waitangi-tribunal.govt.nz/reports/

36 Te Aho, 2010, 'Judicial Creativity', pp.118–9.

37 Waitangi Tribunal, 2007(b), *Final Report on the Impacts of the Crown's Settlement Policy on Te Arawa Waka and Other Tribes* (Wai 1353), Wellington, Waitangi Tribunal, http://www.waitangi-tribunal.govt.nz/reports/

38 Waitangi Tribunal, *Muriwhenua Land Report*.

39 Margaret Mutu, 2007, *Te Rūnanga-ā-Iwi o Ngāti Kahu Land Claims Report for February–March 2007*, Kaitāia, Te Rūnanga-ā-Iwi o Ngāti Kahu.

CHAPTER 14:

2007–08 – The Year of Contrasts: Terror Raids and a Courageous New Treaty Settlements Minister

In the latter part of 2007, Māori–government relations came close to breaking point. A raid carried out by a New Zealand Police Armed Offenders Squad in full combat gear traumatised a small Māori community in the central North Island on 15 October, just weeks after the New Zealand government had joined Australia, Canada and the United States of America to vote against the adoption of the United Nations Declaration on the Rights of Indigenous Peoples. The raid coincided with the release of a government report showing almost 20 percent of Māori were living in Australia with many having left New Zealand for better economic opportunities but also 'to escape the perceived prejudice of Pākehā and mainstream negativity about Māori issues.'[1] Yet by mid-2008, with polls indicating the likelihood of a change of government in the upcoming general election, Māori started reaping the benefits of a government desperate for our support, particularly in the area of settling Māori land claims.

Terror raids on Tūhoe

Early on 15 October 2007, the first reports of early morning police raids around the country started appearing as environmental and Māori sovereignty activists were targeted for alleged terrorist activities. Both the Commissioner of Police and the Prime Minister had been briefed prior to the raids. Several involved single households in urban areas where there was minimal disturbance to neighbours and the wider community. But in Rūātoki, a small, remote Māori community in the Urewera ranges in the heart of Tūhoe tribal territory, media reported a massive police presence. The Māori Party later reported that seventy armed police were in Rūātoki that morning, where three people were arrested.[2] The entire community was locked down and barricaded by police. A roadblock was set up on the only road out of the community. People were forced out of their cars at gunpoint, searched and photographed; cars and a school bus were searched and photographed; women were subjected to intimate body searches in full view of the public; houses and property were searched and some were damaged; people were herded into sheds while property searches were under way; and people were detained for hours without food or water without formal charges being laid.[3] Four rifles and 230 rounds of ammunition were seized. Many people were detained and transported to Rotorua, some 200 kilometers away, only to be subsequently released to find their own way home. The whole community was traumatised, including pre-school children, who referred to the heavily armed combat-ready police in black uniforms, helmets, masks and balaclavas with combat rifles and hand guns strapped to their knees who boarded their school bus as 'the ninja army'.[4]

Raids a chilling reminder of previous government invasions of Tūhoe

Although a general air of disbelief gripped the country and for Māori throughout the country it was a troubling occasion, for many it seemed an all-too-familiar story. It was not the first time Tūhoe had been invaded by state forces. In the nineteenth century Tūhoe's isolation in the mountainous Urewera region had allowed it to resist British settler encroachment for much longer than other tribal groups. But the Crown, driven by British settlers' insatiable greed for land and a dogged determination to force Māori compliance with their white supremacist regime, was insistent, and in 1866 all of Tūhoe's rich agricultural lands were confiscated under the New Zealand Settlements Act 1863. When Tūhoe continued to actively obstruct Crown attempts at surveying, mapping, building roads, public works and mineral prospecting, the Crown adopted a 'scorched earth' policy, burning Tūhoe settlements and destroying cultivations in order to force Tūhoe into submission.[5] Although the Crown eventually succeeded in 'opening up' the Urewera country, Tūhoe have always continued to openly assert their mana motuhake, their right to their own self-determination and sovereignty, and have never been prepared to compromise who they are for the Pākehā hegemony.[6]

Raids a disguise for a fishing expedition?

Rūātoki is the home of the well-known Māori rights campaigner and activist Tame Iti. He was one of the seventeen people from around the country arrested and charged under the Arms Act 1983 and one of six held in custody while the police tried to gather evidence to justify charges under the Terrorism Suppression Act 2002. According to police, those arrested had been running or had attended 'terrorist training camps' in the very remote Urewera ranges, 'learning about civil insurrection, assassination and napalm bombing'.[7] However Māori media quickly identified the so-called 'training camps' as camping sites used by local hunters and forestry workers.[8] The evidence police appeared to have relied on seemed, from the media reports, to be mainly recordings of conversations, including telephone conversations, texts and emails. Many commented at the time that the raids looked like a 'fishing expedition', an indiscriminate searching of homes and property in the hope that damning evidence would be uncovered.[9]

Prime Minister and Commissioner of Police violate rules of *sub judice*; Solicitor-General refuses to allow prosecution for terrorism; evidence leaked to unscrupulous media

In Parliament the Labour minority government's Māori MPs remained silent, claiming it was a police matter.[10] Both the Prime Minister and the Commissioner of Police chose to ignore the fact that the matter was before the courts and commented publicly, with the Prime Minister commenting that those arrested were people 'who at the very least have illicitly used firearms, constructed Molotov cocktails and trained themselves to use napalm'.[11] To the embarrassment of the government, the Solicitor-General refused to allow terrorism charges to be laid and the six people held in custody were released on bail.[12] The next day, in a move that one analyst has described as 'nothing short of breathtaking',[13] Fairfax Media, which publishes www.stuff.co.nz, the *Dominion Post* (Wellington), the *Press* (Christchurch) and the *Waikato Times* (Hamilton), selectively published parts of leaked police evidence that had been suppressed.[14] Six months later they and the editor of the *Dominion Post*, which has a long history of anti-Māori reporting, were charged with contempt of court.[15]

Māori Party comes to defence of Tūhoe; UN asks for an explanation

While government Māori MPs remained silent, maintaining a wait-and-see stance,[16] the Māori Party bitterly attacked the police and the government for violating the community of Rūātoki and leaving the Tūhoe people traumatised. Māori Party MP, Hone Harawira, drew particularly strong personal criticism and abuse from Pākehā for speaking out against the police actions. He responded by issuing a press release citing the full text of his attack in Parliament and refusing to back down.[17] His claim that his statement accurately reflected the feeling in many Māori communities around the country was supported by the results of a survey showing a high level of concern about the raids amongst Māori participants.[18] In his statement he said:

> I will not sit quietly by while state forces terrorise my people. If this requires me to speak out against the rule of law that would impose terror on Māori communities in this country, then I will speak out. I will speak out against it in this chamber, on television, in newspapers, and anywhere else I possibly can.

Nation-wide protests followed. The Human Rights Commissioner received official complaints, as did the United Nations Human Rights Committee, which asked the New Zealand government for an explanation.[19] In November the Police Commissioner conceded that the raids had badly damaged relations with Tūhoe.[20] In March 2008 he acknowledged and expressed regret over the hurt caused.[21]

New Zealand votes against the Declaration on the Rights of Indigenous Peoples

One month before the raids the Māori Party had launched a blistering attack on the government for voting against the Declaration of the Rights of Indigenous Peoples. It had been adopted by the United Nations General Assembly on 13 September by an overwhelming majority of 143 to 4. The four states that voted against it, the United States, Australia, Canada and New Zealand, all share a history of British colonisation which left the indigenous peoples of those countries marginalised, deprived and oppressed minorities in their own lands, stripped of their lands and natural resources, denied sovereignty and subjected to racism and discrimination. The Declaration, in its forty-five articles, is a statement setting out the human rights and fundamental freedoms of indigenous peoples.[22] It sets out the rights to self-determination, cultures, traditions, languages, institutions, world views and ways of life. It calls on states to prevent and redress theft of land and natural resources and forced assimilation, while establishing minimal standards to eliminate racism, discrimination, marginalisation and exploitation that inhibit the development of indigenous peoples.

Māori had been involved in the drafting of the Declaration from the outset in the early 1980s. One of the reasons it took so long to formulate was that the four states that voted against it had consistently impeded its progress, drawing widespread condemnation from the indigenous community. None of them consulted properly with the indigenous peoples they claimed to represent. They did not want the injustices suffered by those peoples scrutinised, nor the fact that ownership of lands now legally owned by states and non-indigenous individuals derives from an initial theft.[23] The declaration urges that land be returned where possible, but where it is not possible it recommends compensation at full value. In New Zealand, Māori have been forced to accept very much less, calculated to be an average of less than 0.1 percent of losses.[24] The New Zealand government did not want to have to admit that its processes of providing restitution were unfair and unjust.

The adoption of the Declaration by the United Nations received scant attention in mainstream media, and the government tried to play down its importance. However Māori Party MP Hone Harawira toured the North Island delivering seminars on it. The New Zealand Human Rights Commission issued a statement saying the Declaration would guide its work.[25] With the change of government in Australia in November 2007, the Australian Human Rights and Equal Opportunities Commission announced that the new government supported the Declaration.[26] And by April 2008 news from Canada's indigenous peoples indicated that the Canadian Parliament now also supported it.[27] With New Zealand becoming more isolated in its stance, a change in the government's attitude to Māori, particularly in respect of its loathed Treaty of Waitangi claims settlement policy and process, became more inevitable.

Waitangi Tribunal criticises government Treaty settlement policy – yet again

In March and again in June 2007, the Waitangi Tribunal issued reports severely critical of the government's settlement policy and process.[28] When the government ignored them, the Federation of Māori Authorities and the New Zealand Māori Council pursued the matter through the courts. At the same time, tribal groupings in various parts of the country continued with the repossession of lands the government had refused to return to them and was trying to sell off.[29] In April 2007 the government had delayed the sale of some of the blocks for three months. It announced in September that several had been withdrawn from sale for four years. But in the House the government was unable to gain sufficient support to pass several of its proposed settlements into law. In September the Minister of Māori Affairs was ridiculed when he tabled the first report in twelve years on the progress of successive governments on implementing the recommendations of the Waitangi Tribunal in respect of Māori Treaty of Waitangi claims against the Crown. Of the forty-eight reports issued by the Tribunal, only twelve had issues addressed or implemented and it was unclear what had happened to the rest.[30]

Deputy Prime Minister and Minister of Finance becomes Treaty settlements Minister

Finally, in October, the Deputy Prime Minister and Minister of Finance took over the portfolio for Treaty of Waitangi Negotiations. Almost immediately, direct negotiations between claimants and the Crown took on a sudden urgency as the meanness of spirit and bad faith on the part of the government that had plagued negotiations for more than a decade appeared to be set aside. In the central North Island where the Waitangi Tribunal issued the first two parts of a seven-part report on the largest inquiry it had made to date,[31] eight iwi groupings came together to develop their own solution for the settlement of their claims to the 176,000 hectares of land under the eight central North Island forests. The forests include the country's largest exotic forest, Kaingaroa. They presented their proposal for the return of the forest lands and related assets in April 2008 and reached agreement with the government in May. The deal was promoted as being worth $419 million, implying that the government was far exceeding the previous largest payouts of $170 million each for the Tainui, fisheries and Ngāi Tahu settlements. Yet $223 million of the $419 million was accumulated rentals from the forests. The rentals belong to the iwi, not the Crown, as a result of the Tribunal upholding their claims to the forest lands. The remaining $196 million is the value the Crown had put on the 176,000 hectares of land under the forests. The amount of land being returned was proportionally larger than had been achieved elsewhere in the country. But it was being returned already encumbered. In purely monetary terms, the settlements of each of the eight iwi were on a par with other Treaty settlements and as such still did not amount to fair, reasonable or just recompense for all the violations they have suffered at the hands of the Crown.

Yet one of the iwi involved, Te Arawa of the Bay of Plenty, was able to use the deal to improve its own proposed settlement significantly, including no longer having to pay for geothermal wells and five school properties.[32]

Mauao returned to its rightful owners – but not really

In the Bay of Plenty, the mountain Mauao, also known as Mount Maunganui, was finally returned to its rightful owners in May 2008. However in a sleight of hand that amazed legal observers, the government managed to retain its historic reserve status and the Minister of Conservation continues to have all the rights and obligations of a freehold owner.[33]

Government abandons its settlement policy to reach agreement on settling Ngāti Kahu's claims

In the Far North, Ngāti Kahu had returned to the Tribunal to seek orders for the return of 12,590 acres of state-owned lands and forests after negotiations failed, and they repossessed the 9,170-acre Rangiputa station to stop the government selling it. In April 2008 the Tribunal gave the government three months to make an offer that was acceptable to Ngāti Kahu. For the first time ever, the Crown apologised to Ngāti Kahu and intensive negotiations with a Chief Negotiator appointed by the Minister followed. Crown policy for settling Treaty claims was largely abandoned. Instead the negotiations focused on the social, economic and spiritual needs and mana whenua considerations of the fifteen hapū and their associated marae that make up Ngāti Kahu. By the end of June the Crown made an offer that broke a lot of new ground in terms of Treaty settlements. It involved the return of the control of more than 24,700 acres of land to Ngāti Kahu, with fee simple title to more than half of it, including Rangiputa station. The rest would come under the control of a statutory board made up of equal Ngāti Kahu/Crown membership, chaired by Ngāti Kahu and all its business conducted according to Ngāti Kahu customary law. The offer also included a cash contribution of $7.5 million to be used to rebuild the fifteen marae and their associated housing, which were either non-existent or in a very poor state of repair. In mid-2008, Ngāti Kahu was in the process of drawing up an Agreement in Principle with the government which they planned to sign off in September, before the general election.

Loss of several Māori icons
Syd Jackson
During the 2007–08 year we lost several Māori icons who had made huge contributions to the well-being of their people. In September 2007 Syd Jackson of Ngāti Kahungunu and Ngāti Porou passed away. He was a prominent Māori leader who had conducted a lifelong campaign for justice for Māori, with a totally unswerving commitment to revolution and freeing Māori from the oppression of British immigrants. He was an outstanding broadcaster, activist, trade unionist and political leader. He completed a Masters degree in political studies in the 1970s before entering trade union work. He was the Secretary of the Clerical Workers' Union in Auckland from 1978 until 1989 when he resigned and co-founded Te Rūnanga o Ngā Kaimahi Māori o Aotearoa as an advocacy agency for those whom the unions would not represent. In the 1970s he was also one of the founders and leaders of the young Māori intellectuals group, Ngā Tamatoa, which fought for tino rangatiratanga (Māori sovereignty), organising protests at Waitangi Day commemorations starting in 1971, forming Matakite to organise the Māori Land March of 1975, and presenting a petition to the government in 1976 demanding legal recognition of the Māori language. He made huge contributions to the Māori renaissance and the creation of the contemporary Māori voice, was one of the country's most radical thinkers and innovators and was a principled and staunch leader to the end.[34]

Archbishop Whakahuihui Vercoe

Later that month Archbishop Whakahuihui Vercoe passed away. He had been a priest for fifty-four years, was a former Bishop of Aotearoa and was Archbishop of the Anglican Church. He was a staunch supporter of Māori rights and status guaranteed under the Treaty of Waitangi. He served as a military chaplain in Malaya between 1961 and 1963 and in South Vietnam in 1968 and 1969. He was part of the radical restructuring of the Anglican Church in 1990 which introduced and implemented a constitution in which Pākehā Anglicans no longer dominate the church, but share equally with their partners, Tikanga Māori and Tikanga Polynesia. He was also one of the leaders of the Hīkoi of Hope in 1998. In his address at Waitangi for the commemoration of the 150th anniversary of the signing of the Treaty of Waitangi in 1990, he took everyone by surprise when, in addressing the visiting British monarch, Queen Elizabeth II, he said very eloquently and simply:

One hundred and fifty years ago, a compact was signed, a covenant made between two people ...

But since the signing of that treaty ... our partners have marginalized us. You have not honoured the treaty ...

The language of this land is yours, the custom is yours, the media by which we tell the world who we are is yours ...

What I have come here for is to renew the ties that made us a nation in 1840. I don't want to debate the treaty; I don't want to renegotiate the treaty. I want the treaty to stand firmly as the unity, the means by which we are one nation ... The treaty is what we are celebrating. It is what we are trying to establish so that my tino rangatiratanga is the same as your tino rangatiratanga.

> And so I have come to Waitangi to cry for the
> promises that you made and for the expectations our
> tupuna [had] 150 years ago … And so I conclude, as
> I remember the songs of our land, as I remember the
> history of our land, I weep here on the shores of the
> Bay of Islands.[35]

Māori reaction to his speech was jubilation. The Governor
General of the day, Sir Paul Reeves, reported the Queen asking
him, 'Is this a radical bishop?' to which he answered 'No,
Ma'am, but he's doing pretty well'. Some Pākehā thought he
got it absolutely right. But most condemned him, there were
denunciations in Parliament of the 'troublesome bishop' and
he was never asked back to Waitangi.[36]

Hone Tūwhare

In January 2008 we lost the towering literary figure, poet and
author, Hone Tūwhare. He wrote the first book of poetry by a
Māori author in English, and will be remembered as a great
artist and philosopher whose real talent was his simplicity.
He was Te Mata poet laureate in 1999, was conferred with
honorary doctorates from both the Universities of Auckland
and Otago, and was one of the ten Icon artists announced
in 2003.[37] His great love of people and the environment is
reflected throughout his work. His most famous poem, 'No
Ordinary Sun', was a passionate cry against nuclear testing and
was published in his first book of poetry in 1964.

> Tree let your arms fall:
> raise them not sharply in supplication
> to the bright enhaloed cloud.
> Let your arms lack toughness and
> resilience for this is no mere axe
> to blunt nor fire to smother.

Your sap shall not rise again
to the moon's pull.
No more incline a deferential head
to the wind's talk, or stir
to the tickle of coursing rain.

Your former shagginess shall not be
wreathed with the delightful flight
of birds nor shield
nor cool the ardour of unheeding
lovers from the monstrous sun.

Tree let your naked arms fall
nor extend vain entreaties to the radiant ball.
This is no gallant monsoon's flash,
no dashing trade wind's blast.
The fading green of your magic
emanations shall not make pure again
these polluted skies ... for this
is no ordinary sun.

O tree
in the shadowless mountains
the white plains and
the drab sea floor
your end at last is written.[38]

Barry Barclay

Then, one month later, it was Barry Barclay. He was a leading light in the world of indigenous film-making, having been the first Māori to direct a feature film. The film, *Ngati*, won best film at the Taormina Film Festival, Italy, in 1987 and also screened at the Cannes festival. Barry made a number of documentaries and was a fierce advocate against injustice, particularly the racism against Māori in the film industry and barriers to telling Māori stories.[39] He was also a dedicated writer and in 2006 published the book *Mana Tūturu: Māori Treasures and Intellectual Property Rights*.

Commemorations for thirty-year anniversaries of Raglan and Takaparawhau

There were also commemorations for the arrests thirty years earlier of Eva Rickard and sixteen others at Raglan for trespassing on their ancestral land taken for an airfield during World War II and never returned. The lands were given instead to the local golf club, but were eventually returned to their rightful owners. Similarly, the arrests of 222 people at Takaparawhau (also known as Bastion Point) in 1978 were commemorated. Those lands were also returned, although not until 1987.

Commemorations at Waitangi peaceful yet again

It was the third year in a row that there were peaceful commemorations at Waitangi on Waitangi Day, although the Prime Minister refused to attend the formal ceremonies,[40] fearing a backlash over the terror raids on Tūhoe. Peaceful commemorations at Waitangi were largely attributed to the Māori Party presence in Parliament and the role they played as the independent Māori voice unafraid to bring Māori issues to the attention of the House and the nation.

Victoria Cross awarded to Corporal Willie Apiata

However the highlight of the Māori year was the award of the Victoria Cross (VC) to Corporal Willie Apiata in July 2007. It was the first time the award had been made to a living Māori – the two previous awards were posthumous. There had been a great deal of bitterness among Māori servicemen that many Māori who should have received VCs, especially during World War II, did not do so even though returned servicemen and their families pursued it for more than fifty years. Corporal

Apiata received his VC for valour in Afghanistan in 2004 in saving the life of a comrade while under heavy fire from opposing forces. Huge hui to celebrate the award were held at Te Kaha on the East Coast and at Waitangi. In April 2008, in a gesture of remarkable generosity, and to mark ANZAC Day, he gifted his Victoria Cross to the nation.[41] In Māori we say, he mahi tino rangatira, a truly noble and selfless deed.

1 Paul Hamer, 2007, *Māori in Australia Ngā Māori i te Ao Moemoeā*, Te Puni Kōkiri, Wellington and Griffith University, Sydney, p. 14, http://www.tpk.govt.nz/en/in-print/our-publications/publications/maori-in-australia/download/tpk-maorinaustralia2007-en.pdf

2 Māori Party, 2007(c), 'Speech: Protected Disclosures Amendment Bill – Hone Harawira', press release, 23 October 2007, http://www.maoriparty.com/index.php?option=com_content&task=view&id=1375&Itemid=28

3 Moana Jackson, 2008, 'Preface – The Constancy of Terror', in Danny Keenan (ed.), *Terror in Our Midst? Searching for Terror in Aotearoa New Zealand*, Wellington, Huia Publishers, p. 6; Danny Keenan, 2008(b), 'Introduction: Searching for Terror', in Keenan (ed.), *Terror in Our Midst?*, p. 19; Teurikore Biddle, 2008, 'Epilogue: Maungapōhatu an Enduring Tūhoetanga', in Keenan (ed.), *Terror in Our Midst?*, p. 256.

4 Sue Abel, 2008, 'Tūhoe and "Terrorism" on Television News', in Keenan (ed.), *Terror in Our Midst?*, p. 119; Keenan, 'Introduction: Searching for Terror', p. 19; Māori Party, 2007(d), 'Tell the Truth about the Bus: Te Ururoa Flavell', press release, 23 October 2007, http://www.maoriparty.com/index.php?option=com_content&task=view&id=1371&Itemid=2

5 Rawinia Higgins, 2008, 'Another Chapter in Our History: Reflections on the Events at Rūātoki, 15 October 2007', in Keenan (ed.), *Terror in Our Midst?*, p. 210; Danny Keenan, 2008(c), 'Autonomy as Fiction: The Urewera Native District Reserve Act 1896', in Keenan (ed.), *Terror in Our Midst?*, pp. 79–83.

6 Higgins, 'Another Chapter in Our History', p. 220.

7 Juliet Rowan, 2007, 'Valley Locked Down After Dawn Raids', *nzherald.co.nz*, 16 October 2007; Jackson, 'Preface – The Constancy of Terror', p. 20.

8 Biddle, 'Epilogue: Maungapōhatu an Enduring Tūhoetanga', p. 256.

9 Danny Keenan, 2008(d), 'The Terror Raids and the Criminalising of Dissent', in Keenan (ed.), *Terror in Our Midst?*, p. 132.

10 Claire Trevett, 2007, 'Defiant Horomia: I Will Not Resign', *nzherald.co.nz*, 29 October 2007.

11 Keenan, Danny, 'Introduction: Searching for Terror', p. 21.

12 NZPA, 2007, 'Last "terror raid" Accused Freed as Hikoi Starts', *nzherald.co.nz*, 12 November 2007.

13 Keenan, 'The Terror Raids and the Criminalising of Dissent', p. 133.

14 Keenan, 'The Terror Raids and the Criminalising of Dissent', p. 133.

15 Keenan, 'Introduction: Searching for Terror', p. 25.

16 Dominic O'Sullivan, 2008, 'Māori MPs and "Operation Eight"', in Keenan (ed.), *Terror in Our Midst?*, p. 140.

17 Māori Party, 2007(e), 'Speech: "I Will Not Sit Quietly by While State Forces Terrorise my People", Hone Harawira', press release, 8 November 2007, http://

www.maoriparty.com/index.php?option=com_content&task=view&id=1415&
Itemid=28

18 Māori Party, 2007(f), 'It's Looking Good for 2008 Says Māori Party', press release, 10 November 2007, http://www.maoriparty.com/index.php?option=com_conte nt&task=view&id=1417&Itemid=2

19 NZPA and NZ Herald Staff, 2008, 'UN Orders Government to Explain Anti-terror Raids', *nzherald.co.nz*, 17 January 2008.

20 Claire Trevett, Stuart Dye and Edward Gay, 2007, 'Tame Iti Seeking Release From Jail', *nzherald.co.nz*, 9 November 2007.

21 Justin Henehan, 2008, 'Raids "hurt" is Regretted', *Herald on Sunday*, 30 March 2008, p. 2.

22 United Nations Declaration on the Rights of Indigenous Peoples, http://www. un.org/esa/socdev/unpfii/en/drip.html

23 Williams, 'Wi Parata is Dead, Long Live Wi Parata'; Rawiri Taonui, 2007, 'Unburdening Future Generations', *New Zealand Herald*, 8 October 2007, p. A13.

24 Mutu, 'Recovering Fagin's Ill-gotten Gains', p. 201.

25 New Zealand Human Rights Commission, 2007, 'Indigenous Rights Declaration to Guide Commission Work', press release, 18 September 2007, http:// www.hrc.co.nz/home/hrc/newsandissues/indigenousrightsdeclaration toguidecommissionwork.php

26 Australia Human Rights and Equal Opportunities Commission, 2008, 'Call for Submissions', http://www.humanrights.gov.au/social_justice/declaration/ comments.html

27 Assembly of First Nations, 2008, 'Fontaine, Simon and Chartier Congratulate Canadian Parliament for Their Support of the United Nations Declaration of the Rights of Indigenous Peoples', press release, 9 April 2008, http://www.afn. ca/article.asp?id=4067

28 Waitangi Tribunal, *Tāmaki Makaurau Settlement Process* and *Final Report on the Impacts of the Crown's Settlement Policy on Te Arawa Waka and Other Tribes*.

29 See chapter 13.

30 MLR, September 2007, p. 8.

31 Waitangi Tribunal, *Report on the Central North Island Claims*.

32 Office of Treaty Settlements, 2008(c), 'Historical Treaty Settlements: Progress Report 2008', *Mana* no. 83, August–September 2008, pp. 16–17.

33 MLR, May 2008, p. 4.

34 Matt McCarten, 2007, 'My First Lesson From a Master in the Gentle Art of Protesting', *nzherald.co.nz*, 9 September 2007; Amokura Panoho, 2008, 'Syd Jackson', *Mana* no. 81, April–May 2008, pp. 6–8.

35 Whakahuihui Vercoe, 1990, 'We Have Not Honoured Each Other's Promises', *New Zealand Herald*, 7 February 1990, p. 9.

36 Alanah May Eriksen, and Yvonne Tahana, 2007, 'Outspoken Anglican Archbishop Dies', *New Zealand Herald*, 14 September 2007, p. A3; 2007–2008, 'Maimai Aroha: Passing of a Soldier Priest', *Mana* no. 79, December 2007–January 2008, p. 9; Lloyd Ashton, 2006, 'The making of a "radical bishop"', *Mana* no. 71, pp. 24–9.

37 Hone Harawira, 2008, 'He Aitua – Hone Tuwhare "No Ordinary Icon"', press release, 17 January 2008; Janet Hunt, 2008, 'Thinking About Tuwhare', *Mana* no. 80, February–March 2008, pp. 8–12.

38 Hone Tūwhare, 1964, *No Ordinary Sun*, Auckland, Blackwood and Janet Paul.

39 Katherine Findlay, 2008, 'Barry Barclay 1945-2008', *Mana* no. 83, August–September 2008, pp. 6–7.

40 John Roughan, 2008, 'Where Clark Fears to Tread', *New Zealand Herald*, 9 February 2008, p. A21.

41 2008, 'Pitopito Korero: Willie's Gift', *Mana* no. 82, June–July 2008, p. 38; Māori Party, 2008(a), 'Willie Apiata's Remarkable ANZAC Day Gift to the Nation', press release, 24 April 2008, http://www.scoop.co.nz/stories/PA0804/S00577.htm

CHAPTER 15

2008–09 – A Year of More Good News than Bad

For the first time since I began writing these reviews on Māori issues in 1994 I could provide a report that in total had more positive aspects than negative. The highlight was the influence the Māori Party had been able to have on the new National-led government. There were also the benefits that were finally starting to flow to Māori after the Labour government, in its dying days, set out to win back Māori support through Treaty of Waitangi claims settlements. The country still has a very long way to go before Māori are accorded the respect owed us as the country's first nation. That includes recognising and upholding our sovereignty guaranteed by Te Tiriti o Wiatangi and reversing the shocking statistical trends in all socio-economic areas. Nevertheless 2008–09 looked like a good start in that direction.

Māori Party wins five seats and receives mandate to become part of the government

The November 2008 election resulted in a landslide victory for the conservative National Party, which won 58 seats in the 120-seat Parliament. With the right-wing ACT Party with five seats, they had sufficient numbers to form a government. However the new Prime Minister, John Key, announced that he would lead a National minority government with confidence-

and-supply support from the ACT, United Future and Māori parties. Although both major parties had been courting the Māori Party in the lead-up to the elections, it came as a surprise that National sought to include them when there was no need to do so. It was also in marked contrast to the Labour Party treatment of the Māori Party after the 2005 election when the then Prime Minister had referred to them as 'the last cab off the rank'.[1] The Māori Party won five of the seven Māori seats in the 2008 elections, with Labour's Ministers of Māori Affairs and Local Government each retaining their Tairāwhiti and Hauraki-Waikato seats.[2] The election delivered six MPs who acknowledge their Māori descent to each of the Labour and National parties, and one to the Green Party, making a total of eighteen MPs of Māori descent in the House. However the only MPs who represent Māori are those in the Māori seats. The rest represent their parties.

Agreement between Māori Party and National covers major issues for Māori

Within days of the election the Māori Party announced that it was prepared to consider John Key's invitation to become part of his government but would only do so after consulting Māori throughout the country. Forty hui were convened and within the week the party reported overwhelming support for them entering into an agreement with National.[3] The agreement covered many issues raised by the Māori Party in the previous Parliament.[4] Both parties were to act in accordance with the Treaty of Waitangi. National had sought to abolish the Māori seats but under the agreement they would not do so without the consent of the Māori people. Māori have long sought constitutional change to embed the Treaty of Waitangi in a written constitution for the country. Under the agreement a group to consider constitutional issues including Māori representation was to be set up by early 2010. The Māori Party was initially created to fight the

Rangiputa repossession. (Margaret Mutu)

Aroha Mead (Ngāti Awa, Ngāti Porou), who, along with Ngāneko Minhinnick and Moana Jackson, worked for more than two decades with other indigenous experts on drafting the United Nations' Declaration on the Rights of Indigenous Peoples. (Gil Hanly)

Ninja army – the name the kohanga reo children gave to the heavily armed, combat-ready members of the police who boarded their bus during the police raid on Rūātoki on 17 October 2007. (Whakatāne Beacon)

Syd Jackson (Ngāti Kahungunu, Ngāti Porou). (Gil Hanly)

Tame Iti (Tūhoe). (New Zealand Herald)

Hone Tūwhare (Ngāpuhi). (Gil Hanly)

Archbishop Whakahuihui Vercoe
(Tūhoe, Te Arawa, Tainui, Whakatōhea,
Ngāi Tai). (Lloyd Ashton)

Barry Barclay (Ngāti Apa). (Mana)

Joe Hawke, who led the Bastion Point protest in the 1970s, addressing the crowd at the thirty-year commemoration at Ōrākei marae, 2008. (Gil Hanly)

Raglan protest 1977. (Mana/John Miller)

Corporal Willie Apiata (Ngāpuhi). (New Zealand Defence Force)

Bastion Point protest, 1978. (New Zealand Herald)

Māori Party MPs 2008: (from left) Hone Harawira, Rāhui Kātene, Hon. Dr Pita Sharples, Hon. Tariana Turia and Te Ururoa Flavell. (New Zealand Herald)

Auckland Supercity protest, May 2009. (Courtesy of the Māori Party)

Auckland Supercity protest, May 2009. (Gil Hanly)

confiscation of the foreshore and seabed from Māori by the Crown, and had a clear mandate to repeal the Foreshore and Seabed Act 2004. Under the agreement a review of the Act was to be conducted before December 2009 and in the event of repeal being necessary, protection would be put in place to ensure that all New Zealanders have access to the foreshore and seabed. In the event the review was completed in June 2009, six months early, and did recommend that the Act be repealed.[5] A government decision on how to proceed with the matter was, in mid-2009, awaited.

Two Māori Party ministers

The most important outcomes of the agreement were the ministerial roles assigned to the leaders of the Māori Party. The consultation hui had indicated that maintaining Māori independence in Parliament remained paramount and that the Māori Party must continue to hold the government to account even though they were part of that government. As such Dr Pita Sharples and Tariana Turia became ministers outside cabinet. Dr Sharples is Minister of Māori Affairs, Associate Minister of Education and Associate Minister of Corrections. Mrs Turia is Minister for the Community and Voluntary Sector, Associate Minister of Health and Associate Minister of Social Development and Employment.

Prime Minister agrees to Māori flag but not to Māori seats on Auckland super city

Within two months the Māori Party was challenging the government about flying a Māori flag on the Auckland Harbour Bridge on Waitangi Day, a request that had been denied repeatedly by the previous government. The Prime Minister answered that he was happy to see that, not only on the Harbour Bridge but also at Parliament, provided Māori could agree which flag was to be flown.[6] As soon as the Foreshore and Seabed hearings were completed in June

2009, the Minister of Māori Affairs started conducting a series of hui around the country to ascertain what Māori wanted. Then when the government announced in April 2009 it would not follow the recommendations of the Royal Commission on Auckland Governance to reserve three seats for Māori on the proposed Auckland super city council,[7] the Māori Party organised a protest march against the government decision that tied up the inner city area for several hours.[8] It also kept needling the government to agree to the United Nations Declaration on the Rights of Indigenous People,[9] when signs appeared indicating that the United States and Canada were moving closer to doing so. In the event of those two nations agreeing to the declaration, New Zealand would be the only country to remain opposed to the international recognition of the human rights of indigenous peoples.

Treaty claims settlements proceed apace …

On the Treaty of Waitangi claims settlements, the pace set by the Deputy Prime Minister in the last government, Dr Michael Cullen, was maintained until the elections. The National government promised to maintain this momentum. Iwi throughout the country, who had suffered interminable delays over several decades at the hands of government officials, found themselves thrown into intense negotiations, with the pace becoming very demanding in the dying days of the Labour government. In its *Four Monthly Report July–October 2008*, the Office of Treaty Settlements reported an unprecedented level of activity in respect of progressing the settlements of historical Treaty of Waitangi claims.[10] Legislation settling the long-running Te Rōroa claim had passed through Parliament. Deeds of Settlement had been signed with the Wellington-based iwi Taranaki Whānui ki Te Upoko o Te Ika, with Waikato-Tainui in respect of the Waikato river and with Ngāti Apa. Agreements in Principle had been reached with Ngāti Kahu, Ngāti Manawa, Tūranganui-a-Kiwa, Ngāti Pahauwera,

Ngāti Makino/Waitaha, Ngāti Maniapoto, Ngāti Raukawa and Te Pūmautanga o Te Arawa.[11]

Taranaki Whānui ki Te Upoko o Te Ika Deed of Settlement

In June 2008, Taranaki Whānui ki Te Upoko o Te Ika of Wellington signed a Deed of Settlement for the return of several small pieces of land including three islands in Wellington harbour, $25 million with which to buy more of their own lands still held by the Crown and a $5 million contribution towards their costs in pursuing the settlement.[12]

Ātihau-Whanganui Incorporation Agreement

In July 2008 Ātihau-Whanganui Incorporation signed an agreement with the Crown for a $24.6 million cash payment to settle a claim for the misuse of their lands in the central North Island. In 1902 101,050 acres of their lands came under the control of the Aotea District Land Board. Pākehā managed to take control of the board and leased the lands to Pākehā at rates and under conditions severely detrimental to its Māori owners, which resulted in them having to pay substantial amounts to those Pākehā once the leases expired. Financial arrangements to resume as many leases as possible when they come up for renewal had cost the incorporation over $30 million, and the settlement will be used mostly to service the incorporation's debts.[13]

Waikato River Deed of Settlement

In August Waikato-Tainui signed a Deed of Settlement for the country's largest and badly polluted river, the Waikato river. The settlement aims to enhance the relationship and partnership between the Crown and Waikato-Tainui regarding the management and use of the river. The main features of the settlement are focused on co-management and collaborative protection of the river. A body made up of iwi and Crown members will have oversight of the clean-up of the river, with the Crown contributing $7 million annually for thirty years. A Waikato River Statutory Board made up of iwi and district council appointees will support the iwi and their relationship with the river,[14] with the Crown contributing $50 million for river initiatives, and a further $1 million per year for thirty years to fund Waikato-Tainui participation in the co-management process. The Crown will also pay $20 million into the Sir Robert Mahuta Endowment.[15] The Office of Treaty Settlements website does not indicate that the Crown recognises that Māori own the river, although a quote from the late Sir Robert Mahuta stating that 'The River belongs to us and we belong to the River. The Waikato tribe and the River are inseparable. It is a gift left to us by our ancestors and we believe we have a duty to protect that gift for future generations' is included. Even so, the settlement appears to give Waikato-Tainui only a limited say in the management of the river.

Ngāti Kahu Agreement in Principle

In September 2008 Ngāti Kahu in the Far North signed an Agreement in Principle for the return of 12,590 acres of their lands and control over a further 12,355 acres through a statutory board made up of equal Ngāti Kahu/Crown membership, chaired by Ngāti Kahu and with all its business conducted according to Ngāti Kahu tikanga. A cash contribution of $7.5 million to rebuild and repair fifteen marae and their associated housing has also been included in the agreement.[16] In 2007 Ngāti Kahu had been forced to repossess parts of their lands when the Crown tried to sell them off.[17] All these lands were returned to Ngāti Kahu.[18]

Hauraki and South Island Commercial Aquaculture Settlement

In October 2008, the Crown signed an Agreement in Principle with iwi of Hauraki and the South Island over resolution of their aquaculture interests. A one-off $97 million cash payment was to be made to settle the Crown's obligations to Māori under the Māori Commercial Aquaculture Claims Settlement Act 2004. The Act obliged the Crown to provide the equivalent of 20 percent of existing aquaculture space for Māori.[19]

Ngāti Porou Agreement

Two days before the elections, on 6 November 2008, the government announced that it had reached agreement with Ngāti Porou to pay a cash sum of $90 million plus interest for up to two years to settle their historical grievances, to gift five properties and possibly a sixth and to afford Ngāti Porou the right to purchase Crown forest lands and land under schools. The agreement also includes considering Crown support for retention and development of Ngāti Porou language, knowledge and customary practices, marae development grants and the use of conservation land to protect and develop Ngāti Porou culture.[20]

Reminder for the Prime Minister that settlements still unjust and unfair

Despite the pace of the settlements they remain neither just nor fair, delivering only a small fraction of what was stolen from each iwi and providing little or no compensation for the extensive damage done to Māori throughout the country since 1840. Two young Ngāti Kahu men reminded the country of this on Waitangi Day at Waitangi when they jostled the Prime Minister and warned him that the vast majority of the injustices perpetrated against Māori remain unaddressed and Māori grievances remain unresolved. They were arrested, but in court had overwhelming support from their whānau and iwi with numerous kaumātua speaking in their defence, including their local MP.[21] It was clear that what the young men had said to the Prime Minister was correct. The community service sentence they received was served amongst their own Ngāti

Kahu iwi, where their past record of extensive voluntary work for kaumātua meant their service was completed in record time.[22]

1 Kevin Taylor, 2005, 'Problems with Holding Hands', *New Zealand Herald*, 10 September 2005, p. B5.

2 Ministry of Justice, Chief Electoral Office, 2008, *Official Count Results – Overall Status*, http://www.electionresults.govt.nz/electionresults_2008/partystatus. html

3 Māori Party, 2008(b), 'Reflections from the Relationship Signing with National Party from Tariana Turia', press release, 16 November 2008, http://www.scoop. co.nz/stories/PA0811/S00181.htm

4 Māori Party, 2008(c), *Relationship and Confidence and Supply Agreement between the National Party and the Māori Party*, http://www.maoriparty.org/index.php? pag=cms&id=153&p=national-party-and-the-māori-party-agreement.html

5 E T Durie, Hana O'Regan and Richard Boast, 2009, *Pākia ki Uta, Pākia ki Tai: Ministerial Review of the Foreshore and Seabed Act*, Wellington, Department of Justice.

6 John Armstrong, 2009, 'Maori to Decide if Flag to Fly on Harbour Bridge – PM', *nzherald.co.nz*, 14 January 2009.

7 Janine Haywood, 2010, 'Local Government Representation' in Malcolm Mulholland and Veronica Tawhai (eds), *Weeping Waters: The Treaty of Waitangi and Constitutional Change*, Wellington, Huia Publishers, pp. 280–4.

8 2009, 'Latest Updates: Super City Hikoi', *nzherald.co.nz*, 25 May 2009.

9 United Nations Declaration on the Rights of Indigenous Peoples, http://www. un.org/esa/socdev/unpfii/en/drip.html

10 Office of Treaty Settlements, 2008(a), *Four Monthly Report July–October 2008*, http://www.ots.govt.nz/frameset-settlementdocs.html

11 Office of Treaty Settlements, *Four Monthly Report July–October 2008.*

12 MLR, August 2008, p. 4.

13 MLR, July 2008, p. 4.

14 MLR, August 2008, pp. 5–6.

15 Office of Treaty Settlements, 2008(b), *Waikato River Settlement Summary*, http:// www.ots.govt.nz/

16 See Chapter 14; Margaret Mutu, 2009(c), 'The Role of History and Oral Traditions in Recovering Fagin's Ill-gotten Gains: Settling Ngāti Kahu's Treaty of Waitangi Claims Against the Crown', in *Te Pouhere Kōrero 3: Māori History, Māori People*, p. 38.

17 See Chapter 13.

18 See Chapter 14; Margaret Mutu, 2009(b), 'Māori Issues in Review: Issues and Events, 2008', *The Contemporary Pacific – A Journal of Island Affairs*, vol. 21 no. 1, p. 166.

19 Te Rūnanga o Ngāi Tahu, 2008, 'Māori Commercial Aquaculture Settlement', http:// www.ngaitahu.iwi.nz/Te-Runanga/He-Kaupapa-Whakahirahira/Aquaculture/; Hauraki Māori Trust Board, 2008, 'Hauraki Fisheries and Aquaculture Settlement', http://www.hauraki.iwi.nz/documents/March09Newsletterweb.pdf

20 Te Haeata, 2008, *Settling Ngāti Porou Historical Treaty Claims*, http://www. ngatiporou.com/myfiles/F1_Latest_news_Te_Haeata_Panui_-High_Level_ Agreement_Summary_05112008.pdf

21 Hone Harawira, 2009, 'Āe Mārika' (weekly column), *Northland Age*, 17 March 2009, p. 5.
22 Te Rūnanga-ā-Iwi o Ngāti Kahu, 2009, Minutes of the Taumata Kaumātua o Ngāti Kahu, 23 February 2009, Te Rūnanga-ā-Iwi o Ngāti Kahu.

Appendix 1

The Declaration of Independence 1835

This table gives the wording of the original document alongside a translation by Dr Margaret Mutu and the 1840 English version, by missionaries, sent by the British Resident, James Busby, to the Under Secretary of State on 2 November 1835.

Original document	Translation by Margaret Mutu	Original English version
He wakaputanga o te Rangatiratanga o Nu Tireni	*A declaration of the paramount authority in respect of New Zealand*	*Declaration of the Independence of New Zealand*
1. Ko matou ko nga Tino Rangatiratanga o nga iwi o Nu Tireni i raro mai o Hauraki kua oti nei te huihui i Waitangi i Tokerau 28 o Okatapa 1835 ka wakaputa i te Rangatiratanga o to matou wenua a ka meatia ka wakaputaia e matou he Wenua Rangatira kia huaina <u>Ko te wakaminenga o nga hapu o Nu Tireni.</u>	*1. We, the paramount chiefs of the tribal groupings of New Zealand north of Hauraki met at Waitangi in the North on 28 October 1835 and declared the paramount authority over our lands and said we would declare a State of Peace to be called <u>The Gathering/ Confederation of the Tribal Groups of New Zealand</u>.*	*1. We, the hereditary chiefs and heads of the tribes of the Northern parts, being assembled at Waitangi, in the Bay of Islands, on this 28th day of October 1835, declare the Independence of our country, which is hereby declared to be an Independent State, under the designation of The United Tribes of New Zealand.*

2. Ko te Kingitanga ko te mana i te wenua o te wakaminenga o Nu Tireni ka meatia nei kei nga Tino Rangatira anake i to matou huihuinga a ka mea hoki e kore e tukua e matou te wakarite ture ki te tahi hunga ke atu, me te tahi Kawanatanga hoki kia meatia i te wenua o te wakaminenga o Nu Tireni ko nga tangata anake e meatia nei e matou e wakaritea ana ki te ritenga o o matou ture e meatia nei e matou i to matou huihuinga.	2. *The kingly authority is the ultimate power, authority and control of the lands of the Confederation of New Zealand and is declared here to lie only with the paramount chiefs at our meeting and we also declare that we will never give over law-making power to any other persons or any other government to have any say over the lands of the Confederation. The only people who we have said are authorised to set down our laws we have spoken of at our meeting.*	2. *All sovereign power and authority within the territories of the United Tribes of New Zealand is hereby declared to reside entirely and exclusively in the hereditary chiefs and heads of tribes in their collective capacity, who also declare that they will not permit any legislative authority separate from themselves in their collective capacity to exist, nor any function of government to be exercised within the said territories, unless by persons appointed by them, acting under the authority of laws regularly enacted by them in Congress assembled.*
3. Ko matou ko nga Tino Rangatira ka mea nei kia huihui ki te runanga ki Waitangi a te Ngahuru i tenei tau i tenei tau ki te wakarite ture kia tika ai te wakawakanga kia mau pu te rongo kia mutu te he kia tika te hokohoko a ka mea hoki ki nga tauiwi o runga kia wakarerea te wawai kia mahara ai ki te wakaoranga o to matou wenua a kia uru ratou ki te wakaminenga o Nu Tireni.	3. *We the paramount chiefs say here that we will meet at the council at Waitangi in the autumn of each year to set down laws so that judgement will be correct, that peace will prevail, that wrong-doing will end, that trading will be conducted properly and correctly, and we also say to the tribal groupings of strangers of the south to abandon fighting so that they can give thought to saving our lands and so that they can join the Confederation of New Zealand.*	3. *The hereditary chiefs and heads of tribes agree to meet in Congress at Waitangi in the autumn of each year, for the purpose of framing laws for the dispensation of justice, the preservation of peace and good order, and the regulation of trade; and they cordially invite the Southern tribes to lay aside their private animosities and to consult the safety and welfare of our common country, by joining the Confederation of the United tribes.*

4. Ka mea matou kia tuhituhia he pukapuka ki te ritenga o tenei o to matou wakaputanga nei ki te Kingi o Ingarani hei kawe atu i to matou aroha nana hoki i wakaae ki te kara mo matou. A no te mea ka atawai matou, ka tiaki i nga pakeha e noho nei i uta e rere mai ana ki te hokohoko, koia ka mea ai matou ki te Kingi kia waiho hei matua ki a matou i to matou Tamarikitanga kei wakakahoretia to matou Rangatiratanga. Kua wakaetia katoatia e matou i tenei ra i te 28 o Oketopa 1835 ki te aroaro o te Reireneti o te Kingi o Ingarani.	4. We have said that a document/letter is to be written to the King of England concerning the compilation of this Declaration of ours to convey our warm acknowledgement that he has agreed with the flag for us. And because we look after and protect the Europeans living ashore here who come here to trade, so therefore do we say to the King that he remain as a mentor to us in our 'childhood' [that is, as we are learning Europeans' ways], lest our paramount authority be denied. We have all agreed on this day, the 28th of October 1835 in the presence of the King of England's Resident.	4. They also agree to send a copy of this Declaration to His Majesty the King of England, to thank him for his acknowledgement of their flag; and in return for the friendship and protection they have shown, and are prepared to show, to such of his subjects as have settled in their country, or resorted to its shores for the purpose of trade, they entreat that he will continue to be a parent of their infant State, and that he will become its Protector from all attempts upon its independence. Agreed to unanimously on this 28th day of October, 1835, in the presence of His Britannic Majesty's Resident.

Paerata	Tareha
Auroa	Kawiti
Hare Hongi	Pumuka
Hemi Kepa Tupe	Kekeao
Ware Poaka	Te Kamara
Waikato	Pomare
Titore	Wiwia
Moka	Te Tao
Warerahi	Marupo
Rewa	Kopiu
Wai	Warau
Reweti Atuahaere	Ngere
Awa	Moetara
Wiremu Teti Taunui	Hiamoe
Te nana	Pukututu
Pi	Te Peka Eruera Pare te kaituhituhi
Kaua	Hone Wiremu Heke

English Witnesses   Henry Williams
James Clendon
George Clarke
Gilbert Mair

Ko matou ko nga Rangatira ahakoa kihai i tae ki te huihuinga nei no to nuinga o te kaipuke no te aha ranei – ka wakaae katoa ki te waka mutunga Rangatiratanga o Nu Tireni a ka uru ki roto ki te whakaminenga.	*We the chiefs, even though we did not reach this meeting because there were so many ships or for whatsoever reason, all agree to the final paramount authority of New Zealand and enter into the Confederation.*	[No translation]

	Nene	
	Huhu	
	Toua	} English witness
	Panakareao	
1836		
13 January	Kiwi Kiwi	
9 February	Tirerau	
29 March	Hamiora Pita – Matangi	No te Popoto
	Tawai	No te Mahurehure
	Mete	No Ngati Moe
	Patuone	No te Ngati Rangi
1837		
25 June	Parore	No te Ngati Apa
	Kahu	No Ngati Tautahi
12 July	Te Morenga	No Te Rarawa
1838	Mahia	No Te Hapouri
Jany 16	Taonui	No te Popoto
Septr 24	Papahia	No te Rarawa
25	Hapuku	No te Watu apiti (Hawkes Bay)
1839		
July 22	Ko te Werowero	Na ko Ngati Mahuta – ko Kakawai he kai tuhituhi

A declaration of
Independence of Native
Chiefs of New Zealand
made in 1835
in the British Resident
in New Zealand.

Appendix 2

The Treaty of Waitangi 1840

This table gives the wording of the original document alongside a translation by Professor Margaret Mutu and the 1840 English version drawn up by William Hobson, representing Victoria, Queen of England.

Original document	Translation by Margaret Mutu	English version
Ko Wikitoria, te Kuini o Ingarani, i tana mahara atawai ki nga Rangatira me nga Hapu o Nu Tirani i tana hiahia hoki kia tohungia ki a ratou o ratou rangatiratanga, me to ratou wenua, a kia mau tonu hoki te Rongo ki a ratou me te Atanoho hoki kua wakaaro ra he mea tika kia tukua mai tetahi Rangatira hei kai wakarite ki nga Tangata maori o Nu Tirani – kia wakaaetia e nga Rangatira maori te Kawanatanga o te Kuini ki nga wahi katoa o te Wenua nei me nga Motu – na te mea hoki he tokomaha ke nga tangata o tona Iwi Kua noho ki tenei wenua, a e haere mai nei.	*Victoria, the Queen of England, in her concern to protect the leaders and groupings of extended families of New Zealand and in her desire to preserve their paramount authority and their lands to them and to maintain peace and good order, considers it necessary to send a chief to arrange with the people of New Zealand so that their leaders will agree to the Queen's government over all parts of this land and (adjoining) islands and also because there are many of her people already living on this land and others yet to come.*	*Her Majesty Victoria Queen of the United Kingdom of Great Britain and Ireland regarding with Her Royal Favour the Native Chiefs and Tribes of New Zealand and anxious to protect their just Rights and Property and to secure to them the enjoyment of Peace and Good Order has deemed it necessary in consequence of the great number of Her Majesty's Subjects who have already settled in New Zealand and the rapid extension of Emigration both from Europe and Australia which is still in progress to constitute and appoint a functionary properly authorised to treat with the Aborigines of New Zealand for the recognition of Her Majesty's Sovereign*

Na ko te Kuini e hiahia ana kia wakarite te Kawanatanga kia kaua ai nga kino e puta mai ki te tangata Maori ki te Pakeha e noho ture kore ana. Na, kua pai te Kuini kia tukua ahau a Wiremu Hopihona he Kapitana i te Roiara Nawi hei Kawana mo nga wahi katoa o Nu Tirani e tukua aianei, amua atu ki te Kuini e mea atu ana ia ki nga Rangatira o te wakaminenga o nga hapu o Nu Tirani me era Rangatira atu enei ture ka korerotia nei.	*So the Queen desires to establish a government so that no evil will come to Maori and to Europeans living in a state of lawlessness.* *So the Queen has seen fit to send me, William Hobson, a Captain in the Royal Navy, to be Governor for all parts of New Zealand (both those) being allocated now and in the future to the Queen and says to the leaders of the Confederation of the tribal groupings of New Zealand, and other leaders these laws spoken of here.*	*authority over the whole or any part of those islands.* *Her Majesty therefore being desirous to establish a settled form of Civil Government with a view to avert the evil consequences which must result from the absence of the necessary Laws and Institutions alike to the native population and to Her Subjects has been graciously pleased to empower and authorise me William Hobson a Captain in Her Majesty's Royal Navy Consul and Lieutenant Governor of such parts of New Zealand as may be or hereafter shall be ceded to Her Majesty to invite the confederated and independent Chiefs of New Zealand to concur in the following Articles and Conditions.*
Ko te tuatahi Ko nga Rangatira o te Wakaminenga me nga Rangatira katoa hoki ki hai i uru ki taua wakaminenga ka tuku rawa atu ki te Kuini o Ingarani ake tonu atu – te Kawanatanga katoa o o ratou wenua.	***The first*** *The leaders of the Confederation and all the Chiefs who have not joined that Confederation give absolutely to the Queen of England forever the complete government over their land.*	***Article the first*** *The Chiefs of the Confederation of the United Tribes of New Zealand and the separate and independent Chiefs who have not become members of the Confederation cede to Her Majesty the Queen of England absolutely and without reservation all the rights and powers of Sovereignty which the said Confederation or Individual Chiefs respectively exercise or possess, or may be supposed to exercise or to possess over their respective Territories as the sole sovereigns thereof.*

Ko te tuarua	The second	Article the second
Ko te Kuini o Ingarani ka wakarite ka wakaae ki nga Rangatira – ki nga hapu ki nga tangata katoa o Nu Tirani te tino rangatiratanga o o ratou wenua o ratou kainga me o ratou taonga katoa. Otiia ko nga Rangatira o te Wakaminenga me nga Rangatira katoa atu ka tuku ki te Kuini te hokonga o era wahi wenua e pai ai te tangata nona te wenua – ki te ritenga o te utu e wakaritea ai e ratou ko te kaihoko e meatia nei e te Kuini hei kai hoko mona.	The Queen of England agrees to protect the leaders, the groupings of extended families and all the people of New Zealand in the unqualified exercise of their paramount authority over their lands, villages and all their treasures. But on the other hand the leaders of the Confederation and all the leaders will allow the Queen to trade for (the use of) those parcels of land which those whose land it is consent to, and at a price agreed to by the person whose land it is and by the person trading for it (the latter being) appointed by the Queen as her trading agent.	Her Majesty the Queen of England confirms and guarantees to the Chiefs and Tribes of New Zealand and to the respective families and individuals thereof the full exclusive and undisturbed possession of their Lands and Estates Forests Fisheries and other properties which they may collectively or individually possess so long as it is their wish and desire to retain the same in their possession; but the Chiefs of the United Tribes and the Individual Chiefs yield to her Majesty the exclusive right of Pre-emption over such lands as the proprietors thereof may be disposed to alienate at such prices as may be agreed upon between the respective Proprietors and persons appointed by Her Majesty to treat with them in that behalf.
Ko te tuatoru	**The third**	**Article the third**
Hei wakaritenga mai hoki tenei mo te wakaaetanga ki te Kawanatanga o te Kuini – Ka tiakina e te Kuini o Ingarani nga tangata maori katoa o Nu Tirani ka tukua ki a ratou nga tikanga katoa rite tahi ki ana mea ki nga tangata o Ingarani.	For this agreed arrangement therefore concerning the Government of the Queen, the Queen of England will protect all the ordinary people of New Zealand [that is, the Māori] and will give them the same rights and duties of citizenship as the people of England.	In consideration thereof Her Majesty the Queen of England extends to the Natives of New Zealand Her royal protection and imparts to them all the Rights and Privileges of British Subjects.

W. Hobson Consul + Lieutenant Governor	*W. Hobson Consul +* *Lieutenant Governor*	*W. Hobson Consul +* *Lieutenant Governor*
Na ko matou ko nga Rangatira o te Wakaminenga o nga hapu o Nu Tireni ka huihui nei ki Waitangi ko matou hoki ko nga Rangatira o Nu Tirani ka kite nei i te ritenga o enei kupu, ka tangohia ka wakaaetia katoatia e matou, koia ka tohungia ai o matou ingoa o matou tohu. Ka meatia tenei ki Waitangi i te ono o nga ra o Pepueri i te tau kotahi mano e waru rau e wa tekau o to tatou Ariki. Ko nga Rangatira o te Wakaminenga	*We the leaders of the* *Confederation of the* *tribal groupings of New* *Zealand who met here* *at Waitangi, along* *with the chiefs of New* *Zealand see the setting* *out of these words,* *they are taken and* *unanimously agreed to* *by us and so our names* *and our signatures are* *indicated. This was done* *at Waitangi on the 6th* *day of February in the* *year of our Lord eighteen* *hundred and forty.* *The chiefs of the* *Confederation*	*Now therefore We* *the Chiefs of the* *Confederation of the* *United Tribes of New* *Zealand being assembled* *in Congress at Victoria* *in Waitangi and We* *the Separate and* *Independent Chiefs of* *New Zealand claiming* *authority over the* *Tribes and Territories* *which are specified after* *our respective names,* *having been made* *fully to understand* *the Provisions of the* *foregoing Treaty, accept* *and enter into the same* *in the full spirit and* *meaning thereof in* *witness of which we have* *attached our signatures* *or marks at the places* *and the dates respectively* *specified.* *Done at Waitangi this* *sixth day of February in* *the year of our Lord one* *thousand eight hundred* *and forty.*

Glossary

ahi kā	'burning fire', those of the whānau or hapū who remain in the home territories and 'keep the home fires burning'
ariki, arikinui	paramount chief
aroha	love, sympathy, pity
hapū	tribal grouping
hīkoi	walk, march
hui	gatherings, discussions, meetings usually on marae
iwi	group of hapū, tribal groupings
kaimoana	seafood
kaitiakitanga	the responsibilities and kaupapa passed down from the ancestors for tangata whenua to take care of the places, natural resources and other taonga in their rohe and the mauri of those places, resources and taonga
karakia	prayer (includes European-introduced Christian prayer)
kaumātua	respected elders, decision-makers for the iwi, hapū or whānau; sometimes includes kuia
kaumātua rangatira	most senior respected elder within an iwi or hapū, paramount chief of elder status
kaupapa	fundamental principles, plan, tactics, strategy, methods
kaupapa Māori	Māori principles, philosophies
kāwanatanga	governance (borrowed from English)
kīngitanga	kingship (borrowed from English)
kōhanga reo	Māori language immersion pre-school
kōiwi	bones, human remains
kuia	respected older woman/women, decision-makers (along with kaumātua) within a hapū or iwi
kura kaupapa Māori	Māori language immersion primary school
mana	power, authority, ownership, status, influence, dignity, respect derived from the gods
manuhiri	visitor(s), guest(s)
marae	local community and its meeting place and buildings

māramatanga	enlightenment
mātauranga	knowledge
mihi	greeting, speech of welcome
mokopuna	grandchildren, those two or more generations below you
muru	plunder; confiscation (Waitangi Tribunal, 1996, *Taranaki Report*)
pā	occupation site, often in a strategic location such as a hilltop
paepae	bird perch (in southern dialects – speakers' bench or seat)
Pākehā	non-Māori of European descent
papakāinga	home lands
poroporoaki	farewell
rāhui	protection of a place or resources by forbidding access or harvest
rangatira	chief or leader, one who has ability to keep the people together
rangatiratanga	the exercise of power and authority derived from the gods; exercise of chieftainship including sovereignty, rights of self-determination, self-government, the authority and power of iwi or hapū to make decisions and to own and control resources
raupatu	confiscation, marginalisation (Taranaki)
te reo	the language (usually denotes the Māori language)
rohe	geographical territories of a hapū or iwi
rūnanga	council of senior decision-makers of an iwi or hapū
tahataha moana	coastal areas
te taha wairua	the spiritual side
take	topic, issue
tangata whenua	people of the land, those who hold mana whenua in an area, Māori people
tangihanga	funerary ceremonies
taniwha	spiritual minder
taonga	valued resources, assets, prized possessions both material and non-material
tapu	sacredness, spiritual power or protective force
tauiwi	stranger, foreigner
teina	younger brother or male cousin of a male, younger sister or female cousin of a female
Te Puni Kōkiri	Ministry of Māori Development
tiaki	look after

tikanga	customary, correct ways of doing things, protocols
tikanga Māori	customary Māori way of doing things correctly, Māori protocol
tino rangatira	paramount chief
tino rangatiratanga	the exercise of paramount authority and power derived from the gods, sovereignty, autonomy
tohunga	person dedicated to a certain purpose and therefore expert in such matters, a person chosen or appointed by the gods to be their representative and agent (Marsden 1992, pp. 128–9)
tuakana	older brother or male cousin of a male, older sister or female cousin of a female
tuku iho	passed down (from the ancestors)
tuku whenua	allocation of land use rights
tūpāpaku	deceased person's body
tūpuna	ancestors
urupā	burial place
wāhi tapu	special and sacred places
wānanga	lore of the tohunga, intellectual debate
whaea	mother, aunt (including any female cousin of a father, mother, aunts and uncles)
whaikōrero	formal speech
whakapapa	genealogy, ancestry, identity to a place, hapū or iwi
whakataukī	proverb
whānau	extended family group
whanaungatanga	kinship, relationship through whakapapa bonds
whānau pani	bereaved family
whare	house, people in a house
whare wānanga	place of higher education, university
whenua	afterbirth, land
whenua rangatira	unchallenged lands
whenua tupuna	ancestral land

References

Abel, Sue, 2008, 'Tūhoe and "Terrorism" on Television News', in Danny Keenan (ed.), *Terror in Our Midst? Searching for Terror in Aotearoa New Zealand*, Wellington, Huia Publishers, pp. 113–28.

Archie, Carol, 1995, *Māori Sovereignty: The Pakeha Perspective*, Auckland, Hodder Moa Beckett.

Archive of Executive Government, http://www.executive.govt.nz/minister/

Armstrong, John, 2000, 'Slow Shove to Point of no Return', *New Zealand Herald*, 15 April 2000, p. A15.

Armstrong, John, 2002, 'PM's Tip to Turia: "Bite your lip"', *New Zealand Herald*, 11 March 2002, p. A7.

Arotahi News Service, 2003, 'Māori TV Passed', item 20, May 2003, edition 6.

Ashton, Lloyd, 2006, 'The making of a "radical bishop"', *Mana* no. 71, pp. 24–9.

Assembly of First Nations, 2008, 'Fontaine, Simon and Chartier Congratulate Canadian Parliament for Their Support of the United Nations Declaration of the Rights of Indigenous Peoples', press release, 9 April 2008, http://www.afn.ca/article.asp?id=4067

Australia Human Rights and Equal Opportunities Commission, 2008, 'Call for Submissions', http://www.humanrights.gov.au/social_justice/declaration/comments.html

Ballara, Angela, 1986, *Proud to be White? A Survey of Pakeha Prejudice in New Zealand*, Auckland, Heinemann.

Barclay, Barry, 2005, *Mana Tūturu: Māori Treasures and Intellectual Property Rights*, Auckland, Auckland University Press.

Bassett, Michael, 2002, 'Halt the Treaty Gravy Train', *Dominion*, 6 February 2002, p.12.

Bay of Plenty Times, 2002, 'Parties in Wahi Tapu Row Could Meet Before Christmas', *nzherald.co.nz*, 29 November 2002.

Bennion, Tom (ed.), 1994–2008, *Māori Law Review: A Monthly Review of Law Affecting Māori*, Wellington, Tom Bennion.

Berry, Ruth, 2003(a), 'Māori MPs Could Revolt Over Government Foreshore Plan', *nzherald.co.nz*, 19 August 2003.

Berry, Ruth, 2003(b), 'Angry Voices Won't be Far From Foreshore Hui', *nzherald.co.nz*, 4 September 2003.

Berry, Ruth, 2003(c), 'Clark Rebukes Turia Over Foreshore Speech', *nzherald.co.nz*, 16 December 2003.

Berry, Ruth, 2003(d), 'Iwi Leaders Call for Foreshore Protests', *nzherald.co.nz*, 19 December 2003.

Berry, Ruth, 2004(a), 'No Surrender Vows te Heuheu as she Loses Role', *nzherald.co.nz*, 4 February 2004.

Berry, Ruth, 2004(b), 'Māori Party Victors Turn Their Fire on Labour', *nzherald.co.nz*, 12 July 2004.

Berry, Ruth, 2004, and NZPA, 'Helen Clark Hits Out at Judge over East Coast Claim', *nzherald.co.nz*, 13 March 2004.

Berry, Ruth, 2004, and Ainsley Thomson, 'Government Faces Second Defection', *nzherald.co.nz*, 4 May 2004.

Biddle, Teurikore, 2008, 'Epilogue: Maungapōhatu an Enduring Tūhoetanga', in Danny Keenan (ed.), *Terror in Our Midst? Searching for Terror in Aotearoa New Zealand*, Wellington, Huia Publishers, pp. 245–58.

Bidois, Vanessa, 2000(a), 'Tears Flow as MP Says Sorry for Drugs Slur', *New Zealand Herald*, 15 May 2000, p. A3.

Bidois, Vanessa, 2000(b), 'Troubled Waters Loom for Maori Fisheries', *New Zealand Herald*, 4 July 2000, p. A11.

Bingham, Eugene, 2000(a), 'Angry Tamihere Names "thieves"', *New Zealand Herald*, 29 March 2000, p. A2 .

Bingham, Eugene, 2000(b), 'Tamihere Sorry for Thief, Addict Gibe', *New Zealand Herald*, 6 April 2000, p. A5.

Bingham, Eugene, 2001, 'The Grounding of Qantas NZ: a Blow That Came in the Dark', *New Zealand Herald*, 28 April 2001, pp. B6–7.

Boast, Richard, 2007, 'Foreshore and Seabed in New Zealand Law: A Legal-Historical Introduction', in Claire Charters and Andrew Erueti (eds), *Māori Property Rights and the Foreshore and Seabed: The Last Frontier*, Wellington, Victoria University Press, pp. 14–29.

Brash, Don, 2004, 'Nationhood', speech to the Orewa Rotary Club, http://www.scoop.co.nz/stories/PA0401/S00220.htm

Brook, Kip (NZPA), 1995, 'Kaikoura on Whale's Back', *New Zealand Herald*, 18 February 1995, p. 24.

Brookfield, FM (Jock), 2003, 'Māori Customary Title to Foreshore and Seabed', *New Zealand Law Journal*, August 2003, pp. 295–7.

Brooking, Tom, 1996, 'The Year that Broke the Mould: MMP the Highlight of a Year of Triumph and Disappointment', *New Zealand Herald*, 31 December 1996, p. D2.

Burns, Derek, 1997, *Public Money, Private Lives: Aotearoa Television – the Inside Story*, Auckland, Reed.

Byrnes, Giselle, 2004, *The Waitangi Tribunal and New Zealand History*, Melbourne, Australia, Oxford University Press.

Calder, Peter, 2002, 'Te Tangata Whai Rawa o Weniti', *New Zealand Herald*, 16 February 2002, p. E6.

Campbell, Michael, his website, http://www.cambogolf.com/profile.cfm?pageid=my-journey

Carter, Bridget, 2002, 'Jail Activists Vow to Battle On', *New Zealand Herald*, 5 June 2002, p. A2.

Chapple, Irene, 2002, 'Tribes Swap Dissent For Profit', *New Zealand Herald*, 29 October 2002, p. C1.

Charters, Claire 2007, and Erueti, Andrew (eds), *Māori Property Rights and the Foreshore and Seabed: The Last Frontier*, Wellington, Victoria University Press.

Cleave, Louisa, 2002, 'Mai FM Steals Newstalk ZB's Mantle as No.1', *New Zealand Herald*, 18 April 2002, p. A1.

Collins, Simon, 2002, 'One Man's Poll: Maori in the New Millenium', *New Zealand Herald*, 9 July, 2002, p. A9.

Controller and Auditor-General, 2000, 'Part 3.6: Student Loan Debt', in *Report of the Results of the 1999–2000 Central Government Audits*, Wellington, Office of the Controller and Auditor-General, http://www.oag.govt.nz/central-govt/3rd-report/docs/part3-6.pdf

References

Crown Forestry Rental Trust, 2006, 'Forest Rental Proceeds Held in Trust at 31 March 2006', in *Notes to the Financial Statement for the Year Ended 31 March 2006*, http://www.cfrt.org.nz/doclibrary/public/thestorehouse/rta2005-2006/RentalProceeds0506.pdf

Daes, Erica-Irene A, 1988, *Confidential Report by Professor Erica-Irene A Daes, Chairman-Rapporteur of the United Nations Working Group on Indigenous Populations, on Visit to New Zealand, 2–7 January, 1988*, Athens, E A Daes.

Daily Post (Rotorua), 2004, 'Te Arawa Hit Back at PM's Hikoi Comments', *nzherald. co.nz*, 4 May 2004.

de Boni, Dita, 2001, 'BIL Chief Looks on Brighter Side', *New Zealand Herald*, 18 March 2001, D1.

Department of the Prime Minister and Cabinet, 2003, *The Foreshore and Seabed of New Zealand: Protecting Public Access and Customary Rights: Government Proposals for Consultation*, Wellington, New Zealand Government.

Diamond, Paul, 2003, *A Fire in Your Belly: Māori Leaders Speak*, Wellington, Huia Publishers.

Drent, Rob, 1997, 'Public View of SFO All Wrong, Say Staff', *Sunday Star Times*, 16 March 1997, p. 5.

Durie, E T, 1994, 'Keynote Address', in *Kia Pūmau Tonu: Proceedings of the Hui Whakapūmau*, Department of Māori Studies, Massey University.

Durie, E T, 2000, 'The Treaty in the Constitution', in Colin James (ed.), *Building the Constitution*, Wellington, Institute of Policy Studies, Victoria University of Wellington, pp. 201–4.

Durie, E T, 2010, 'Treaty Claims and Self-Determination', Manu-Ao Lecture Series, 3 March 2010, http://www.manu-ao.ac.nz/

Durie, E T, Hana O'Regan and Richard Boast, 2009, *Pākia ki Uta, Pākia ki Tai: Ministerial Review of the Foreshore and Seabed Act*, Wellington, Department of Justice.

Durie, Mason, 1998, *Te Mana, Te Kāwanatanga: The Politics of Māori Self-Determination*, Auckland, Oxford University Press.

Durie, Mason, 2000, 'A Framework for Considering Constitutional Change and the Position of Māori in Aotearoa', in Colin James (ed.), *Building the Constitution*, Wellington, Institute of Policy Studies, Victoria University of Wellington, pp. 414–25.

Durie, Mason, 2005, *Ngā Tai Matatū*, Melbourne, Oxford University Press.

Easton, Brian, 1997, 'Accounting for Difference: How Should we Judge Jeff Chapman?', *New Zealand Listener*, 3 May 1997, http://www.eastonbh.ac.nz/?p=31

Eriksen, Alanah May, 2007, and Yvonne Tahana, 'Outspoken Anglican Archbishop Dies', *New Zealand Herald*, 14 September 2007, p. A3.

Field, Michael, 1991, *Mau: Samoa's Struggle for Freedom*, Auckland, Polynesian Press.

Findlay, Katherine, 2008, 'Barry Barclay 1945–2008', *Mana* no. 83, August–September 2008, pp. 6–7.

Foote, Jeff, Maria Hepi, Marara Rogers-Koroheke and Hone Taimona, 2005, *Urban Water Decision Making Project: Learning from the Stories of Nga Puna Wai o Hokianga*, Environmental Science and Research Ltd, http://www.ocvs.govt.nz/documents/work-programme/building-good-practice/good-practice-in-action/whirinaki-water-project-evaluation-report.pdf

Fox, Derek, 1995(a), 'No Difference from the Tauiwi', *Mana* no. 8, February–April 1995, p. 36.

Fox, Derek, 1995(b), 'Te Raupatu Number Two?', *Mana* no. 8, February–April 1995, p. 37.

Fox, Derek, 2002, 'Politics: Who'll speak up for Māori?', *Mana* no. 47, August–September 2002, p. 24.

Fox, Derek, 2006(a), 'Feature: I Told Them I Wasn't Ready', *Mana* no. 69, April–May 2006, pp. 20–3.

Fox, Derek, 2006(b), 'Education: Te Wananga o Aotearoa: Who's at the Helm Now?', *Mana* no. 69, April–May 2006, p. 67.

Fox, Derek, 2006(c), 'Cover Story: "The Lady"', *Mana* no. 72, October–November 2006, pp. 6–27.

Frame, Alex, 2007, 'Te Heuheu Tukino VII 1919–1997', in *Dictionary of New Zealand Biography*, http://www.dnzb.govt.nz/

Gamble, Warren, 1997(a), 'Mansfield Denies Being Pushed Out', *New Zealand Herald*, 18 January 1997, p. A3.

Gamble, Warren, 1997(b), 'Chapman "guilty" on 10 Charges', *New Zealand Herald*, 1 March 1997, p. A3.

Gamble, Warren, 1997(c), 'Defendant in Child Sex Case is a Judge', *New Zealand Herald*, 8 March 1997, p. A3.

Gardiner, Wira, 1996, *Return to Sender: What Really Happened at the Fiscal Envelope Hui*, Auckland, Reed.

Gibson, Anne, 2002, 'Iwi Wins Bid to Appeal on Sylvia Park', *nzherald.co.nz*, 26 November 2002.

Gifford, Adam, 1995, 'Fires at Takahue: The Corruption of the Occupation Strategy', originally published to NATIVE-L, a now-defunct mailing list; republished at http://groups.yahoo.com/group/worlds-indigenous-people/message/8053, accessed 2010.

Gleeson, Shenagh, 1995, 'Backing for PM on Sovereignty', *New Zealand Herald*, 15 May 1995, p. 7.

Graham, Douglas, 1997, *Trick or Treaty*, Wellington, Institute of Policy Studies, Victoria University of Wellington.

Gregory, Angela, 2001, 'Treaty Settlement Success Stories: How They Did It', *New Zealand Herald*, 10 January 2001, p. A13.

Gregory, Angela, 2002, 'Treaty Experts Sceptical Over Kahu Kidnap Link', *New Zealand Herald*, 17 April 2002, p. A3.

Hamer, Paul, 2004, 'A Quarter-century of the Waitangi Tribunal', in Janine Haywood and Nicola R Wheen (eds), *The Waitangi Tribunal: Te Roopu Whakamana i te Tiriti o Waitangi*, Wellington, Bridget Williams Books, pp. 3–14.

Hamer, Paul, 2007, *Māori in Australia Ngā Māori i te Ao Moemoeā*, Te Puni Kōkiri, Wellington and Griffith University, Sydney, http://www.tpk.govt.nz/en/in-print/our-publications/publications/maori-in-australia/download/tpk-maorinaustralia2007-en.pdf

Harawira, Hone, 1995, 'Te Reo o te Kawariki', series of columns published in *Northland Age*.

Harawira, Hone, 1995, 'Te Reo o te Kawariki: Sovereignty must come soon', *Northland Age*, 18 May 1995, p. 3.

Harawira, Hone, 2008, 'He Aitua – Hone Tuwhare "No Ordinary Icon"', press release, 17 January 2008.

Harawira, Hone, 2009–2010, 'Āe Mārika' (weekly column), *Northland Age*.

Harawira, Wena, 1997, 'You Can Blow it All', *Mana* no. 15, Autumn 1997, pp. 72–4.

Harawira, Wena and Nevak Ilolahia, 1997, 'What Makes Tau Tick?', *Mana* no.15, Autumn 1997, p. 28.

Harris, Aroha, 2004, *Hīkoi: Forty Years of Māori Protest*, Wellington, Huia Publishers.

Harris, Ricci, Martin Tobias, Mona Jeffreys, Kiri Waldegrave, Saffron Karlsen and James Nazroo, 2006, 'Effects of Self-reported Racial Discrimination and Deprivation on Māori Health and Inequalities in New Zealand: Cross-sectional Study', *The Lancet*, vol. 367, 17 June 2006, pp. 2005–9.

Harrison, Noel, 2002, *Graham Latimer*, Wellington, Huia Publishers.

Hauraki Māori Trust Board, 2008, 'Hauraki Fisheries and Aquaculture Settlement', http://www.hauraki.iwi.nz/documents/March09Newsletterweb.pdf

Haywood, Janine (ed.), 2003, *Local Government and the Treaty of Waitangi*, Melbourne, Oxford University Press.

Haywood, Janine, 2010, 'Local Government Representation' in Malcolm Mulholland and Veronica Tawhai (eds), *Weeping Waters: The Treaty of Waitangi and Constitutional Change*, Wellington, Huia Publishers, pp. 269–84.

Haywood, Janine and Nicola R Wheen (eds), 2004, *The Waitangi Tribunal: Te Roopu Whakamana i te Tiriti o Waitangi*, Wellington, Bridget Williams Books.

Hemi, Murray, 2003, 'The Good Oil', *Mana* no. 52, June–July 2003, p. 60.

Henare, Denese, 2000, 'Can or Should the Treaty be Replaced?', in Colin James (ed.), *Building the Constitution*, Wellington, Institute of Policy Studies, Victoria University of Wellington, pp. 207–13.

Hendery, Simon, 2001, 'Buyout of Qantas NZ Tipped; Takeover an Option to Boost Aussie's Share', *New Zealand Herald*, 6 April 2001, p. C1.

Henehan, Justin, 2008, 'Raids "hurt" is Regretted', *Herald on Sunday*, 30 March 2008, p. 2.

Herbert, Patricia, 1997, 'Maori "spoon-fed like imbeciles"', *New Zealand Herald*, 27 February 1997, p. A5.

Hide, Rodney, 1997, 'Another MP Bites the Dust as Taxi Meter Ticks Over', *National Business Review*, 11 April 1997, p. 26.

Higgins, Rawinia, 2008, 'Another Chapter in Our History': Reflections on the Events at Rūātoki, 15 October 2007', in Danny Keenan (ed.), *Terror in Our Midst? Searching for Terror in Aotearoa New Zealand*, Wellington, Huia Publishers.

Howden-Chapman, Philippa, Simon Hales, Ralph Chapman and Ilmo Keskimaki, 2005, *The Impact of Economic Recession on Youth Suicide: Report 4: Social Explanations for Suicide in New Zealand*, Wellington, Ministry of Health.

Hunt, Graeme, 1996, *Scandal at Cave Creek: A Shocking Failure in Public Accountability*, Auckland, Waddington in association with the *National Business Review*.

Hunt, Graeme, 2005, 'Weight of Evidence', *New Zealand Listener*, vol. 198 no. 3390, April 30–May 6 2005, http://www.listener.co.nz/issue/3390/features/3907/weight_of_evidence.html;jsessionid=DCC5CCC0F1FDF49A223DF7D72A55A1A1

Hunt, Janet, 2008, 'Thinking About Tuwhare', *Mana* no. 80, February–March 2008, pp. 8–12.

Jackson, Daniel, 2001(a), 'Lawyers to Watch Whangarei Police', *New Zealand Herald*, 18 October 2001, p. A5.

Jackson, Daniel, 2001(b), 'Top Officer Will Investigate Whangarei police', *New Zealand Herald*, 19 October 2001, p. A5.

Jackson, Daniel and Scott MacLeod, 2001, 'Judge Says Women Forced to Confess', *New Zealand Herald*, 27 October 2001, p. A3.

Jackson, Moana, 1988, *Maori and the Criminal Justice System: He Whaipaanga Hou – A New Perspective*, Wellington, Ministry of Justice.

Jackson, Moana, 1997, 'What do Maori Want?', *Mana* no. 16, June–July 1997, p. 20.

Jackson, Moana, 1998, 'The Good, the Bad and the Ugly', *Mana* no. 25, December 1997–January 1998, pp. 16–17.

Jackson, Moana, 2000, 'Where Does Sovereignty Lie?', in Colin James (ed.), *Building the Constitution*, Wellington, Institute of Policy Studies, Victoria University of Wellington, pp. 196–200.

Jackson, Moana, 2001, 'Terror and Democracy', *Mana* no. 42, October–November 2001, p. 50.

Jackson, Moana, 2002, 'The English Text', *Mana* no. 46, June–July 2002, p. 51.

Jackson, Moana, 2002–3, 'Highs and Lows', *Mana* no. 49, December 2002–January 2003, p. 45.

Jackson, Moana, 2008, 'Preface – The Constancy of Terror', in Danny Keenan (ed.), *Terror in Our Midst? Searching for Terror in Aotearoa New Zealand*, Wellington, Huia Publishers, pp. 1–10.

James, Colin (ed.), 2000, *Building the Constitution*, Wellington, Institute of Policy Studies, Victoria University of Wellington.

Jobs Research Trust, 1995, 'Diary', *The Jobs Letter* no. 25, 26 September 1996, http://www.jobsletter.org.nz/jbl02501.htm

Jobs Research Trust, 2000, 'The Jobs Budget 2000', *The Jobs Letter* no. 126, 23 June 2000, http://www.jobsletter.org.nz/jbl12610.htm

Johnston, Kerensa and Nin Tomas, 2003, 'Who Owns the Foreshore and Seabed of Aotearoa', Part III, *New Zealand Law Review*, pp. 462–83.

Justice and Electoral Select Committee, 2003, Report to Parliament on the Supreme Court Bill, http://www.parliament.nz/NR/rdonlyres/710D1400-725F-47DC-8713-29F0407D9199/47916/DBSCH_SCR_2552_28191.pdf

Kawharu, Merata (ed.), 2002, *Whenua: Managing our Resources*, Auckland, Reed.

Keenan, Danny, 2000, '*Dialogue*: Whose Holocaust? That Is Still a Good Question', *New Zealand Herald*, 7 September 2000, p. A13.

Keenan, Danny (ed.), 2008(a), *Terror in Our Midst? Searching for Terror in Aotearoa New Zealand*, Wellington, Huia Publishers.

Keenan, Danny, 2008(b), 'Introduction: Searching for Terror', in Danny Keenan (ed.), *Terror in Our Midst? Searching for Terror in Aotearoa New Zealand*, Wellington, Huia Publishers, pp. 17–34.

Keenan, Danny, 2008(c), 'Autonomy as Fiction: The Urewera Native District Reserve Act 1896', in Danny Keenan (ed.), *Terror in Our Midst? Searching for Terror in Aotearoa New Zealand*, Wellington, Huia Publishers, pp. 79–94.

Keenan, Danny, 2008(d), 'The Terror Raids and the Criminalising of Dissent', in Danny Keenan (ed.), *Terror in Our Midst? Searching for Terror in Aotearoa New Zealand*, Wellington, Huia Publishers, pp. 129–38.

Keith, Sir Kenneth, 1995, 'The Roles of the Tribunal, the Courts and the Legislature', in Geoff McLay (ed.), *Treaty Settlements: The Unfinished Business*, Wellington, New Zealand Institute of Advanced Legal Studies and Victoria University of Wellington Law Review.

Kelsey, Jane, 1993, *Rolling Back the State*, Wellington, Bridget Williams Books.

MacLeod, Scott and Reuters, 2001, 'Global Chorus for Peace', *New Zealand Herald*, 1 October 2001, p. A4.

Manuera, Tuhoe, 1995, 'Ngati Kahu Spokesmen', *Northland Age*, 29 June 1995, p. 2.

Māori Affairs Select Committee, 2002, press release, 'Inquiry into the Crown Forestry Rental Trust', 19 September 2002, http://www.scoop.co.nz/stories/PA0209/S00337.htm

Māori Party, 2007(a), 'Poroporoaki: Don Selwyn', press release, 16 April 2007, http://www.scoop.co.nz/stories/PA0704/S00272.htm

Māori Party, 2007(b), 'Flavell: Ngati Mutunga', press release, 27 July 2007, http://www.scoop.co.nz/stories/PA0607/S00483.htm

Māori Party, 2007(c), 'Speech: Protected Disclosures Amendment Bill – Hone Harawira', press release, 23 October 2007, http://www.maoriparty.com/index.php?option=com_content&task=view&id=1375&Itemid=28

Māori Party, 2007(d), 'Tell the Truth about the Bus: Te Ururoa Flavell', press release, 23 October 2007, http://www.maoriparty.com/index.php?option=com_content&task=view&id=1371&Itemid=2

Māori Party, 2007(e), 'Speech: "I Will Not Sit Quietly by While State Forces Terrorise my People", Hone Harawira', press release, 8 November 2007, http://www.maoriparty.com/index.php?option=com_content&task=view&id=1415&Itemid=28

Māori Party, 2007(f), 'It's Looking Good for 2008 Says Māori Party', press release, 10 November 2007, http://www.maoriparty.com/index.php?option=com_content&task=view&id=1417&Itemid=2

Māori Party, 2008(a), 'Willie Apiata's Remarkable ANZAC Day Gift to the Nation', press release, 24 April 2008, http://www.scoop.co.nz/stories/PA0804/S00577.htm

Māori Party, 2008(b), 'Reflections from the Relationship Signing with National Party from Tariana Turia', press release, 16 November 2008, http://www.scoop.co.nz/stories/PA0811/S00181.htm

Māori Party, 2008(c), *Relationship and Confidence and Supply Agreement between the National Party and the Māori Party*, http://www.maoriparty.org/index.php?pag=cms&id=153&p=national-party-and-the-māori-party-agreement.html

Māori Party website, http://www.maoriparty.org/index.php

Marsden, Māori, 1992, 'God, Man and Universe: A Maori View' in Michael King (ed.) *Te Ao Hurihuri*, Wellington, Hicks Smith (2nd edition).

Matiu, McCully and Margaret Mutu, 2003, *Te Whānau Moana: Ngā Kaupapa me Ngā Tikanga: Customs and Protocols*, Auckland, Reed.

McCarten, Matt, 2007, 'My First Lesson from a Master in the Gentle Art of Protesting', *nzherald.co.nz*, 9 September 2007.

McCurdy, Diana and Renee Kiriona, 2004, 'Te Reo Comes to Prime Time', *nzherald.co.nz*, 27 March 2004.

McFadden, Suzanne, 1997, 'Chanting as Cup Smashed', *New Zealand Herald*, 15 March 1997, p. A1.

McLay, Geoff (ed.), 1995, *Treaty Settlements: The Unfinished Business*, Wellington, New Zealand Institute of Advanced Legal Studies and Victoria University of Wellington Law Review.

Minister of Māori Affairs, 1996, 'Tribunal Interim Report on Taranaki Claims Welcomed', 14 June 1996, http://www.beehive.govt.nz/release/tribunal+interim+report+taranaki+claims+welcomed

Ministry for Culture and Heritage, 2009, 'Waitangi Day in the 21st Century', http://www.nzhistory.net.nz/politics/treaty/waitangi-day/21st-century-waitangi-day

Ministry of Education, 2005, 'Māori Students in Formal Tertiary Education by Subsector 1994–2004', in *Māori in Tertiary Education*, Wellington, Ministry of Education, http://www.educationcounts.govt.nz/publications/maori_education/maori_in_tertiary_education

Ministry of Health and University of Otago, 2006, *Decades of Disparity III: Ethnic and Socioeconomic Inequalities in Mortality, New Zealand 1981–1999*, Wellington, Ministry of Health.

Ministry of Justice, Chief Electoral Office, 2008, *Official Count Results – Overall Status*, http://www.electionresults.govt.nz/electionresults_2008/partystatus.html

Misa, Tapu, 1995, 'Cover Story: A Migrant Story', *Mana* no. 10, Spring 1995, pp. 14–16.

Misa, Tapu, 2002(a), 'The Spoiling of Samoa', *New Zealand Herald*, 1 June 2002, p. B5.

Misa, Tapu, 2002(b), 'Parliamentary Colour in Quantity, but Quality in Doubt', *New Zealand Herald*, 31 July 2002, p. A13.

Misa, Tapu, 2002(c), 'Media Perceptions of Māori Still Pretty Distorted', *nzherald. co.nz*, 27 November 2002.

Misa, Tapu, 2002(d), 'Let's Catch Racism Early and Hit it Where it Counts', *nzherald. co.nz*, 11 December 2002.

Mulholland, Malcolm (ed.), 2006, *State of the Māori Nation: Twenty-first Century Issues in Aotearoa*, Auckland, Reed.

Mulholland, Malcolm and Veronica Tawhai (eds), 2010, *Weeping Waters: The Treaty of Waitangi and Constitutional Change*, Wellington, Huia Publishers.

Mutu, Margaret, 1991, *Rating and Valuation of Māori Land in Te Taitokerau*, Auckland, Department of Māori Studies, University of Auckland.

Mutu, Margaret, 1995, *Report to the Minister of Māori Affairs on the New Zealand Conservation Authority*, Wellington, New Zealand Conservation Authority.

Mutu, Margaret, 1998, 'Māori Customary Fishing Rights', in L Pihama and C W Smith (eds), *Economics, Politics, and Colonisation Volume Three: Fisheries and Commodifying Iwi*, Auckland, International Research Institute for Māori and Indigenous Education, University of Auckland.

Mutu, Margaret, 2002, 'Barriers to Tangata Whenua Participation in Resource Management', in Merata Kawharu (ed.), *Whenua: Managing Our Resources*, Auckland, Reed, pp. 75–95.

Mutu, Margaret, 2005(a), 'Recovering Fagin's Ill-Gotten Gains: Settling Ngāti Kahu's Treaty of Waitangi Claims against the Crown', in Michael Belgrave, Merata Kawharu and David Williams (eds), *Waitangi Revisited: Perspectives on the Treaty of Waitangi*, Melbourne, Oxford University Press.

Mutu, Margaret, 2005(b), 'Research Ethics Associated with Treaty of Waitangi Claims and the Foreshore and Seabed Legislation', in *Tikanga Rangahau: Mātauranga Tuku Iho – The Proceedings of the Traditional Knowledge and Research Ethics Conference 2004*, Auckland, Ngā Pae o te Māramatanga: New Zealand's Māori Centre of Research Excellence, University of Auckland.

Mutu, Margaret, 2007, *Te Rūnanga-ā-Iwi o Ngāti Kahu Land Claims Report for February–March 2007*, Kaitāia, Te Rūnanga-ā-Iwi o Ngāti Kahu.

Mutu, Margaret, 2008, 'Maori Issues in Review: Issues and Events, 1 July 2006 to 30 June 2007', *The Contemporary Pacific – A Journal of Island Affairs*, vol. 20 no. 1, pp. 232–8.

Mutu, Margaret, 2009(a), 'Media and Literature: Depictions of Māori and Chinese', in Manying Ip (ed.), *The Dragon and the Taniwha: Māori and Chinese in New Zealand*, Auckland, Auckland University Press, pp. 236–74.

Mutu, Margaret, 2009(b), 'Māori Issues in Review: Issues and Events, 2008', *The Contemporary Pacific – A Journal of Island Affairs*, vol. 21 no. 1, pp. 162–9.

Mutu, Margaret, 2009(c), 'The Role of History and Oral Traditions in Recovering Fagin's Ill-gotten Gains: Settling Ngāti Kahu's Treaty of Waitangi Claims Against the Crown', in *Te Pouhere Kōrero 3: Māori History, Māori People*, pp. 23–44.

Mutu, Margaret, 2010, 'Constitutional Intentions: The Treaty of Waitangi Texts', in Malcolm Mulholland and Veronica Tawhai (eds.), 2010, *Weeping Waters: The Treaty of Waitangi and Constitutional Change*, Wellington, Huia Publishers, pp. 13–40.

National Party website, http://www.national.org.nz/

New Zealand Executive Government News Release Archive, http://www.beehive. co.nz/release/

New Zealand Government, 1994, *Crown Proposals for the Settlement of Treaty of Waitangi Claims: Detailed Proposals*, Wellington, Office of Treaty Settlements.

New Zealand Government, 1995, *Report of Submissions: Crown Proposals for the Treaty of Waitangi Claims*, December 1995, Wellington, New Zealand Government.

New Zealand History online, 2008(a), 'Eva Rickard', http://www.nzhistory.net.nz/ people/eva-rickard

New Zealand History online, 2008(b), 'Matiu Rata', http://www.nzhistory.net.nz/people/matiu-rata

New Zealand Human Rights Commission, 2007, 'Indigenous Rights Declaration to Guide Commission Work', press release, 18 September 2007, http://www.hrc.co.nz/home/hrc/newsandissues/indigenousrightsdeclarationtogindigenousrightsde.php

NZPA, 1995, 'Tourism Coup for Kaikoura Whales', *New Zealand Herald*, 10 February 1995, p 5.

NZPA, 2002(a), 'Judge Rebukes Police Over Marae Fracas', *New Zealand Herald*, 12 February 2002, p. A7.

NZPA, 2002(b), 'Clark Making Right Noises Says Samuels', *nzherald.co.nz*, 2 June 2002.

NZPA, 2002(c), 'ACT Wants End of Year Deadline for Lodging Treaty Claims', *nzherald.co.nz*, 3 July 2002.

NZPA, 2002(d), 'Land Claim Puts Tycoon's Resort on Hold', *nzherald.co.nz*, 4 August 2002.

NZPA, 2002(e), 'MP Slams Prison Costs', *nzherald.co.nz*, 4 September 2002.

NZPA, 2002(f), 'Protestors Occupy Prison Site, Warn of Taniwha Trouble', *nzherald.co.nz*, 2 December 2002.

NZPA, 2002(g), 'Pakeha settlers "like Taleban vandals"', *New Zealand Herald*, 4 December 2002, p. A1.

NZPA, 2004(a), 'Protestors Bring Capital's Traffic to Standstill', *nzherald.co.nz*, 6 May 2004.

NZPA, 2004(b), 'Hikoi Estimates Range From 10,000 to 30,000', *nzherald.co.nz*, 6 May 2004.

NZPA, 2006(a), 'Urban Maori? UN Envoy "stunned"', *nzherald.co.nz*, 6 April 2006;

NZPA, 2006(b), 'UN Man Answers Back on Cullen Jibe', *nzherald.co.nz*, 6 April 2006.

NZPA, 2007, 'Last "terror raid" Accused Freed as Hikoi Starts', *nzherald.co.nz*, 12 November 2007.

NZPA and NZ Herald Staff, 2008, 'UN Orders Government to Explain Anti-terror Raids', *nzherald.co.nz*, 17 January 2008.

New Zealand Press Council, 2001, *Case Number 815: John Gamby Against the New Zealand Herald*, http://www.presscouncil.org.nz/display_ruling.php?case_number=815

NewstalkZB and Herald online staff, 2006, 'UN Man Advises Overhaul or Scrapping of Foreshore Act', *nzherald.co.nz*, 4 April 2006.

Norquay, Kevin, of NZPA, 2000, 'Tamihere Promises to Expose Cost of Claims', *New Zealand Herald*, 12 May 2000, p. A5.

Office of the Deputy Prime Minister, 2003, *Foreshore and Seabed: A Framework*, Wellington, Office of the Deputy Prime Minister.

Office of Treaty Settlements, 1994, *Crown Proposals for the Settlement of Treaty of Waitangi Claims*, Wellington, Office of Treaty Settlements.

Office of Treaty Settlements, 2005, *Summary of the Te Roroa Deed of Settlement*, http://www.ots.govt.nz/

Office of Treaty Settlements, 2006, *Deed to Amend Deed of Settlement of the Te Arawa Lakes Historical Claims and Remaining Annuity Issues*, http://www.ots.govt.nz/

Office of Treaty Settlements, 2008(a), *Four Monthly Report July–October 2008*, http://www.ots.govt.nz/frameset-settlementdocs.html

Office of Treaty Settlements, 2008(b), *Waikato River Settlement Summary*, http://www.ots.govt.nz/

Office of Treaty Settlements, 2008(c), 'Historical Treaty Settlements: Progress Report 2008', *Mana* no. 83, August–September 2008, pp. 16–17.

Oliver, Paula, 2002, 'Details of Kahu Kidnap Revealed', *New Zealand Herald*, 25 May 2002, p. A2.

Oliver, W H, 1991, *Claims to the Waitangi Tribunal*, Wellington, Department of Justice.

Orsman, Bernard, 1997, 'MP Relative Incurred Car Fines', *New Zealand Herald*, 20 February 1997, p. A3.

O'Sullivan, Dominic, 2008, 'Māori MPs and "Operation Eight"', in Danny Keenan (ed.), *Terror in Our Midst? Searching for Terror in Aotearoa New Zealand*, Wellington, Huia Publishers, pp.139–50.

O'Sullivan, Fran, 2002, 'Forest Action Begins – Touch Wood', *New Zealand Herald*, 6 May 2002, p. D2.

Palmer, Sir Geoffrey, 1995, 'Where to from Here?', in Geoff McLay (ed.), *Treaty Settlements: The Unfinished Business*, Wellington, New Zealand Institute of Advanced Legal Studies and Victoria University of Wellington Law Review, pp. 151–4.

Panoho, Amokura, 2008, 'Syd Jackson', *Mana* no. 81, April–May 2008, pp. 6–8.

Peace Movement Aotearoa, 2000(a), *The Shooting of Steven Wallace*, http://www.converge.org.nz/pma/steven.htm#articles

Peace Movement Aotearoa, 2000(b), 'Relationships in Taranaki', http://www.converge.org.nz/pma/steven.htm#articles

Public Health Advisory Committee, 2006, *Health is Everyone's Business*, Wellington, Public Health Advisory Committee.

Radio New Zealand Sound Archives, 1995(a), 'Waitangi Day – 1955', *Treaty of Waitangi: Events – 1990s*, 7 February 1995, http://www.radionz.co.nz/popular/treaty/events-1990s

Radio New Zealand Sound Archives, 1995(b), 'Māori Activism', *Treaty of Waitangi: Events – 1990s*, April–May 1995, http://www.radionz.co.nz/popular/treaty/events-1990s

Rangiheua, Tania, 2003, 'Time for Talk', *Mana* no. 52, June–July 2003, p. 61.

Reweti, Debra, 2006, 'Māori and Broadcasting', in Malcolm Mulholland (ed.), 2006, *State of the Māori Nation: Twenty-first Century Issues in Aotearoa*, Auckland, Reed, 179–86.

Ritchie, James, 2001, 'Robert Te Kotahi a Koroki Mahuta', *Mana* no. 39, April–May 2001, pp. 70–1.

Rivers, Kaio, 1995, 'Future Maori leadership', *Northland Age*, 18 July 1995, p. 2.

Robb, Andrew, 1993, 'Going to the Top', *Mana*, April/May 1993, pp. 58–61.

Robb, Andrew, 1995, 'No Need to Lose Heart', *Mana* no. 5, February–March 1995, pp. 51–2.

Rooney, Edward, 1997, 'Chief Admits Mistakes in Battle to Kill Moths', *Sunday Star Times*, 12 January 1997, p. A4.

Roughan, John, 2008, 'Where Clark Fears to Tread', *New Zealand Herald*, 9 February 2008, p. A21.

Rowan, Juliet, 2007, 'Valley Locked Down After Dawn Raids', *nzherald.co.nz*, 16 October 2007.

Ruru, Jacinta, 2004, 'A Politically Fuelled Tsunami: The Foreshore/Seabed Controversy in Aotearoa me te Waipounamu/New Zealand', *Journal of the Polynesian Society*, vol. 113 no. 1, pp. 57–72.

Samuels, Dover, 2000, 'Capacity Building Boost for Māori Affairs', press release, http://www.executive.govt.nz/budget2000/gaps-samuels.htm

Scion, 1998, 'Every Moth Matters – the Eradication of the White-spotted Tussock Moth', *Forest Health News* no. 72, March 1998.

Snedden, Pat, 2005, *Pakeha and the Treaty: Why it's Our Treaty Too*, Auckland, Random House.

Solomon, Maui, 2000, 'An affront from ERMA', *Mana* no. 35, August–September 2000, pp. 52–3.

Spoonley, Paul, 1995, *Racism and Ethnicity*, Auckland, Oxford University Press.

Statistics New Zealand, 1998, *New Zealand Now: Income*, Wellington, Statistics New Zealand.

Stavenhagen, Rodolfo, 2006, *Report of the Special Rapporteur on the Situation of Human Rights and Fundamental Freedoms of Indigenous People*. Mission to New Zealand. E/CN.4/2006/78/Add.3, 13 March 2006, Geneva, United Nations Human Rights Commission.

Stevenson, Philippa, 2001, 'Apple Growers Biting Back at ENZA Dispute', *New Zealand Herald*, 2 July 2001, p. D4.

Stewart, Kerry, 1995, 'Tension Remains High On Waahi Tapu Site', *New Zealand Herald*, Auckland, 23 February 1995, p. 9.

Stokes, Jon, 2004, 'Non-Maori Fans of Maori TV', *nzherald.co.nz*, 25 June 2004.

Sullivan, Ann, 2003, 'Māori Representation in Local Government', in Janine Haywood (ed.), *Local Government and the Treaty of Waitangi*, Melbourne, Oxford University Press, pp. 150–3.

Sykes, Annette, 2000, 'Te Tiriti o Waitangi: A Vision of Respect of Civilisations and Cultures', in Colin James (ed.), *Building the Constitution*, Wellington, Victoria University of Wellington Institute of Policy Studies, pp. 144–52.

Sykes, Annette, 2003, 'Let's Get it Right', *Mana* no. 51, April–May 2003, p. 48.

Taonui, Rawiri, 2007, 'Unburdening Future Generations', *New Zealand Herald*, 8 October 2007, p. A13.

Tataurangi, Phil, his website, http://www.philtataurangi.com/main.cfm?id=13

Taylor, Kevin, 2005, 'Problems with Holding Hands', *New Zealand Herald*, 10 September 2005, p. B5.

Te Aho, Linda, 2010, 'Judicial Creativity' in Malcolm Mulholland and Veronica Tawhai (eds), *Weeping Waters: The Treaty of Waitangi and Constitutional Change*, Wellington, Huia, pp. 109–126.

Te Ara Encyclopedia of New Zealand, 'The End of a "white New Zealand" Policy', http://www.teara.govt.nz/NewZealanders/NewZealandPeoples/HistoryOfImmigration/15/en

Te Aratai Productions, 2006, *Darling of Dubai*, broadcast on Māori Television 3 July 2006.

Te Haeata, 2008, *Settling Ngāti Porou Historical Treaty Claims*, http://www.ngatiporou.com/myfiles/F1_Latest_news_Te_Haeata_Panui_-High_Level_Agreement_Summary_05112008.pdf

Te Puni Kōkiri, 1998, *Progress Towards Closing the Social and Economic Gaps between Māori and non-Māori: a Report to the Minister of Māori Affairs*, Wellington, Ministry of Māori Affairs.

Te Puni Kōkiri, 2006, *Te Kotahitanga o te Whakahaere Rawa: Māori and Council Engagement Under the Resource Management Act 1991*, Wellington, Te Puni Kōkiri.

Te Rūnanga-ā-Iwi o Ngāti Kahu, 2009, Minutes of the Taumata Kaumātua o Ngāti Kahu, 23 February 2009, Kaitāia, Te Rūnanga-ā-Iwi o Ngāti Kahu.

Te Rūnanga o Ngāi Tahu, 2008, 'Māori Commercial Aquaculture Settlement', http://www.ngaitahu.iwi.nz/Te-Runanga/He-Kaupapa-Whakahirahira/Aquaculture/

Te Rūnanga o Ngāi Tahu, 2009, 'About Ngāi Tahu', http://www.ngaitahu.iwi.nz/About-Ngai-Tahu/

Te Wānanga o Aotearoa website, http://www.twoa.ac.nz/

Treaty of Waitangi Fisheries Commission, 2002, *Statement of Financial Position of the Treaty of Waitangi Fisheries Commission Group, Annual Report to Parliament for the Year Ended 30 September 2002*, p. 36, http://teohu.maori.nz/te_ohu/archive/reports/Treaty%20of%20Waitangi%20Annual%20Report%202003.pdf

Trevett, Claire, 2007, 'Defiant Horomia: I Will Not Resign', *nzherald.co.nz*, 29 October 2007.

Trevett, Claire, Stuart Dye and Edward Gay, 2007, 'Tame Iti Seeking Release From Jail', *nzherald.co.nz*, 9 November 2007.

Turia, Tariana, 2002, 'Politics: Election 2002: A Pathway of Change', *Mana* no. 46, June–July 2002, p. 41.

Tuuta, Dion, 2003, *Maori Experiences of the Direct Negotiations Process*, Wellington, Crown Forestry Rental Trust.

Tūwhare, Hone, 1964, *No Ordinary Sun*, Auckland, Blackwood and Janet Paul.

United Nations Committee on the Elimination of Racial Discrimination, 2005, *Report on the New Zealand Foreshore and Seabed Act 2004*, Decision 1(66), 66th Session, 11th March 2005. UN Doc CERD/C/66/NZL/Dec.1.

United Nations Declaration on the Rights of Indigenous Peoples, http://www.un.org/esa/socdev/unpfii/en/drip.html

Vercoe, Whakahuihui, 1990, 'We Have Not Honoured Each Other's Promises', *New Zealand Herald*, 7 February 1990, p. 9.

Waaka, Maureen, 2006, 'Local Government', in Malcolm Mulholland (ed.), *State of the Māori Nation: Twenty-first Century Issues in Aotearoa*, Auckland, Reed, pp. 219–25.

Wairaka.net, 1998, 'Media statement for Hīkoi of Hope follow-up delegation visit to Parliament', 9 December 1998, http://www.wairaka.net/ubinz/Hikoi/

Waitangi Tribunal website, http://www.waitangi-tribunal.govt.nz

Waitangi Tribunal, 1983, *The Report of the Waitangi Tribunal on the Motunui-Waitara claim* (Wai 6), Wellington, Waitangi Tribunal. All Waitangi Tribunal reports are also available from the Tribunal's website, at http://www.waitangi-tribunal.govt.nz/reports/

Waitangi Tribunal, 1984, *Report of the Waitangi Tribunal on the Kaituna River Claim* (Wai 4), Wellington, Waitangi Tribunal.

Waitangi Tribunal, 1985, *Report of the Waitangi Tribunal on the Manukau Claim* (Wai 8), Wellington, Waitangi Tribunal.

Waitangi Tribunal, 1986, *Report of the Waitangi Tribunal on the Te Reo Maori Claim* (Wai 11), Wellington, Waitangi Tribunal.

Waitangi Tribunal, 1988(a), *Report of the Waitangi Tribunal on the Muriwhenua Fishing Claim* (Wai 22), Wellington, Waitangi Tribunal.

Waitangi Tribunal, 1988(b), *Report of the Waitangi Tribunal on the Mangonui Sewerage Claim* (Wai 17), Wellington, Waitangi Tribunal.

Waitangi Tribunal, 1992(a), *Ngai Tahu Sea Fisheries Report* (Wai 27), Wellington, Waitangi Tribunal.

Waitangi Tribunal, 1992(b), *The Te Roroa Report 1992* (Wai 38), Wellington, Waitangi Tribunal.

Waitangi Tribunal, 1994, *Māori Electoral Option Report* (Wai 413), Wellington, Brooker's.

Waitangi Tribunal, 1996, *Taranaki Report: Kaupapa Tuatahi: Te Muru me te Raupatu* (Wai 143), Wellington, GP Publications.

Waitangi Tribunal, 1997, *Muriwhenua Land Report* (Wai 45), Wellington, GP Publications.

Waitangi Tribunal, 1998(a), *The Turangi Township Remedies Report* (Wai 84), Wellington, GP Publications.

Waitangi Tribunal, 1998(b), *Te Ika Whenua Rivers Report* (Wai 212), Wellington, GP Publications.

Waitangi Tribunal, 1999(a), *The Ngati Awa Raupatu Report* (Wai 46), Wellington, Legislation Direct.

Waitangi Tribunal, 1999(b), *Radio Spectrum Management and Development Final Report* (Wai 776), Wellington, GP Publications.

Waitangi Tribunal, 1999(c), *The Wananga Capital Establishment Report* (Wai 718), Wellington, GP Publications.

Waitangi Tribunal, 1999(d), *The Whanganui River Report* (Wai 167), Wellington, GP Publications.

Waitangi Tribunal, 2002, *Ahu Moana: The Aquaculture and Marine Farming Report* (Wai 953), Wellington, GP Publications.

Waitangi Tribunal, 2003, *The Petroleum Report* (Wai 796), Wellington, GP Publications.

Waitangi Tribunal, 2004, *Report on the Crown's Foreshore and Seabed Policy* (Wai 1071), Wellington, Legislation Direct.

Waitangi Tribunal, 2007(a), *Tāmaki Makaurau Settlement Process* (Wai 1362), Wellington, Waitangi Tribunal.

Waitangi Tribunal, 2007(b), *Final Report on the Impacts of the Crown's Settlement Policy on Te Arawa Waka and Other Tribes* (Wai 1353), Wellington, Waitangi Tribunal.

Waitangi Tribunal, 2008, *He Maunga Rongo: The Report on the Central North Island Claims, Stage 1* (Wai 1200), Wellington, Waitangi Tribunal.

Wakefield, Roger, 1997, 'Cup "Symbol of Everything Accused Hated"', *New Zealand Herald*, 15 March 1997, A3.

Walker, Ranginui, 2002, 'Māori News is Bad News', in Judy McGregor and Margie Comrie (eds), *What's News: Reclaiming Journalism in New Zealand*, Palmerston North, Dunmore Press, pp. 215–32.

Walker, Ranginui, 2004, *Ka Whawhai Tonu Matou: Struggle Without End*, Auckland, Penguin.

Wall, Tony, 1997, 'Drug Trespass Notice Sent to Minister's Son', *New Zealand Herald*, 22 March 1997, p. A1.

Wall, Tony, 2001(a), 'Strong Arm of the Law Put in the Dock', *New Zealand Herald*, 3 November 2001, p. A1.

Wall, Tony, 2001(b), 'Police defy judge's rebuke', *New Zealand Herald*, 4 November 2001, p. A1.

Ward, Alan, 1999, *An Unsettled History: Treaty Claims in New Zealand Today*, Wellington, Bridget Williams Books.

Watkins, Tracy, 2003, 'Pandora's Box Warning for Oil', *Dominion Post*, 22 May 2003, p. A2.

Watkins, Tracy, 2010, 'NZ Does U-turn on Rights Charter', *Stuff*: http://www.stuff.co.nz/national/politics/3599153/NZ-does-U-turn-on-rights-charter, 20 April 2010.

Wickliffe, Caren, 2000, 'Multiculturalism and the Constitution – Lessons from Another Country: Fiji', in Colin James (ed.), *Building the Constitution*, Wellington, Institute of Policy Studies, pp. 244–58.

Wikipedia contributors, 'Eva Rickard', http://en.wikipedia.org/wiki/Eva_Rickard accessed 2009.

Wikipedia contributors, 'Taranaki', http://en.wikipedia.org/wiki/Taranaki accessed 2009.

Wikipedia contributors, 2009, 'Tau Henare', http://en.wikipedia.org/wiki/Tau_Henare accessed 2009.

Williams, D V, 2005, 'Myths, National Origins, Common Law and the Waitangi Tribunal', *Murdoch University Electronic Journal of Law*, vol. 11 no. 4, http://www.murdoch.edu.au/elaw/issues/v11n4/williams114nf.html

Williams, D V, 2007, 'Wi Parata is Dead, Long Live Wi Parata', in C Charters and A Erueti (eds), *Māori Property Rights and the Foreshore and Seabed: The Last Frontier*, Wellington, Victoria University Press.

Williams, Joe, 2000, 'Building the Constitution Conference', in Colin James (ed.), *Building the Constitution*, Wellington, Institute of Policy Studies, pp. 44–7.

Winiata, Whatarangi, 1998, 'Reducing the Socio-economic Disparities in Housing, Employment, Health and Education', in Ian Ritchie (ed.), *1998 Hikoi of Hope* website, http://www.wairaka.net/ubinz/Hikoi/

Winiata, Whatarangi, 2000, 'How Can or Should the Treaty be Reflected in Institutional Design?', in Colin James (ed.), *Building the Constitution*, Wellington, Institute of Policy Studies, pp. 205–6.

Wycherley, Greg and Richard Knight, 2002, 'Whangai Adoption a Grey Area', *New Zealand Herald*, 17 April 2002, p. A3.

Young, Audrey, 1995, 'Bolger Adamant on Maori Claims: Sovereignty Issue a Distraction Away From Treaty Discussions says PM', *New Zealand Herald*, 19 September 1995, p. 1.

Young, Audrey, 1996, 'PM "Grumpy" as Peters Skips Talks: Restaurant Incident "Not Responsible"', *New Zealand Herald*, 31 October 1996, p. A1.

Young, Audrey, 2000(a), 'PM Insists on Full-Value Maori Policy', *New Zealand Herald*, 29 February 2000, p. A3.

Young, Audrey, 2000(b), 'Turia Accepts Edict on Holocaust Term', *New Zealand Herald*, 7 September 2000, p. A5.

Young, Audrey, 2002(a), 'Greens move to defend Maori sovereignty stand', *New Zealand Herald*, 9 February 2002, p. A7.

Young, Audrey, 2002(b), 'NZ First Will Campaign on Treaty, Race Issues', *New Zealand Herald*, 19 April 2002, p. A6.

Young, Audrey, 2002(c), 'Fish Accord Backed by 91pc of Tribes', *New Zealand Herald*, 4 December 2002, p. A6.

Young, Audrey, 2003(a), 'Quick Move Blocks Maori Bid to Claim Rights Over Seabed', *nzherald.co.nz*, 24 June 2003.

Young, Audrey, 2003(b), 'National Caucus Suspends Williamson', *nzherald.co.nz*, 22 July 2003.

Young, Audrey, 2004, 'Tribunal Report Disappointing and Flawed, Says Cullen', *nzherald.co.nz*, 8 March 2004.

Young, Audrey, 2006(a), 'UN Foreshore Report "unbalanced"', *nzherald.co.nz*, 5 April 2006.

Young, Audrey, 2006(b), 'Heat on Horomia Over Absence of Budget Bid', *nzherald. co.nz*, 25 May 2006.

Unattributed articles

Evening Post
1997, 'Chapman Gets Six Months', *Evening Post*, 14 March 1997, p. 1.

Mana magazine
1993, 'The Privy Council', *Mana* no. 2, April–May 1993, p. 61.

1995, 'He Pitopito Korero: Not Over Yet', *Mana* no. 9, Winter 1995, p. 9.

1995, 'Eva Rickard: Still has a Job to do', *Mana* no. 9, Winter 1995, pp. 24–5.

1995, 'Te Rito: Peter Loughlin: Kaitātai Kākahu', *Mana* no. 10, Spring 1995, pp. 50–1.

1996, 'Popular Guest', *Mana* no. 11, Summer 1996, p. 6.

1996, 'Maori Political Muscle – *at last*', *Mana* no. 14, Summer 1996–97, pp. 38–9.

1997, 'He Maimai Aroha: Hepi te Heuheu', *Mana* no. 18, October–November 1997, p. 6.

1998, 'The Judge Opts for Iwi', *Mana* no. 23, August–September 1998, pp. 51–4.

1998, 'The Hīkoi of Hope', *Mana* no. 24, October–November 1998, pp. 22–3.

1999, 'He Pitopito Korero: Pakaru Pangaru', *Mana* no. 26, February–March 1999, p. 17.
1999, 'Politics: A Call for *Change*', *Mana* no. 26, February–March 1999, pp. 46–7.
2001, 'He Maimai Aroha: Bob Mahuta', *Mana* no. 38, February–March 2001, pp. 6–7.
2002, 'Money-back Guarantee?', *Mana* no. 47, August–September 2002, p. 27.
2007–2008, 'Maimai Aroha: Passing of a Soldier Priest', *Mana* no. 79, December 2007–January 2008, p. 9.
2008, 'Pitopito Korero: Willie's Gift', *Mana* no. 82, June–July 2008, p. 38.

New Zealand Herald/nzherald.co.nz
1996, 'Henare Shoots from the Lip', *New Zealand Herald*, 19 November 1996, p. A12.
2000, 'MPs Drop Investigation into Waipareira Trust', *New Zealand Herald*, 7 June 2000, p. A5.
2001, 'Maori Seats on BOP Council Could be a Reality by October', *nzherald.co.nz*, 10 May 2001.
2002, '*Chatterbox*: Picking up Good Vibes, and Bryan', *nzherald.co.nz*, 16 November 2002.
2002, 'Protestors Occupy Young Nick's Head', *nzherald.co.nz*, 15 July 2002.
2002, 'Chief Justice Sends Steven Wallace Case Back to Court', *nzherald.co.nz*, 14 June 2002.
2003, 'Question time: Metiria Turei, Green list MP', *New Zealand Herald*, 8 January 2003, p. A8.
2003, 'Row Brewing Over Urewera Pa Site', *nzherald.co.nz*, 14 April 2003.
2003, 'Revolt by Maori MPs Over Foreshore', *New Zealand Herald*, 25 June 2003, p. A1.
2003, 'Majority Opposed to Customary Ownership', *nzherald.co.nz*, 18 August 2003.
2004, 'Clark to Take Another Look at Maori Policies', *nzherald.co.nz*, 24 February 2004.
2004, 'Reality Check', *nzherald.co.nz*, 8 May 2004.
2006, 'Claims Hewitt's Miracle Survival a "hoax" Rubbished', *nzherald.co.nz*, 12 February 2006.
2009, 'Latest Updates: Super City Hikoi', *nzherald.co.nz*, 25 May 2009.

Northland Age
1995, 'Takahue Occupiers Support Ngawha Stand', *Northland Age*, 27 April 1995, p. 1.
1995, 'Muriwhenua Claimants "treated like mushrooms"', *Northland Age*, 1 June 1995, p. 1.
1995, 'Hone Harawira a Lone Voice says Rata', *Northland Age*, 6 June 1995, p. 9.
1995, 'Taemaro not Part of Muriwhenua Claims', *Northland Age*, 6 June 1995, p. 9.
1995, 'No Mandate from Te Rarawa', *Northland Age*, 15 June 1995, p. 1.
1995, 'No Confidence Vote in Matiu Rata', *Northland Age*, 22 June 1995, p. 1.
1995, 'Te Rarawa's Version of Waimanoni Hui', *Northland Age*, 6 July 1995, p. 1.
1995, 'No Mandate from Five Tribes', *Northland Age*, 20 July 1995, pp. 1–2.
1995, 'Occupation Ends with Abuse and Arrests', *Northland Age*, 15 August 1995, p. 1.
1995, 'Te Rarawa Moves to Conduct Own Land Claims', *Northland Age*, 19 September 1995, p. 6.
1995, 'Support Rolls in for Takahue Rebuilding', *Northland Age*, 26 September 1995, p. 1.

1995, 'From Cries of Traitor to Applause', *Northland Age*, 12 October 1995, p. 1.

1996, 'New Hopes for Settlement of Muriwhenua Claims', *Northland Age*, 11 January 1996, p. 1.

1996, 'Three Tribes Press Ahead with Tribunal Claims', *Northland Age*, 15 February 1996, p. 1.

1996, 'Auckland Claimants Support New Order', *Northland Age*, 20 February 1996, p. 1.

1996, 'Ngati Kuri Votes for Muriwhenua', *Northland Age*, 22 February 1996, p. 1.

1996, 'Two Singled out for Suspended Sentences', *Northland Age*, 11 April 1996, p. 3.

1996, 'Support for Runanga and Rata', *Northland Age*, 28 May 1996, p. 1.

1996, 'Ngati Kuri Votes to Stand Alone', *Northland Age*, 28 May 1996, p 1.

1996, 'No Renewed Faith for Te Rarawa', *Northland Age*, 30 May 1996, p. 1.

1997, 'Grief and Anger at Matauri Bay', *Northland Age*, 24 June 1997, p. 1.

1998, 'East Coast Youth "Abused by Police"', *Northland Age*, 22 January 1998, p. 1.

1998, 'Provocation and Harrassment', *Northland Age*, 29 January 1998, p. 2.

1998, 'The Audacity of It', *Northland Age*, 3 February 1998, p. 2.

1999, 'Whaddya Reckon About This Lot, Augie', *Northland Age*, 26 January 1999, p. 1.

1999, 'Gary Baty's Leaving – But He's Staying', *Northland Age*, 26 January 1999, p. 3.

Acts of Parliament

Bay of Plenty Regional Council (Maori Constituency Empowering) Act 2001
Conservation Act 1987
Crown Forest Assets Act 1989
Foreshore and Seabed Act 2004
Local Government Act 2002
Local Government Amendment Act 2002
Maori Fisheries Act 1989
New Zealand Settlements Act 1863
Ngaa Rauru Kiitahi Claims Settlement Act 2005
Ngai Tahu Claims Settlement Act 1998
Ngati Awa Claims Settlement Act 2005
Ngati Mutunga Claims Settlement Act 2006
Ngati Ruanui Claims Settlement Act 2003
Ngati Tama Claims Settlement Act 2003
Ngati Turangitukua Claims Settlement Act 1999
Ngati Tuwharetoa (Bay of Plenty) Claims Settlement Act 2005
Pouakani Claims Settlement Act 2000
Race Relations Act 1971
Resource Management Act 1991
State-owned Enterprises Act 1986
State-owned Enterprises Amendment Act 1988
Te Arawa Lakes Settlement Act 2006
Te Roroa Claims Settlement Act 2008
Te Ture Whenua Maori Act/Maori Land Act 1993
Te Uri o Hau Claims Settlement Act 2002
Terrorism Suppression Act 2002

Treaty of Waitangi (Fisheries Claims) Settlement Act 1992
Treaty of Waitangi (State Enterprises) Act 1988
Waitangi Tribunal Act 1975
Waikato-Tainui Raupatu Claims Settlement Act 1995

Legal decisions

Atawhai Taiaroa and Others v The Hon. the Minister of Justice, The Chief Registrar of Electors and the Attorney-General, High Court, McGechan, J, CP No 99/94, 4 October 1994
Attorney-General v Ngati Apa [2003] 3 NZLR 643 (Court of Appeal)
Huakina Development Trust v Waikato Development Authority [1987] 2 NZLR 188
New Zealand Maori Council v Attorney-General [1987] 1 NZLR 641
New Zealand Maori Council v Attorney-General [1992] 2 NZLR 576
Taiaroa v Minister of Justice [1995] 1 NZLR 411 (Court of Appeal)
Te Heuheu Tukino v Aotea District Maori Land Board [1941] AC 308 (Privy Council)
Wellington International Airport v AVR NZ [1991] 1 NZLR 671
Wi Parata v Bishop of Wellington [1877] 3 NZ Jur (NS) 72

Newspapers and magazines

Horowhenua-Kapiti Chronicle, Horowhenua/Kapiti, New Zealand
Mana: The Maori Magazine for Everyone, Auckland, New Zealand
Nelson Mail, Nelson, New Zealand
Nga Korero o te Wa: A monthly summary of Maori news and views from throughout Aotearoa, Auckland, New Zealand
The Belfast Telegraph, Belfast, Ireland
The Dominion, Wellington, New Zealand
The Dominion Post, Wellington, New Zealand
The Evening Post, Wellington, New Zealand
The Independent, London, England
The New Zealand Herald, Auckland, New Zealand
The New Zealand Listener, Auckland, New Zealand
The Northland Age, Kaitāia, New Zealand
The Press, Christchurch, New Zealand
The Otago Daily Times, Dunedin, New Zeland
The Waikato Times, Hamilton, New Zealand

Index

Bold type indicates photographs and information in captions between the numbered pages. There may be more than one relevant photograph in the block.

References in the form 52n30 are to information in chapter endnotes, showing page and note number.